WITHDRAWN

The Scarecrow Author Bibliographies

WALT WHITMAN
and the critics

A Checklist of Criticism,
1900-1978

Jeanetta Boswell

**The Scarecrow Author Bibliographies,
No. 51**

 **The Scarecrow Press, Inc.
Metuchen, N.J., & London
1980**

Other Scarecrow Titles by
Jeanetta Boswell:

Ralph Waldo Emerson and the Critics: A Checklist
of Criticism

Herman Melville and the Critics: A Checklist
of Criticism

What Men or Gods Are These?

Library of Congress Cataloging in Publication Data

Boswell, Jeanetta, 1922-
    Walt Whitman and the critics.

    (The Scarecrow author bibliographies ; no. 51)
    Includes indexes.
    1. Whitman, Walt, 1819-1892--Bibliography.
I. Title.
Z8971.5.B65   [PS3231]   016.811'3   80-20528
ISBN 0-8108-1355-6

Copyright © 1980 by Jeanetta Boswell

Manufactured in the United States of America

This one is for
my brother Perry
and my sister Wynelle

CONTENTS

INSCRIPTIONS

I. "A Pact, " by Ezra Pound

I make a pact with you, Walt Whitman--
I have detested you long enough.
I come to you as a grown child
Who has had a pig-headed father;

I am old enough now to make friends.
It was you that broke the new wood,
Now is a time for carving.
We have one sap and one root--
Let there be commerce between us.

From Personae: The Collected
Poems. New Directions
Press, 1926.

II. From Emerson to Walt Whitman:

".... I give you joy of your free and brave thought.
I have great joy in it. I find incomparable things said
incomparably well, as they must be. I find the courage of treatment which so delights us, and which large
perception only can inspire.
"I greet you at the beginning of a great career
...."

Letter from Ralph Waldo Emerson to Whitman, July 21,
1855.

III. "With a Voice as Big as America, " by Waldo Frank

"In the century since the first, slim, privately printed

volume of <u>Leaves of Grass</u> appeared, Walt Whitman has become throughout the world America's most widely read, most deeply discussed poet. But the hundred years have not removed the ambiguities of his place in his own country. He sang for the American people, who remain indifferent. By a consensus of intellectual opinion, he is our greatest poet, yet the fashionable critics and most of the biographers do not understand him, and in many cases actually dislike him...."

> From the <u>New York Times Book Review</u>, July 3, 1955, p. 1.

IV. A Review, by Henry James, of <u>Drum-Taps</u>

"It has been a melancholy task to read this book; and it is a still more melancholy one to write about it.... It exhibits the effort of an essentially prosaic mind to lift itself, by a prolonged muscular strain, into poetry...."

> From <u>The Nation</u>, November 16, 1865.

V. <u>Letters to Walt Whitman</u>, by Ronald Johnson

I, too, have plucked a stalk of grass

from your ample prairie, Walt,
& have savored whole fields of a summer's hay in it--

I have known your Appalachian length, the heights
of your Sierra
--I have unearthed the roots of calamus
you left at the margin

of many, hidden ponds,
& have exchanged it with the few, select,
lovers.

I have lain in the open night,

till my shoulders felt twin roots, & the tree of
my sight swayed
among the stars.

I, too, have plucked a stalk of grass

from your ample prairie, Walt.

From <u>Valley of the Many-
colored Grasses.</u> W. W.
Norton and Company, 1969.

PREFATORY REMARKS

Although Henry James complained of the "melancholy task" of reading Drum-Taps, Edith Wharton records an entirely different view of James when she comments on his habit of reading aloud and his marvelous ability to do so in spite of a stammer in speech. In her book A Backward Glance (1934), Wharton recalls,

> ... some one spoke of Whitman, and it was a joy to me to discover that James thought him, as I did, the greatest of American poets. Leaves of Grass was put into his hands, and all that evening we sat rapt while he wandered from "The Song of Myself" to "When lilacs last in the dooryard bloomed" (when he read "Lovely and soothing Death" his voice filled the hushed room like an organ adagio), and thence let himself be lured on to the mysterious music of "Out of the Cradle, " reading, or rather crooning it in a mood of subdued ecstasy till the five-fold invocation to Death tolled out like the knocks in the opening bars of the Fifth Symphony.

Whatever this passage says of James, it says a great deal more about Whitman, evoking the emotional and musical qualities of the poet. No poet in American literature so much deserves to be read aloud, and I doubt that any teacher of Whitman has not experienced an awakening of student interest in the poet when he is read aloud.

In putting this checklist of criticism together, I have tried to include every article, book, and essay that I could possibly find, preferring not to be selective and therefore running the risk of being wrong in a value judgment. Admittedly there are too many "notes" in the field of literary criticism, and too few really spacious studies. However, the notes and short pieces take on acquired significance when they are viewed in the total context of Whitman criticism.

Although this work is principally based on criticism since 1900, there are a few exceptions to this rule. Nineteenth-century criticism is listed if it has been reprinted recently; if the author's life and career ran significantly into the twentieth century; or if the work has been used in the bibliography of a recent article, book, or dissertation. Very few foreign works are included, and these because they have been recently used or translated.

As always there are more debts of gratitude to acknowledge than there is space in which to acknowledge them: The University of Texas at Arlington is my rock in a storm, and especially the interlibrary loan department has been immensely helpful. My friends continue to wish me well; my family provides enthusiasm and interest. But perhaps above all I owe thanks to Sarah Crouch and to Dan Young, my assistants, who are able to find all the missing parts in some obscure corner of the library.

"A Pact" by Ezra Pound is reprinted with permission of New Directions Press of New York and Faber and Faber of of London.

"Letters to Walt Whitman" by Ronald Johnson is reprinted with permission of W. W. Norton.

Jeanetta Boswell

Arlington, Texas

December 31, 1979

A NOTE
ON USING THIS BOOK

The first 50 entries are of anonymous authorship and are listed chronologically.

Subarrangements under authors' names are chronological.

THE CHECKLIST

1 "Walt Whitman's 'Grandee Spain Succumbing.'" Monthly Review, May, 1903, pp. 151-157.

2 "English Appreciation of Whitman." Atlantic, 92 (November, 1903), 714-716.

3 "An American Primer." Atlantic, 93 (April, 1904), 460-470.

4 "A Poet of the Cosmic Consciousness." Brotherhood (London), 19 (April 14, 1906), 142-148.

5 "A Precursor of Whitman." North American Review, 185 (June 21, 1907), 463-464.

6 "New England Nature Studies: Thoreau, Burroughs, Whitman." Edinburgh Review, 208 (October, 1908), 343-366.

7 "Walt Whitman as Musical Prophet." Musical America, 16 (April 15, 1917), 12-14.

8 "With Walt Whitman in Camden." Seven Arts, 2 (September, 1917), 627-637.

9 "Walt Whitman's America." Conservator, 28 (November, 1917), 134-136.

10 "Whitmania." Conservator, 29 (May, 1918), 40-42.

11 "Walt Whitman's Vogue in Europe." Current Opinion, 64 (May, 1918), 349-350.

12 "A Lonely Whitmanite." Literary Digest, 57 (June 15, 1918), 29-30.

13 "Walt Whitman and His Noblest Woman-Friend. " Current
    Opinion, 65 (December, 1918), 394-395.

14 "Celebrating Walt Whitman as a Liberator. " Current
    Opinion, 67 (June, 1919), 392-393.

15 "Walt for Our Day. " Literary Digest, 61 (June 21, 1919),
    28-29.

16 "New Light on Whitman's Contradictory Gospel. " Current
    Opinion, 67 (October, 1919), 246-247.

17 "DeTocqueville and Whitman. " Nation, 109 (November
    22, 1919), 655.

18 "Whitman and Traubel as Prophets Rejected. " Current
    Opinion, 69 (August, 1920), 233-236.

19 "Whitman's Home to Be Preserved as a Literary Shrine. "
    Current Opinion, 69 (October, 1920), 527-529.

20 "Walt Whitman as an Old Fashioned Conservative. " Cur-
    rent Opinion, 70 (March, 1921), 383-385.

21 "Edward Carpenter. " Manchester Guardian Weekly, 21
    (July 5, 1929), 18.

22 "In The Week an Incident Relative to Walt Whitman's
    Being Placed in the Hall of Fame. " New Republic, 67
    (May 27, 1931), 30.   Refers to work by Thoreau.

23 "A Canadian Interview with Walt Whitman. " American
    Notes and Queries, 3 (May, June, 1943), 19-24, 35-36.

24 "The Whitman Collection: Some New Manuscripts. "
    Library Chronicle of the University of Pennsylvania,
    14 (April, 1947), 29-31.

25 "Poets in Politics. " Times Literary Supplement, May
    10, 1947, p. 225.

26 "Backward Glances. " Times Literary Supplement, Octo-
    ber 4, 1947), p. 507.

27 "Whitman's Birthplace. " American Notes and Queries,
    8 (January, 1950), 160.

28 "Prophet-Poet of America." Times Literary Supplement,
    July 31, 1953, p. 492.

29 "Walt Whitman: The Oscar Lion Collection." Bulletin
    of the New York Public Library, 58 (May, June, July,
    August, September, October, 1954), 213-229, 305-308,
    348-359, 397-410, 455-461, 497-514.

30 Walt Whitman: A Catalog Based upon the Collection of
    the Library of Congress (With Notes). Washington,
    D. C.: Library of Congress, 1955. Reprinted, Boston:
    J. S. Canner, 1967.

31 "Poet of Democracy: Walt Whitman." Anonymous re-
    view, translated from the Russian by Stephen Stepan-
    chev, in Allen, Gay Wilson, ed., Walt Whitman Abroad
    (1955), pp. 158-169.

32 "A Word About the Whitman Exhibition by the Whitman
    Exhibition Committee," in Allen, ed., Walt Whitman
    Abroad (1955), pp. 257-259.

33 "Walt Whitman, poète insolite." Informations et Docu-
    ments, 25 (March 15, 1955), 29-38. In French.

34 "Two Civil War Letters." American Heritage, 8 (Octo-
    ber, 1957), 62-64.

35 "'Kentucky': An Unpublished Poem." Walt Whitman
    Newsletter, 4 (June, 1958), 99. Also printed in
    Prairie Schooner, 32 (September, 1958), 170-171.

36 "Sketches of the Sidewalks and Levee: With Glimpses
    into the New Orleans Bar (Rooms). Mrs. Giddy Gay
    Butterfly." Walt Whitman Newsletter, 4 (September,
    1958), 87-90.

37 "Selections from Walt Whitman's Leaves of Grass."
    Folkway Records, FL 9750, 1958.

38 "The First Words of Warm Approval." Walt Whitman
    Review, 5 (1959), 30-33.

39 "Last Words." Walt Whitman Review, 5 (1959), 39.

40 "A Letter to Grant." Walt Whitman Review, 6 (March,
    1960), 19.

41 "Criticism." Literary Review, 4 (August, 1960), 49-59.
    Facsimile of holograph of unpublished Whitman essay.

42 "Unpublished Whitman Poem Found in California Attic."
    Walt Whitman Bulletin, 4 (January, 1961), 12.

43 "A Variorum 'Leaves of Grass.'"   American Book Col-
    lector, 11 (May, 1961), 5.

44 "The Bird of Freedom." Times Literary Supplement,
    June 2, 1961, p. 340. Review article.

45 "(Bernard) O'Dowd to Whitman: Whitman to O'Dowd."
    Overland, 23 (April, 1962), 8-18.

46 "Poet of the 'Modern.'" Times Literary Supplement,
    November 2, 1962, p. 840.

47 Leaves of Grass. Garden City, N.Y.: Doubleday Dol-
    phin Books, 1965. Reprint of 1855 edition.

48 Leaves of Grass. New York: Eakins Press, 1966.

49 "Walt Whitman--The Man and the Poet." Quarterly
    Journal of the Library of Congress, 27 (1970), 171-176.
    Feinberg Collection exhibited in Library of Congress,
    May, 1969-January, 1970.

50 "Walt Whitman in the News." American Transcendental
    Quarterly, 13 (1972), 77-83. Reprinted news items
    from Whitman's times.

END OF ANONYMOUS ENTRIES

51 AARON, Daniel. "Whitman: The 'Parturition Years,'"
    in Aaron, The Unwritten War: American Writers and
    the Civil War. New York: Knopf, 1973. Pp. 56-74.

52 ABBOTT, L. D. "The Democracy of Whitman and the
    Democracy of Socialism." Conservator, 13 (Novem-
    ber, 1902), 136.

53 _____. "Walt Whitman and His Influence in American
    Poetry." Poetry Review, 1 (October, 1912), 473-
    475.

54 ABEL, Darrel. A Simplified Approach to Walt Whitman.
    Great Neck, N.Y.: Barron's, 1964.

55 ABERNETHY, Peter L. Jr.   "The Journey Image in
    Walt Whitman's Poetry."   Ph.D. diss., North Caro-
    lina (Chapel Hill), 1972.   DA, 34 (1973), 2602A.

56 _____ . "Frank Lloyd Wright, Walt Whitman: The
    Expatriate's Dream of Home." American Studies,
    18 (1977), 45-53.

57 ABRAMS, M. H. "The Correspondent Breeze: A Ro-
    mantic Metaphor." Kenyon Review, 19 (1957), 113-
    130. The aeolian harp in Romantic poetry. See also
    article by Kalita (1975).

58 _____ . Natural Supernaturalism: Tradition and Rev-
    olution in Romantic Literature. New York: Norton,
    1971. Whitman, passim.

59 ABRAMS, Robert E. "The Function of Dreams and
    Dream-Logic in Whitman's Poetry." Texas Studies
    in Literature and Language, 17 (1975), 599-616.

60 _____ . "An Early Precursor of 'The Sleepers':
    Whitman's 'The Last of the Sacred Army.'" Walt
    Whitman Review, 22 (1976), 122-125.

61 ACKERMAN, Catherine A. "The Mysticism of Walt
    Whitman." Lock Haven Bulletin, 1 (1959), 66-72.

62 ADAMS, Charles M. "Whitman's Use of 'Grass.'"
    American Notes and Queries, 6 (February, 1947),
    167-168.

63 ADAMS, George Matthew. "Gaity of Heart," in Adams,
    Better Than Gold. New York: Duell, Sloane, 1949.
    Pp. 191-192.

64 ADAMS, Richard P. "Whitman: A Brief Re-valuation."
    Tulane Studies in English, 5 (1955), 111-149.

65 _____ . "Romanticism and the American Renaissance."
    American Literature, 23 (January, 1952), 419-432.

66 _____ . "Whitman's 'Lilacs' and the Tradition of
    Pastoral Elegy." PMLA, 72 (June, 1957), 479-487.

67 _____ . "Whitman and the Rhythms of Life." Calamus,
    14 (1977), 17-24.

68 ADICKS, Richard R. "The Sea-Fight Episode in 'The Song of Myself.'" Walt Whitman Review, 13 (1967), 16-21.

69 ADIMARI, Ralph. "Leaves of Grass--First Edition." American Book Collector, 5 (May-June, 1934), 150-152.

70 ADKINS, Nelson F. "Walt Whitman and William Motherwell: 'Goodbye, My Fancy.'" Notes and Queries, 169 (October 12, 1935), 268-269.

71 AGRAWAL, I. N. "Whitman, Van Wyck Brooks, and the American Tradition." Indian Journal of American Studies, 1 (1971), 95-101.

72 AHLERS, Alice. "Cinematographic Technique in Leaves of Grass." Walt Whitman Review, 12 (1966), 93-97.

73 AHLUWALIA, Harsharon Singh. "Walt Whitman's Concept of the Poet: A Study of the Poetic Persona in His Major Poems." Ph.D. diss., Wisconsin, 1971. DA, 32 (1972), 4598A.

74 _____. "The Private Self and the Public Self in Whitman's 'Lilacs.'" Walt Whitman Review, 23 (1977), 166-174.

75 AHNEBRINK, Lars. "Whitman and Sweden." Walt Whitman Review, 6 (1960), 43-44.

76 ALBRECHT, Robert C. "The Theological Response of the Transcendentalists to the Civil War." New England Quarterly, 38 (March, 1965), 21-34. Reprinted in Barbour, Brian M., ed. American Transcendentalists: An Anthology of Criticism. Notre Dame: Notre Dame University Press, 1973. Pp. 211-221.

77 ALEGRÍA, Fernando. "The Whitman Myth in Latin America." Américas, 6 (February, 1954), 9-11, 41-42.

78 _____. "El Whitman de José Martí." Humanismo, 3 (October, 1954), 239-247. In Spanish.

79 ALEXANDER, C. C. "A Note on Walt Whitman." American Literature, 9 (May, 1937), 242-243.

80 ALLEN, Charles A. "The Whitman Centenary: A Pub-

lisher's View." New Mexico Quarterly, 25 (Winter 1955-1956), 387-392.

81 ALLEN, Evie Allison (wife of Gay Wilson Allen). "Some Recent Whitman Items." Walt Whitman Bulletin, 2 (October, 1958), 9-10.

82 ALLEN, Gay Wilson. "Biblical Analogies for Walt Whitman's Prosody." Revue Anglo-Américaine, 10 (August, 1933), 490-507.

83 _____. "Biblical Echoes in Whitman's Works." American Literature, 6 (November, 1934), 302-315.

84 _____. "Walt Whitman Bibliography, 1918-1934." Bulletin of Bibliography, 15 (September, December, 1934), 84-88, 106-109. Also published as Bulletin of Bibliography Pamphlet, No. 30.

85 _____. American Prosody. New York: American Book Company, 1935. Whitman, pp. 217-243.

86 _____. "Walt Whitman--Nationalist or Proletarian?" English Journal (College Edition), 26 (January, 1937), 48-52.

87 _____. "Walt Whitman and Jules Michelet." Etudes Anglaises, 1 (May, 1937), 230-237. Refers to Michelet's The People, trans. G. H. Smith. New York: Appleton, 1846.

88 _____. "Walt Whitman's 'Long Journey' Motif." Journal of English and Germanic Philology, 38 (January, 1939), 76-95.

89 _____. "Walt Whitman Bibliography, 1935-1942." Bulletin of Bibliography, 24 (January-April, 1943), 209-210.

90 _____. Twenty-Five Years of Walt Whitman Bibliography, 1918-1942. Boston: Faxon, 1943. Also published as Bulletin of Bibliography Pamphlet, No. 38.

91 _____. "Walt Whitman in Comparative Literature." Comparative Literature Newsletter, 2 (December, 1943), 4-5. Bibliography notes.

92 _____. Walt Whitman Handbook. Chicago: Hen-
dricks House, 1946. Reissued, 1962.

93 _____. "Walt Whitman's Reception in Scandinavia."
Papers of the Bibliographical Society of America, 40
(1946), 259-275.

94 _____. "On the Trochaic Meter of 'Pioneers! O,
Pioneers!'" American Literature, 20 (January,
1949), 449-451.

95 _____. "Whitman's 'When Lilacs Last in the Dooryard Bloom'd.'" Explicator, 10 (June, 1952), item
55.

96 _____. "The Man," in Allen, Gay Wilson, Mark Van
Doren, and David Daiches, contributors, Walt Whitman: Man, Poet, Philosopher. Three lectures presented under the auspices of Gertrude Clarke Whittall
Poetry and Literature Fund. Washington, D.C.: Library of Congress, 1955. Pp. 1-14.

97 _____. The Solitary Singer: A Critical Biography
of Walt Whitman. New York: Macmillan, 1955,
1960. Reprinted with revisions, New York: New
York University Press, 1967.

98 _____. "Walt Whitman: 'Cosmos-Inspired,'" in
New World Writing: Eighth Mentor Selection. New
York: New American Library of World Literature,
1955.

99 _____. "Regarding the 'Publication' of the First
Leaves of Grass." American Literature, 28 (March,
1956), 78-79.

100 _____. "Whitman in Japan, China, and Finland."
Walt Whitman Newsletter, 3 (1957), 26-27.

101 _____. "Whitman Edition: Progress Report." Walt
Whitman Newsletter, 4 (1958), 71-72.

102 _____. "The Problem of Metaphor in Translating
Walt Whitman's Leaves of Grass." English Studies
Today, 2 (1961), 269-280.

103 _____. Walt Whitman as Man, Poet, and Legend.

Carbondale: Southern Illinois University Press, 1961.
Contains a checklist of Whitman publications, 1945-
1960, by Evie Allison Allen. Reprinted with revisions,
Detroit: Wayne State University Press, 1969.

104 _____. "Editing the Writings of Walt Whitman: A
Million Dollar Project Without a Million Dollars."
Arts and Sciences, 1 (Winter, 1963), 7-12.

105 _____. "A Note on Comparing Whitman and
Nietzsche." Walt Whitman Review, 11 (1965), 74-76.
Review of book by C. N. Stavrou, 1964.

106 _____. "The Two Poets of Leaves of Grass," in
La France, M., ed., Patterns of Commitment. Toronto: University of Toronto Press, 1967. Pp. 53-
72.

107 _____. "The Influence of Space on the American
Imagination," in Gohdes, C., ed. Essays on Amer-
ican Literature in Honor of Jay B. Hubbell. Durham,
N.C.: Duke University Press, 1967. Pp. 329-342.

108 _____. "The 'Blue Book' in Facsimile." Walt Whitman Review, 14 (1968), 28-29.

109 _____. "Walt Whitman's Inner Space," in Partlow,
Robert, ed., Studies in American Literature. Edwardsville: Southern Illinois University, 1969. Pp.
7-17. Published by Papers on Language and Literature, 5 supplement, Summer, 1969.

110 _____. "The Iconography of Walt Whitman," in
Miller, E. H., ed., The Artistic Legacy (1970),
pp. 127-152. Contains 24 pictures and drawings of
Whitman.

111 _____. A Reader's Guide to Walt Whitman. New
York: Farrar, Straus, and Giroux, 1970.

112 _____. "Whitman and Michelet--Continued." American Literature, 45 (1973), 428-432.

113 _____. The New Walt Whitman Handbook. New
York: New York University Press, 1975.

114 _____, ed. Walt Whitman Abroad: Foreign Crit-

icism in Translation. Syracuse, New York: Syracuse University Press, 1955. Critical evaluations
from Germany, France, Scandinavia, Russia, Italy,
Spain, Latin America, Israel, Japan, and India.

115 _____, ed. Walt Whitman. New York: Grove Press;
London: Evergreen, 1961. Biographical sketch with
selections.

116 _____, and Charles T. Davis, eds. with Introduction.
Walt Whitman's Poems: Selections with Critical Aids.
New York: New York University Press, 1955.

117 _____, et al., eds. "Special Symposium Issue--Walt
Whitman, 1960." Walt Whitman Review, 6 (1960),
3-16.

118 ALLEN, Walter. "Kosmos, of Manhattan the Sun."
New Statesman, 58 (September 12, 1959), 326-327.

119 ALLISON, The Honorable John M. (Ambassador of the
United States to Japan). "Statement from the Catalog
of the 1953 Walt Whitman Exhibition in Tokyo," in
Allen, G. W., ed., Walt Whitman Abroad (1955),
pp. 256-257.

120 AMACHER, Richard E. "Whitman's 'Passage to India.'"
Explicator, 9 (December, 1950), item 2.

121 AMERICAN DIALOG. Special Whitman Issue, 5 (Spring-
Summer, 1969), 1-38. Joseph North, Walter Lowenfels, and Hugo Gellert, eds. Contains 36 items.

122 AMERICAN TRANSCENDENTAL QUARTERLY. Special
Whitman Issue, 12 (Fall, 1971), 1-98.

123 AMUR, G. S. "Whitman's Song of Man: A Humanistic
Approach to 'Song of Myself.'" Walt Whitman Review, 18 (1972), 50-56.

124 AMYOT, Gerald F. "Contrasting Visions of Death in
the Poetry of Poe and Whitman." Walt Whitman
Review, 19 (1973), 103-111.

125 _____. "Walt Whitman's 'Language Experiment.'"
Walt Whitman Review, 20 (1974), 97-103.

126 ANDERSON, D. D. "Walt Whitman's Poetic Philosophy."
     Walt Whitman Review, 4 (1960), 3-7.

127 ANDERSON, Quentin. The Imperial Self: An Essay in
     American Literary and Cultural History. New York:
     Knopf, 1971. "Consciousness and Form in Whitman,"
     pp. 88-118; "The World in the Body," pp. 119-165;
     and "Coming Out of Culture," pp. 201-244.

128 _____. "Whitman's New Man," in Railton, Stephen,
     ed., Walt Whitman's Autograph Revision (1974), pp.
     11-52.

129 _____. "Practical and Visionary Americans." Amer-
     ican Scholar, 45 (1976), 405-418.

130 ANDERSON, Sherwood, ed. with Introduction. Leaves
     of Grass. New York: Crowell, 1933. Illustrations
     by Charles Cullen.

131 ANDREWS, Linda L. "'I am the Poet of the Woman
     the same as the Man': Whitman's View of Women
     as Depicted in 'Song of Myself.'" Ball State Uni-
     versity Forum, 16 (1975), 68-76.

132 ANDREWS, Thomas F. "Walt Whitman and Slavery:
     A Reconsideration of One Aspect of His Concept of
     the American Common Man." College Language As-
     sociation Journal, 9 (1966), 225-233.

133 ANGELO, Valenti, illustrator. Leaves of Grass. New
     York: Random House Modern Library, 1936. 1891-
     92 text with woodcuts by Valenti Angelo.

134 ARBUR, Rosemarie. "'Lilacs' and 'Sorrow': Whitman's
     Effect on the Early Poems of D. H. Lawrence."
     Walt Whitman Review, 24 (1978), 17-21.

135 ARMAND, E. "Resurrexit Walt Whitman." L'Unique,
     117 (January-February, 1955), 16-18. In French.

136 ARMISTEAD, J. M. "Ending with Whitman," Journal
     of English Teaching Techniques, 7 (1974), 14-21.

137 ARMS, George W. "Whitman's 'To a Locomotive in
     Winter.'" Explicator, 5 (November, 1946), item 14.

138 _____ . The Fields Were Green. Palo Alto, Calif.:
Stanford University Press, 1953. A study of Longfellow; Whitman, passim.

139 ARVIN, Newton. "Whitman's Individualism." New Republic, 71 (July 6, 1932), 221-213.

140 _____ . Whitman. New York: Macmillan, 1938.
Reprinted, New York: Russell and Russell, 1969.

141 ASKEW, Melvin W. "Whitman's 'As I Ebb'd with the
Ocean of Life.'" Walt Whitman Review, 10 (1964),
87-92.

142 ASKIN, Denise Theresa. "Prophet of the Square Deific: Savior and Satan in the Works of Walt Whitman."
Ph.D. diss., Notre Dame, 1975. DA, 36 (1975),
265A.

143 ASPIZ, Harold. "Educating the Cosmos: 'There Was
a Child Went Forth.'" American Quarterly, 18
(1966), 655-666. Relates poem to phrenology.

144 _____ . "Unfolding the Folds." Walt Whitman Review, 12 (1966), 81-87. "Unfolded Out of the Folds"
and phrenology.

145 _____ . "Envelope Structure in 'Spirit That Formed
This Scene.'" Explicator, 28 (1969), item 25.

146 _____ . "'Children of Adam' and Horace Greeley."
Walt Whitman Review, 15 (1969), 49-51.

147 _____ . "A Reading of Whitman's 'Faces.'" Walt
Whitman Review, 19 (1973), 37-48.

148 _____ . "Mrs. Davis's 'Drab Love.'" Walt Whitman Review, 22 (1976), 162-163. Refers to Whitman's housekeeper.

149 _____ . "'The Body Electric': Science, Sex, and
Metaphor." Walt Whitman Review, 24 (1978), 137-
142.

150 ASSELINEAU, Roger. "A propos Walt Whitman." Les
Langues Modernes, 42 (August-October, 1948), 446-
449. In French.

151 _____. "Walt Whitman, Child of Adam? Three Unpublished Letters." Modern Language Quarterly, 10
(March, 1949), 91-95.

152 _____. "Le Thème de la mort dans l'oeuvre de Walt
Whitman." Lettres Modernes, 10 (November, 1954),
132-148. In French.

153 _____. L'Evolution de Walt Whitman: The Creation
of a Book, 2 vols. Paris: Didier, 1954. Work
trans. and revised by Richard P. Adams and the
author. Cambridge: Harvard University Press,
Vol. I, The Creation of a Personality, 1960; Vol.
II, The Creation of a Book, 1962.

154 _____. "Whitman's Fundamental Aesthetics," trans.
from L'Evolution by the author, in Allen, ed., Walt
Whitman Abroad (1955), pp. 90-109.

155 _____. "Whitman Agonistes." Walt Whitman Newsletter, 3 (March, 1957), 3-5.

156 _____. "Walt Whitman--or Nature Imitates Art,"
trans. from French by Edward P. Grier. Walt
Whitman Newsletter, 3 (June, 1957), 22-24.

157 _____. "A Footnote to Whitman's Essay on Taine."
Walt Whitman Newsletter, 4 (September, 1958), 93-
94.

158 _____. "Walt Whitman to Gabriel Sarrazin: Four
Unpublished Pieces." Walt Whitman Review, 5 (1959),
8-11.

159 _____. "Three Uncollected 'Leaves of Grass.'"
Huntington Library Quarterly, 22 (May, 1959), 255-
259.

160 _____. "Whitman in France in 1960." Walt Whitman Review, 6 (1960), 4-5.

161 _____. "A Poet's Dilemma: Walt Whitman's Attitude to Literary History and Literary Criticism,"
in Edel, Leon, ed., International Federation of Modern Language and Literature. New York: New York
University Press, 1965. Pp. 50-61.

162 _____. "Camerado, This Is No Book: Who Touches This Touches a Bomb." American Dialogue, 5 (1969), 16-17.

163 _____. "Walt Whitman: From Paumanok to More Than America," in Partlow, Robert, ed., Studies in American Literature. Edwardsville: Southern Illinois University Press, 1969. Pp. 18-39. Published by Papers on Language and Literature, 5 supplement, Summer, 1969.

164 _____. "Walt Whitman," in Woodress, James, ed., Eight American Authors, revised edition. New York: Norton, 1971. Pp. 225-272.

165 _____. "Walt Whitman's Humor." American Transcendental Quarterly, 22 (1974), 86-91.

166 _____. "From Whitman's 'Yawp' to Ginsberg's 'Howl,' or the Poetry of the Large Cities in American Literature." Revue des Langues Vivantes (Brussels), 42 (United States Bicentennial Issue, 1976), 23-35.

167 _____. "Jack London et Walt Whitman." Europe: Revue Littéraire Mensuelle, 76 (1976), 561-562. In French.

168 _____. "'Dreaming in the Grass' ou la constante Transcendentalists de la littérature américaine." Etudes anglaises, 29 (1976), 331-340. In French.

169 _____. "Whitman in France in 1976," in The Long-Islander's Annual Walt Whitman Page, July 1976. Reprinted in Walt Whitman Review, 22 supplement (1976), 13-14.

170 _____, ed. The Long Islander's Annual Walt Whitman Page, May 27, 1971.

171 _____, and Richard H. Rupp, eds. Critics on Whitman. Coral Gables: University of Miami Press, 1972. Reprinted criticism.

172 _____ and William White, eds. Walt Whitman Today. Detroit: Wayne State University Press, 1972.

173 ATKINSON, J. B. "Walt Whitman's Democracy."
     Freeman, 3 (April 13, 1921), 106-108.

174 ATKINSON, W. W. "My Recollections of Whitman."
     New Thought Magazine, January, 1910, pp. 6-9.

175 AUDEN, W. H. The Enchaféd Flood: Romantic Icono-
     graphy of the Sea. New York: Random House,
     1950. Reprinted, Charlottesville: University Press
     of Virginia, 1979. Principally on Melville; Whitman,
     passim.

176 _____, and Norman Holmes Pearson, eds. Poets of
     the English Language. New York: Viking Press,
     1950. Whitman, passim.

177 AUSLANDER, Joseph. Five American Immortals.
     Worcester, Mass.: St. Onge, 1940.

178 AUSTIN, Mary. The American Rhythm: Studies and
     Re-expressions of Amerindian Songs. New edition,
     Boston: Houghton Mifflin, 1930. Refers to chants
     and song of American Indians.

179 AZARNOFF, Roy S. "Walt Whitman's Concept of the
     Oratorical Ideal." Quarterly Journal of Speech, 47
     (April, 1961), 169-172.

180 _____. "Walt Whitman's Lecture on Lincoln in Had-
     donfield." Walt Whitman Review, 9 (1963), 65-66.

181 _____. "Walt Whitman's Rhetorical Theory and Prac-
     tices." Ph.D. diss., Missouri, 1965.

182 BABIC, Ljiljana. "Walt Whitman in Yugoslavia." Acta
     Neophilologica, 9 (1976), 9-58. In English.

183 BAILEY, Elmer James. Religious Thought in the
     Greater American Poets (1922). Reprinted, Free-
     port, N.Y.: Books for Libraries Press, 1968.
     Whitman, pp. 183-228.

184 BAILEY, John Cann. Walt Whitman. New York: Mac-
     millan, 1926. Reprinted, St. Clair Shores, Mich.:
     Scholarly Press, 1970.

Baker   16

185 BAKER, Carlos. "The Road to Concord: Another Mile-
     stone in the Whitman-Emerson Friendship." Prince-
     ton University Library Chronicle, 7 (April, 1946),
     100-117. An Emerson letter.

186 BAKER, John D. "Whitman and Dos Passos: A Sense
     of Communion." Walt Whitman Review, 20 (1974),
     30-33.

187 BAKER, Portia. "The Development of Walt Whitman's
     Literary Reputation in the United States and England
     from 1855 to 1892." Ph.D. diss., Chicago, 1933.

188 _____. "Walt Whitman and The Atlantic Monthly."
     American Literature, 6 (November, 1934), 283-301.

189 _____. "Walt Whitman's Relations with Some New
     York Magazines." American Literature, 7 (Novem-
     ber, 1935), 274-301.

190 BALÁZES, Mary Elizabeth Webber. "Walt Whitman
     and William James: Stirres of the Long Silent Amer-
     ican Mind." Ph.D. diss., Pennsylvania State, 1965.
     DA, 27 (1966), 764A-65A.

191 BALDENSPERGER, F. "Walt Whitman and France."
     Columbia University Quarterly, 21 (July, 1919),
     298-309.

192 BALKE, Rev. Victor H. "Walt Whitman: An American
     Surrealist." Ph.D. diss., St. Louis, 1973. DA,
     34 (1974), 5089A.

193 BALSEIRO, José A. "Emerson y Whitman." Atlántico
     (Madrid), 2 (1956), 49-71. In Spanish.

194 _____. "Walt Whitman." Carrell, 7 (1966), 1-7.

195 BARAC, Vladimir. "'Song of Myself' as Myth and
     Reality: An American Quest for Epic." Ph.D. diss.,
     Texas (Austin), 1971. DA, 32 (1972), 5772A.

196 BARKER, Elsa. "What Whitman Learned from the
     East." Canada Monthly, 10 (October, 1911), 438-443.

197 BARRUS, Clara. The Life and Letters of John Bur-
     roughs, 2 vols. Boston: Houghton Mifflin, 1925.

198 _____. "Whitman and Burroughs as Comrades."
     Yale Review, 15 (October, 1925), 59-81.

199 _____. Whitman and Burroughs: Comrades. Bos-
     ton: Houghton Mifflin, 1931. Reprinted, Port Wash-
     ington, N. Y.: Kennikat, 1968. Editorial comments
     by Dr. Clara Barrus and Clifford J. Furness.

200 BARTLETT, I. H. "The Democratic Imagination," in
     Bartlett, The American Mind in the Mid-Nineteenth
     Century. New York: Crowell, 1967. Pp. 94-113.

201 BARTON, William Eleazar. Abraham Lincoln and Walt
     Whitman. Indianapolis: Bobbs-Merrill, 1928. Re-
     printed, Port Washington, N. Y.: Kennikat, 1965.

202 BASLER, Roy P. "Out of the Cradle Endlessly Rock-
     ing." Explicator, 5 (June, 1947), item 59.

203 _____. "Walt Whitman in Perspective," in White,
     William, ed., Walt Whitman in Our Time (1970),
     pp. 5-8.

204 _____, ed. Walt Whitman's Memoranda During the
     War and Death of Abraham Lincoln. Reproduced in
     facsimile, with Introduction. Bloomington: Indiana
     University Press, 1962.

205 BATCHELOR, Sally Ann. "Whitman's Yawp and How
     He Yawped It." Walt Whitman Review, 18 (1972),
     97-101.

206 BATTEN, Charles L. Jr. "Unpublished Whitman Letter
     to Dr. Bucke." Walt Whitman Review, 20 (1974),
     115-116.

207 BAUDOUIN, Charles. Studies in Psychoanalysis.
     Trans. from French by Eden and Cedar Paul. Lon-
     don: George Allen and Unwin, 1922; New York:
     Dodd, Mead, 1924. Whitman not discussed; back-
     ground material for Whitman's symbolism.

208 BAYLEN, Joseph O., and Robert B. Holland. "Whit-
     man, W. T. Stead, and the Pall Mall Gazette: 1886-
     1887." American Literature, 33 (March, 1961), 68-
     72.

209 BAYTOP, Adrianne. "'Song of Myself,' Sec. 52:

Motion as Vehicle for Meaning." Walt Whitman Review, 18 (1972), 101-103.

210   BAZALGETTE, Léon. Walt Whitman: The Man and His Work. Paris: Mercure de France, 1908. Trans. from French by Ellen Fitzgerald and published, New York: Doubleday, Page, 1920. Reprinted, New York: Cooper Square, 1971.

211   _____. Le Poème-Evangile de Walt Whitman. Paris: Mercure de France, 1921. In French; has not been translated.

212   BEACH, Joseph Warren. The Concept of Nature in Nineteenth Century English Poetry. New York: Pageant, 1936. Whitman, pp. 370-394.

213   BEARDSHEAR, William M. "Charge to a Walt." Palimpsest, 51 (1970), 349-352.

214   BEATTY, Richmond C. "Whitman's Political Thought." South Atlantic Quarterly, 46 (January, 1947), 72-83. Reprinted in Hamilton, William Baskeville, ed., SAQ: Fifty Years of the South Atlantic Quarterly. Durham, N.C.: Duke University Press, 1952. Pp. 319-330.

215   BEAVER, Joseph C. "Walt Whitman: Star Gazer." Journal of English and Germanic Philology, 48 (July, 1949), 307-319.

216   _____. "Walt Whitman--Poet of Science." Ph.D. diss., New York University, 1950.

217   _____. Walt Whitman--Poet of Science. New York: King's Crown Press, 1951. Reprinted, New York: Octagon, 1974.

218   BECK, Maximilian. "Walt Whitman's Intuition of Reality." Ethics, 53 (October, 1942), 14-24.

219   BECK, Ronald. "The Structure of 'Song of Myself' and the Critics." Walt Whitman Review, 15 (1969), 32-38.

220   BEERBOHM, Max. The Poet's Corner (A Book of Caricatures). London: William Heinemann, 1904. Re-

issued, 1922. Reprinted, New York: Penguin, 1943.
"Whitman Inciting the Bird of Freedom to Soar,"
plate 11.

221 BEERS, Henry Augustin. Four Americans: Roosevelt,
     Hawthorne, Emerson, Whitman. New Haven: Yale
     University Press, 1919. Reprinted, Freeport, N.Y.:
     Books for Libraries Press, 1968. Whitman, pp. 85-
     90.

222 BEGG, Edleen. "Larks, Purple Cows, and Whitmania."
     University of Texas Library Chronicle, 2 (Spring,
     1947), 190-192.

223 BELSON, Joel Jay. "Whitman's 'Overstaid Fraction.'"
     Walt Whitman Review, 17 (1971), 63-65.

224 BEMROSE, Clive. "A Whitman Poem and an 1890 Eng-
     lish School's Song." Walt Whitman Review, 22 (1976),
     168-170.

225 BENNETT, Frances H. "'Starting from Paumanok' as
     Functional Poetry." Walt Whitman Review, 15 (1969),
     117-120.

226 BENNETT, James O'Donnell. "Whitman's Leaves of
     Grass," in Much Loved Books. New York: Liveright,
     1927. Pp. 339-344. Shorter version reprinted,
     Greenwich, Conn.: Fawcett, 1959. Whitman, pp.
     204-209.

227 _____. "Whitman and Certain Curiosities of Criti-
     cism," in Much Loved Books (1927), pp. 345-351.
     In shorter version (1959), pp. 210-216.

228 BENNETT, Josiah Q. "Whitman Loses His Ego: or
     'Not I, said the fly.'" Serif, 7 (1970), 35-36. Dis-
     cusses 1855 Leaves of Grass.

229 BENOIT, Raymond. "The Mind's Return: Whitman,
     Teilhard, and Jung." Walt Whitman Review, 13
     (1967), 21-28. Reprinted in Benoit, Single Nature's
     Double Name. Atlantic Highlands, N.J.: Humanities
     Press, 1973. Pp. 67-76.

230 BENSON, Adolph B. "Walt Whitman's Interest in Swed-
     ish Writers." Journal of English and Germanic Phil-
     ology, 31 (July, 1932), 332-345.

231 BENSON, Arthur Christopher. Escape and Other Essays. New York: Appleton-Century, 1915. Whitman, pp. 63-90.

232 BERBRICH, Joan Dolores. "The Influence of Long Island on Three Major Writers." Ph.D. diss., New York University, 1964. DA, 26 (1965), 364-365.

233 _____. Three Voices from Paumanok: The Influence of Long Island on James Fenimore Cooper, William Cullen Bryant, and Walt Whitman. Port Washington, N.Y.: Ira J. Friedman, 1969. Whitman, pp. 111-196.

234 BERCOVITCH, Sacvan. The American Jeremiad. Madison: University of Wisconsin Press, 1978. Whitman and other Renaissance figures, passim.

235 BERGMAN, Herbert. "Whitman on Politics, Presidents, and Hopefuls." American Notes and Queries, 8 (May, 1948), 19-26.

236 _____. "Whitman in June, 1885: Three Uncollected Interviews." American Notes and Queries, 8 (July, 1948), 51-56.

237 _____. "Whitman's Parodies." American Notes and Queries, 8 (August, 1948), 74.

238 _____. "Sir Edwin Arnold and Walt Whitman." Notes and Queries, 193 (August 21, 1948), 366.

239 _____. "A Poet's Western Visit." Missouri Historical Review, 8 (January, 1949), 74.

240 _____. "Whitman on His Poetry and Some Poets: Two Uncollected Interviews." American Notes and Queries, 10 (February, 1950), 103-105.

241 _____. "'Chicago' An Uncollected Poem, Possibly by Whitman." Modern Language Notes, 65 (November, 1950), 478-481.

242 _____. "Whitman on Beethoven and Music." Modern Language Notes, 66 (December, 1952), 556-557.

243 _____. "Whitman and Tennyson." Studies in Philology, 51 (July, 1954), 492-504.

244 _____. "'Walt Whitman' by Ezra Pound." American Literature, 27 (March, 1955), 59-61. Original
title by Pound, "What I Feel About Walt Whitman,"
dated February, 1909. Reprinted in Pearce, Roy
Harvey, ed., Whitman: A Collection of Criticism
(1962), pp. 8-10.

245 _____. "The Whitman-Twain Enigma Again." Mark
Twain Journal, 10 (Winter, 1956), 22-23; continued
in 11 (Summer, 1957), 3-9.

246 _____. "The Influence of Whitman's Journalism on
Leaves of Grass." American Literary Realism, 3
(1970), 399-404.

247 _____. "On Editing Whitman's Journalism." Walt
Whitman Review, 16 (1970), 104-109.

248 _____. "Walt Whitman: Self Advertiser." Bulletin
of New York Public Library, 74 (1970), 634-639.

249 _____. "Walt Whitman as a Journalist: 1831-1848."
Journalism Quarterly, 48 (1971), 195-204.

250 _____. "Whitman on Editing, Newspapers and Journalism." Journalism Quarterly, 48 (1971), 345-348.

251 _____. "Walt Whitman as a Journalist, March 1848-
1892." Journalism Quarterly, 48 (1971), 431-437.

252 _____, ed. "Walt Whitman on New Jersey: An Uncollected Essay." Proceedings of the New Jersey
Historical Society, 66 (October, 1948), 139-154.

253 _____, and William White, eds. "Walt Whitman's
Lost 'Sun-Down Papers,' Numbers 1-3." American
Book Collector, 20 (1970), 17-20.

254 _____, and William White, eds. The Journalism,
5 vols. in Collected Writings. New York: New
York University Press, projected date of publication,
early 1980's.

255 BERKOVE, Lawrence I. "Biblical Influence on Whitman's Concept of Creatorhood." Emerson Society
Quarterly, 47 (1967), 34-37.

256 BERNARD, Edward G. "Some New Whitman Manuscript

Notes." American Literature, 8 (March, 1936), 59-63.

257 BERNBROCK, John, S.J. "Whitman's Language Study: Work in Progress." Walt Whitman Review, 6 (1960), 69-72.

258 _____. "Walt Whitman and 'Anglo-Saxonism.'" Ph.D. diss., North Carolina, 1961. DA, 22 (1962), 2789-2790.

259 _____. "George H. Colton, Whitman, and 'By Blue Ontario's Shore.'" Walt Whitman Review, 8 (1962), 38-40.

260 BERRY, Edmund G. "Whitman's Canadian Friend." Dalhousie Review, 24 (April, 1944), 77-82. Refers to Dr. Richard M. Bucke.

261 BERRYHILL, Michael Kenneth. "Walt Whitman and Post Modern Consciousness." Ph.D. diss., Minnesota, 1975. DA, 38 (1977), 1376A.

262 BERRYMAN, John. "'Song of Myself': Intention and Substance," in Berryman, The Freedom of the Poet. New York: Farrar and Straus, 1976.

263 BERTHOLF, Robert. "Poetic Epistemology of Whitman's 'Out of the Cradle.'" Walt Whitman Review, 10 (1964), 73-77.

264 BETSKY, Seymour. "Whose Walt Whitman? French Scholars and American Critics." English Studies, 47 (June, 1966), 199-208.

265 BETT, W. R. "Walt Whitman, the Invert Who Sought to Redeem Democracy," in Bett, The Infirmities of Genius. New York: Philosophical Library, 1952. Pp. 45-56.

266 BICKMAN, Martin Elliott. "Voyages of the Mind's Return: A Jungian Study of Poe, Emerson, Whitman, and Emily Dickinson." Ph.D. diss., Pennsylvania, 1974. DA, 36 (1975), 266A.

267 _____. "Occult Traditions and American Romanticism: A Jungian Perspective," in Frank, Luanne,

ed., Literature and the Occult. Arlington: University of Texas, 1977. Pp. 54-64.

268 BICKNELL, P. F. "The Real and the Ideal Whitman." Dial, 40 (March 1, 1906), 144-146.

269 _____. "An Aged Poet in His Daily Talk." Dial, 56 (June 16, 1914), 493-494.

270 BINNS, Henry Bryan. A Life of Walt Whitman. New York: E. P. Dutton; London: Methuen, 1905. Reprinted, New York: Haskell House, 1969; also reprinted New York: AMS Press, 1972.

271 BIRDSALL, Eric Reed. "Translating the Hints: Walt Whitman's Poetry of Indirection." Ph.D. diss., Johns Hopkins, 1977. DA, 37 (1977), 6482A-6483A.

272 BIRSS, John Howard. "A Note on 'O Captain! My Captain!'" Notes and Queries, 161 (September 26, 1931), 233.

273 _____. "Whitman on Arnold: An Uncollected Comment." Modern Language Notes, 47 (May, 1932), 316-317.

274 _____. "Notes on Whitman." Notes and Queries, 163 (October 29, 1932), 311-312.

275 _____. "A Satire on Whitman." Notes and Queries, 164 (January 7, 1933), 6-7.

276 _____. "Whitman and Herman Melville." Notes and Queries, 164 (April 22, 1933), 280.

277 BLACK, A. "The Desk," in The Latest Thing and Other Things. New York: Harper, 1922. Pp. 161-167.

278 BLACK, Stephen Ames. "Whitman and the Failure of Mysticism: Identity and Identification in 'Song of Myself.'" Walt Whitman Review, 15 (1969), 223-230.

279 _____. "Review of Edwin H. Miller, ed., A Century of Whitman Criticism." West Coast Review, 5 (Fall, 1970), 40-41.

280 _____. "Whitman and Psychoanalytic Criticism."
Literature and Psychology, 20 (1970), 79-82. A
reply to Arthur Golden's review of Edwin H. Miller's
Walt Whitman's Poetry (1968).

281 _____. "Radical Utterances from the Soul's Abysms:
Toward a New Sense of Whitman." PMLA, 88 (1973),
100-111.

282 _____. "Journeys into Chaos: A Psychoanalytic
Study of Whitman, His Literary Processes, and His
Poems." Literature and Psychology, 24 (1974), 47-
54.

283 _____. Whitman's Journeys into Chaos: A Psychoanalytic Study of the Poetic Process. Princeton,
N.J.: Princeton University Press, 1975.

284 BLACKWELL, Louise. "'Song of Myself' and the Organic Theory of Poetry." Walt Whitman Review,
12 (1966), 35-41.

285 BLACKWOOD, R. T. "William James and Walt Whitman." Walt Whitman Review, 21 (1975), 78-79.

286 BLANCK, Jacob. "News from the Rare Book Sellers."
Publishers' Weekly, 153 (September 27, 1947), 201-
202.

287 BLANCO, Manuel Garcia. "Walt Whitman y Unamuno."
Cultura Universitaria (Venezuela), 52 (November-
December, 1955), 76-102. In Portuguese.

288 BLASER, Kent. "Walt Whitman and American Art."
Walt Whitman Review, 24 (1978), 108-118.

289 BLASING, Mutlu Konuck. "'The Sleepers': The Problem of Self in Whitman." Walt Whitman Review, 21
(1975), 111-119.

290 _____. "Walt Whitman, a Kosmos, of Manhattan the
Son," in Blasing, The Art of Life: Studies in Amer-
ican Autobiographical Literature. Austin and London:
University of Texas Press, 1977. Pp. 25-53.

291 BLODGETT, Harold W. "Walt Whitman in England."
Ph.D. diss., Cornell, 1929.

292 _____ . "Walt Whitman in England." <u>American</u>
<u>Mercury</u>, 17 (August, 1929), 490-496.

293 _____ . "Whitman and Dowden." <u>American Litera-</u>
<u>ture,</u> 1 (May, 1929), 171-182.

294 _____ . "Whitman and Buchanan." <u>American Litera-</u>
<u>ture,</u> 2 (May, 1930), 131-140. Refers to Robert
Buchanan, late-19th-century English poet and essay-
ist.

295 _____ . "Walt Whitman's Dartmouth Visit." <u>Dart-</u>
<u>mouth</u> Alumni Magazine, 25 (February, 1933), 13-15.

296 _____ . <u>Walt Whitman in England.</u> Ithaca, N.Y.:
Cornell University Press, 1934.

297 _____ . "Bibliographical Description as a Key to
Whitman." <u>Walt Whitman Newsletter</u>, 2 (March-
June, 1956), 8-9.

298 _____ . "A Note on Whitman's Poetic Fragments."
<u>Walt Whitman Newsletter</u>, 2 (September, 1956), 26-
27.

299 _____ . "Toward the Second Edition of <u>Leaves of</u>
<u>Grass</u>: An Unpublished Whitman Notebook, 1855-1856."
<u>Walt Whitman Newsletter</u>, 2 (December, 1956), 35-
53.

300 _____ . "An Early Whitman Manuscript." <u>Walt</u>
<u>Whitman Newsletter</u>, 4 (March, 1958), 73-74.

301 _____ . "Whitman and the Linton Portrait." <u>Walt</u>
<u>Whitman Newsletter</u>, 4 (September, 1958), 90-92.

302 _____ . "Walt Whitman in 1960," in "Special Symposium Issue." <u>Walt Whitman Review</u>, 6 (1960),
23-24.

303 _____ . "Whitman in Iran." <u>Walt Whitman Review</u>,
5 (1959), 11-12.

304 _____ . "Teaching 'Song of Myself,'" in "Walt Whitman Symposium." <u>Emerson Society Quarterly</u>, 22
(1961), 2-3.

305 _____. "Whitman's 'Whisperings.'" Walt Whitman
     Review, 8 (1962), 12-16.

306 _____. "Editing Leaves of Grass: The Manuscript
     Problems." Center of Editions of American Authors
     Newsletter, 1 (1968), 3-4.

307 _____. "Who Listens to Him Today?" American
     Dialogue, 5 (1969), 10-12, 36-38.

308 _____. "Democratic Vistas: 100 Years After," in
     Schubert, Karl, and Ursula Müller-Richter, eds.,
     Geschichte und Gesellschaft in der amerikanischen
     Literatur. Heidelberg: Quelle and Mayer, 1975.
     In English. Pp. 114-131.

309 _____, ed. with Introduction and Notes. The Best
     of Whitman. New York: Ronald Press, 1953.

310 _____, ed. with Introduction. An 1855-1856 Note-
     book Toward the Second Edition of Leaves of Grass.
     Carbondale: Southern Illinois University Press, 1959.

311 _____, ed. "Special Symposium Issue--Whitman,
     1960." Walt Whitman Review, 6 (1960), 23-35.

312 _____, ed. Long-Islander Annual Walt Whitman
     Page, May 25, 1961.

313 _____, and Sculley Bradley, eds. with Introduction
     and Notes. Leaves of Grass: Comprehensive Read-
     er's Edition, in Collected Writings. New York: New
     York University Press 1965. Text reprinted as
     Norton Critical Edition, New York: Norton, 1973.

314 _____, et al., eds., "Walt Whitman Symposium."
     Emerson Society Quarterly, 22 (1961), 2-28.

315 BLOOM, Harold. "The Central Man: Emerson, Whit-
     man, Wallace Stevens." Massachusetts Review, 7
     (Winter, 1966), 23-42.

316 _____. "Emerson and Whitman: The American Sub-
     lime," in Bloom, Poetry and Repression: Revision-
     ism from Blake to Stevens. New Haven: Yale Uni-
     versity Press, 1976. Pp. 235-266.

317 _____. "Whitman, The Native Strain," in Bloom,

Figures of Capable Imagination. New York: Sea-
brook Press, 1976. Pp. 68-88.

318 _____. Wallace Stevens: The Poems of Our Cli-
mate. Ithaca, N.Y.: Cornell University Press,
1977. Influence of Whitman and Emerson discussed.

319 BLOOR, Ella Reeve. We Are Many: An Autobiography.
New York: International Publishers, 1940. Introduction by Elizabeth Gurley Flynn. Whitman, pp.
43, 303, et passim.

320 BLUESTEIN, E. Gene. "The Advantages of Barbarism:
Herder and Whitman's Nationalism." Journal of the
History of Ideas, 24 (January-March, 1963), 115-126.

321 _____. "The Emerson-Whitman Tradition: Whitman,"
in Bluestein, The Voice of the Folk: Folklore and
American Literary Theory. Amherst: University of
Massachusetts Press, 1972. Pp. 37-64.

322 BO, Carlo. "Whitman." Paragoné, 22 (October, 1951),
37-52. In Spanish.

323 BOATRIGHT, Mody C. "Whitman and Hegel." University of Texas Studies in English, 9 (1929), 134-150.

324 BOCHNER, Martin J. "Profond Aujourd' hui: Blaise
Cendrars and the Whitman Tradition in France."
Ph.D. diss., Columbia, 1971. DA, 33 (1972), 301A.

325 BODE, Carl. "Whitman at Oxbridge," in Bode, The
Half-World of American Culture. Carbondale:
Southern Illinois University Press, 1965. Pp. 63-65.
Preface by C. P. Snow.

326 BOLLER, Paul F., Jr. American Transcendentalism,
1830-1860: An Intellectual Inquiry. New York:
Putnam's, 1974. Whitman, pp. 178-180 et passim.

327 BOLLIER, E. P. "Against the American Grain: William Carlos Williams Between Whitman and Poe."
Tulane Studies in English, 23 (1978), 123-142.

328 BOLTON, Whitney French, and D. Crystal, eds. The
English Language: Essays by Linguists and Men of
Letters, 1858-1964, 2 vols. Cambridge, England:

Cambridge University Press, 1969. "Whitman: Slang in America," Vol. II, pp. 54-58.

329 BOND, Reece A. "Whitman's Visual Imagination." Ph.D. diss., Minnesota, 1972. DA, 33 (1973), 3631A-3632A.

330 BORGES, Jorge Luis. "The Achievements of Walt Whitman." Texas Quarterly, 5 (Spring, 1962), 43-48.

331 _____. "Note on Walt Whitman," in Borges, Other Inquisitions, 1937-1952. Austin: University of Texas Press, 1964. Pp. 66-72.

332 _____. "Walt Whitman: Man and Myth." Critical Inquiry, 1 (1975), 707-721. Transcription of a lecture given at University of Chicago, January 30, 1968.

333 _____, ed. with Foreword. Homage to Walt Whitman: A Collection of Poems to Whitman. Trans. from Spanish and annotated by Didier Tisdel Jaén. University: University of Alabama Press, 1969.

334 BORN, Helena. Whitman's Ideal Democracy and Other Writings, ed. with biographical sketch of Born by Helen Tufts. Boston: Everett Press, 1902.

335 BOROFF, David. "Walt Whitman's Brooklyn and Mine." Nocturne, 7 (Spring, 1955), 29-32.

336 BOVÉ, Paul Anthony. "A 'New Literary History' of Modern Poetry: History and Deconstruction in the Works of Whitman, Stevens, and Olson." Ph.D. diss., New York (Binghamton), 1976. DA, 36 (1975), 3682A-3683A.

337 BOWEN, Dorothy, and Philip Durham, eds. "Walt Whitman Materials in the Huntington Library." Huntington Library Quarterly, 19 (November, 1955), 81-96.

338 BOWERING, George. "The Solitary Everything." Walt Whitman Review, 15 (1969), 13-26.

339 BOWERS, Fredson. "Whitman's Manuscripts for the Original 'Calamus' Poems." Studies in Bibliography (University of Virginia), 6 (1953-1954), 257-265.

340 _____. "The Manuscript of Walt Whitman's 'A Carol
of Harvest for 1867.'" Modern Philology, 52 (August, 1954), 29-51.

341 _____. "The Manuscripts of Whitman's 'Song of the
Redwood Tree.'" Papers of the Bibliographical Society of America, 50 (1956), 53-85.

342 _____. "The Earliest Manuscript of Whitman's
'Passage to India' and Its Notebook." Bulletin of
the New York Public Library, 61 (July, 1957), 319-
352.

343 _____. Textual and Literary Criticism. Cambridge,
Mass.: Harvard University Press, 1959. The
Sanders Lectures in Bibliography, 1957-1958.

344 _____. "The Facsimile of Whitman's Blue Book,"
in Bowers, Essays in Bibliography, Text, and Editing. Charlottesville: University Press of Virginia,
1976. Published for the Bibliographical Society of
the University of Virginia.

345 _____, ed. with Introduction. Whitman's Manuscripts:
Leaves of Grass (1860). A parallel text with notes
and introduction. Chicago: University of Chicago
Press, 1955.

346 BOYD, Ernest A. "The Father of Them All." American Mercury, 6 (December, 1925), 451-458.

347 _____. "Walt Whitman," in Literary Blasphemies.
New York: Harpers, 1927. Pp. 186-212.

348 BOYNTON, Percy H. "Whitman's Idea of the State."
New Republic, 7 (June 10, 1916), 139-141.

349 _____. "I, Walt Whitman." New Republic, 19 (May
31, 1919), 141-143.

350 _____. "Walt Whitman--A Centenary View." Nation,
108 (May 31, 1919), 866-867.

351 _____. "Soil Preparation and Grass Seed." New
Republic, 31 (July 19, 1922), 225-226.

352 BOZARD, John F. "Walt Whitman in America: 1855-
1892." Ph.D. diss., Cornell, 1937.

353 _____. "Horace Traubel's Socialistic Interpretation of Whitman." Furman University Bulletin, 20 (January, 1938), 35-45.

354 _____. "Richard Maurice Bucke and Whitman." Appalachian State Teachers College Faculty Publication, 1957. Pp. 20-31.

355 BRACKER, Jon. "The Christopher Morley Collection." Library Chronicle of University of Texas (Austin), 7 (Summer, 1962), 19-35.

356 _____. "The Conclusion of 'Song of Myself.'" Walt Whitman Review, 10 (1964), 21-22.

357 BRADFORD, Gamaliel. "Portraits of American Authors." Bookman, 42 (January, 1916), 533-548.

358 _____. "Walt Whitman," in Bradford, Biography and the Human Heart. Boston: Houghton Mifflin, 1932. Pp. 65-93.

359 _____. "Walt Whitman," in Johnson, A. Theodore, and Allen Tate, eds., America Through the Essay: An Anthology for English Courses. New York: Oxford University Press, 1938.

360 BRADLEY, E. Sculley. "Mr. Walter Whitman." Bookman, 76 (March, 1933), 227-232.

361 _____. "Walt Whitman on Timber Creek." American Literature, 5 (November, 1933), 235-246.

362 _____. "The Fundamental Metrical Principle in Whitman's Poetry." American Literature, 10 (January, 1939), 437-459.

363 _____. "The Problem of a Variorum Edition of Whitman's Leaves of Grass," in English Institute Annual for 1941. New York: Columbia University Press, 1942. Pp. 129-158.

364 _____. "Walt Whitman, Poet of the Present War." General Magazine and Historical Chronicle, 45 (October, 1942), 7-14.

365 _____. "Walt Whitman and the Postwar World."

South Atlantic Quarterly, 42 (July, 1943), 220-224.

366 _____. "Whitman and the Charcoal Burner." Walt Whitman Newsletter, 2 (September, 1956), 21-23.

367 _____. "Whitman and John Quincy Adams: A Review." Walt Whitman Review, 8 (1962), 19-20.

368 _____. "The Teaching of Whitman." College English, 23 (May, 1962), 618-622.

369 _____. "Whitman." Review of Current Scholarship in American Literary Scholarship, 1963. Pp. 41-52.

370 _____. "Physical Evidence in Textual Collation." Center for Editions of American Authors Newsletter, 1 (1968), 9.

371 _____. "The Controlling Sexual Imagery in Whitman's 'Song of Myself,'" in Deakin, Motley, and Peter Lisca, eds., From Irving to Steinbeck: Studies of American Literature in Honor of Harry R. Warfel. Gainesville: University of Florida Press, 1972. Pp. 45-54.

372 _____, and John A. Stevenson. "Origin of 'A Backward Glance O'er Travel'd Roads,'" in Backward Glances (1947), pp. 1-13.

373 _____, and John A. Stevenson. "A Note on the Texts," in Backward Glances (1947), pp. 14-16.

374 _____, ed. with Introduction. Walt Whitman's Leaves of Grass and Selected Prose. New York: Holt, Rinehart, 1949. Rinehart Edition.

375 _____, ed. With Walt Whitman in Camden, by Horace Traubel, Vol. IV. Philadelphia: University of Pennsylvania Press, 1953.

376 _____, and John A. Stevenson, eds., with Introduction on the Evolution of the Text. Walt Whitman's Backward Glances: A Backward Glance O'er Travel'd Roads and Two Contributing Essays Hitherto Uncollected. Philadelphia: University of Pennsylvania Press, 1947. Reprinted, Freeport, N.Y.: Books for Libraries Press, 1968.

377 _____, and Harold Blodgett, eds. with Introduction
      and Notes. Leaves of Grass: Comprehensive Read-
      er's Edition, in Collected Writings. New York: New
      York University Press, 1965. Text reprinted as
      Norton Critical Edition, New York: Norton, 1973.

378 BRADSHAW, Harold D. "Walt Whitman's Physicians in
      Camden." Transactions and Studies of the College
      of Physicians and Surgeons of Philadelphia, 4th Se-
      ries, 31 (1964), 227-230.

379 BRADSHER, E. L. "Walt Whitman and a Modern
      Problem." Sewanee Review, 22 (January, 1914), 86-
      95.

380 BRADY, Sister Mary W. "Walt Whitman's Revisions of
      'Song of Myself.'" Ph.D. diss., Chicago, 1948.

381 BRAGMAN, Louis J. "Walt Whitman, Hospital Attend-
      ant and Medical Critic." Medical Life, 39 (1932),
      606-615.

382 BRASHER, Thomas Lowber. "'To All the People of
      Brooklyn': Walt Whitman as Editor of The Brooklyn
      Daily Eagle, 1846-1848." Ph.D. diss., Louisiana
      State, 1955. DA, 16 (1956), 1681-1682.

383 _____. "Whitman and The Crescent: A Conjecture."
      Walt Whitman Newsletter, 3 (June, 1957), 24-25.

384 _____. "Whitman and Universalism." Walt Whit-
      man Newsletter, 3 (September, 1957), 40-42.

385 _____. "Whitman and Emma Willard's 'Rocked in
      the Cradle of the Deep.'" Walt Whitman Newsletter,
      4 (March, 1958), 78.

386 _____. "Whitman's Conversion to Phrenology."
      Walt Whitman Newsletter, 4 (June, 1958), 95-97.

387 _____. "Whitman's Conversion to Opera." Walt
      Whitman Newsletter, 4 (June, 1958), 109-110.

388 _____. "Whitman, Robert Owen, and Radical Re-
      form." Walt Whitman Review, 5 (1959), 72-73.

389 _____. "Organized Labor Versus Whitman's 'Im-

mutable Truth.'" Walt Whitman Review, 6 (1960), 63-66.

390 _____. "A Modest Protest Against Viewing Whitman as Pantheist or Reincarnationist." Walt Whitman Review, 13 (1967), 92-94.

391 _____. "'Be --, Be --, Be Not Too Damned.'" Walt Whitman Review, 14 (1968), 60.

392 _____. Whitman as Editor of 'The Brooklyn Daily Eagle.' Detroit: Wayne State University Press, 1970.

393 _____. "Walt Whitman in League with Women." Walt Whitman Review, 17 (1971), 62-63.

394 _____, ed. with Introduction and Notes. The Early Poems and the Fiction, in Collected Writings. New York: New York University Press, 1963.

395 BREDVOLD, L. I. "Walt Whitman." Dial, 53 (November 1, 1912), 323-325.

396 BRENNAN, Joseph Gerard. "Delius and Whitman." Walt Whitman Review, 18 (1972), 90-96.

397 BRENNER, George A. "Whitman and You." Nassau Review, 1 (Spring, 1965), 84-98.

398 BRENNER, Rica. Twelve American Poets Before 1900. New York: Harcourt, Brace, 1933. Reprinted, Freeport, N.Y.: Books for Libraries Press, 1968.

399 BRESLIN, James E. "William Carlos Williams and the Whitman Tradition," in Damon, Phillip, ed., Literary Criticism and Historical Understanding. Selected papers from the English Institute, 1965. New York: Columbia University Press, 1966. Pp. 151-179.

400 _____. "The Poetry of Celebration: William Carlos Williams and Walt Whitman." Ph.D. diss., Minnesota, 1966. DA, 28 (1967), 224A.

401 _____. "Whitman and the Early Development of William Carlos Williams." PMLA, 82 (1967), 613-621. Williams from 1902 to 1914.

402 BREWER, Frances J., ed. Walt Whitman: A Selection
     of the Manuscripts, Books, and Associated Items
     Gathered by Charles E. Feinberg. Detroit: Wayne
     State University Press, 1955.

403 BRIDGES, William E., ed. Spokesmen for the Self:
     Emerson, Thoreau, and Whitman. Scranton, Pa.:
     Chandler, 1971. Whitman, pp. 151-208. Quotations,
     excerpts, passages from the works of the authors.

404 BRIDGMAN, Richard. "Whitman's Calendar Leaves."
     College English, 25 (March, 1964), 420-425.

405 _____, ed. with Introduction. Leaves of Grass:
     First Edition. San Francisco: Chandler, 1968.
     Chandler Facsimile edition.

406 BRIEN, Dolores Elise. "A Study of the Poetry of
     Robert Creeley and Robert Duncan in Relation to the
     Emerson-Whitman Tradition." Ph.D. diss., Brown,
     1969. DA, 35 (1975), 5388A-5389A.

407 _____. "Robert Duncan: A Poet in the Emerson-
     Whitman Tradition." Centennial Review, 19 (1975),
     308-316.

408 BRIGGS, Arthur E. Walt Whitman--Thinker and Artist.
     New York: Philosophical Library, 1952.

409 BRINTON, Daniel G., and Horace L. Traubel. "A
     Visit to West Hills." Walt Whitman Fellowship
     Papers, 10 (December, 1894), 62.

410 BRISTOL, James. "Literary Criticism in Specimen
     Days." Walt Whitman Review, 12 (1966), 16-19.

411 BRODERICK, John C. "An Unpublished Whitman Letter
     and Other Manuscripts." American Literature, 37
     (January, 1966), 475-478. Prints letter of 1867.

412 _____. "Whitman's Earliest Known Notebook: A
     Clarification." PMLA, 84 (1969), 1657.

413 _____. "The Greatest Whitman Collector and the
     Greatest Whitman Collection." Quarterly Journal of
     the Library of Congress, 27 (1970), 109-128. Il-
     lustrated.

414 _____. "Walt Whitman's Earliest Letter." Quarterly
      Journal of the Library of Congress, 30 (1973), 44-
      47. With biographical commentary on Whitman's as-
      sociation with Whitestone School.

415 _____, ed. Whitman the Poet: Materials for
      Study. Belmont, Calif.: Wadsworth Publish-
      ing Company, 1962. Reprints criticism.

416 BROMER, E. S. "Is Walt Whitman the Best Repre-
      sentative of America's Independent Spirit in Poetry?"
      Reformed Church Review, 16 (July, 1912), 346-366.

417 BROMWICH, David. "Suburbs and Extremities." Prose,
      8 (1974), 25-38. Emerson, Whitman, Wallace Stev-
      ens, and the American sublime.

418 BROOKS, Van Wyck. America's Coming of Age. New
      York: Huebach Publishing, 1915. "Whitman: Pre-
      cipitant," pp. 109-129. Reprinted in Brooks, Three
      Essays on Americans. New York: Dutton, 1934.
      Pp. 77-97.

419 _____. "A Lost Prophet." Freeman, 1 (March 24,
      1920), 46-47.

420 _____. "A French View of Whitman." Freeman,
      1 (March 31, 1920), 68-69.

421 _____. "The Influence of Whitman," in Brooks,
      Sketches in Criticism. New York: Dutton, 1932.
      Pp. 178-183.

422 _____. "Whitman: Sixty Years After," in Sketches
      (1932), pp. 184-189.

423 _____. "Walt Whitman's Youth," in The Times of
      Melville and Whitman. New York: Dutton, 1947.
      Pp. 122-141. Everyman's Library edition, pp. 125-
      144.

424 _____. "Whitman: Leaves of Grass," in Brooks,
      The Times (1947), pp. 176-191. Everyman's Library
      edition, pp. 180-196.

425 _____. "Washington: Lincoln and Whitman," in
      Brooks, The Times (1947), pp. 217-233. Everyman's
      Library edition, pp. 233-240.

426 _____ . "After the Civil War, " in Brooks, The
Times (1947), pp. 234-257. Everyman's Library
edition, pp. 241-265.

427 _____ . "Farm and Country, " in Brooks, The Times
(1947), pp. 429-447. Everyman's Library edition,
pp. 440-458.

428 BROPHY, John. "The Walt Whitman Legend. " John
O'London's Weekly, 40 (July 15, 1938), 12.

429 BROWN, Bahngrell W. "T. Sterry Hunt, the Man
Who Brought Walt Whitman to Canada. " Southern
Quarterly, 10 (1971), 43-48.

430 BROWN, Calvin S. "The Musical Development of Symbols: Whitman, " in Brown, Music and Literature.
Athens: University of Georgia Press, 1948. Pp.
178-194. Reprinted in Feidelson, Charles, and Paul
Brodtkorb, eds., Interpretations of American Literature. New York: Oxford University Press, 1959.
Pp. 186-196.

431 BROWN, Charles H. "Young Editor Whitman: An In-
dividualist in Journalism. " Journalism Quarterly,
27 (Spring, 1950), 141-148.

432 _____ , and Joseph Jay Rubin, eds. Walt Whitman of
the New York Aurora. State College, Pa.: Bald
Eagle Press, 1950.

433 BROWN, Clarence A. "Walt Whitman and Lincoln. "
Journal of Illinois State Historical Society, 47 (Summer, 1954), 176-184.

434 _____ . "Walt Whitman and the 'New Poetry.' "
American Literature, 33 (March, 1961), 33-45.

435 BROWN, H. D. "Whitman and the American of Today. "
Conservator, 28 (August, 1917), 86-88.

436 BROWNE, Ray B., and Donald Pizer, eds. Themes and
Directions in American Literature: Essays in Honor of
Leon Howard. West Lafayette, Indiana: Purdue Re-
search Foundation, 1969.

437 BRUCCOLI, Mathew J., ed. The Chief Glory of Every

People: Essays on Classic American Writers. Car-
bondale: Southern Illinois University Press, 1973.
"Walt Whitman's Omnisexual Vision, " by James E.
Miller, pp. 231-262.

438 BRUÈRE, R. W. "Walt Whitman." Reader, 5 (March,
     1905), 490-494.

439 BRUMLEVE, Sister Barbara A., S.S., N.D. "Whit-
     man and Stevens: From an Organic to a Process
     Metaphor. " Ph.D. diss., St. Louis, 1969. DA,
     30 (1970), 3450A-3451A.

440 BRUNNER, Edward. "'Your Hands, Whitman, in My
     Hands Are Deeds': Poems of Love in The Bridge."
     Iowa Review, 4 (1973), 105-126. Refers to poem by
     Hart Crane.

441 BRUNO, Giordano (1548-1600, burned at the stake).
     Cause, Principle, and Unity, trans. from German
     by Jack Lindsay. London: International Publishers,
     1962; New York, 1964. Whitman similar in panthe-
     istic doctrine; see article by Lowenfels (1963).

442 BRYANT, Arthur. "Emerson and Whitman, " in Bryant,
     ed., American Ideal. Boston: Allan Press, 1934.
     Pp. 106-138.

443 BUCHANAN, Robert W. "Walt Whitman, " in David
     Gray and Other Essays, Chiefly on Poetry. London:
     Sampson Low, Son, and Marston, 1868. Pp. 203-
     220.

444 _____. "The American Socrates, " in A Look Round
     Literature. London: Ward and Downey, 1887. Pp.
     341-346.

445 BUCK, Philo Melvin. "Vociferous Faith: Walt Whit-
     man, " in The World's Great Age. New York: Mac-
     millan, 1936. Pp. 113-141.

446 BUCKE, Richard Maurice, M.D. Man's Moral Nature:
     An Essay. New York: G. P. Putnam's Sons, 1879.
     Whitman not discussed by name, but the poet's posi-
     tion in the moral order is unequivocal; book is dedi-
     cated to Whitman. See articles by Lozynsky (1975,
     1977).

447 _____. Walt Whitman. Philadelphia: David McKay, 1883. Appendix with The Good Gray Poet, by William Douglas O'Connor (1866 pamphlet). Introduction by William Douglas O'Connor. Edited by Edward Dowden and published in Glasgow: Wilson and McCormick, 1884.

448 _____. Catalogue to the Exposition, June 10-14, 1963. Toronto: University of Toronto Press, 1963. 23 page pamphlet of Maurice Bucke Collection of Whitman.

449 _____. Autograph Revision of the Analysis of Leaves of Grass, first printed in Dr. Richard Maurice Bucke's Walt Whitman (1883). New York: New York University Press, 1974. Contents include: Anderson, Quentin, "Introductory Essay"; Kinnell, Galway, "Whitman's Indicative Words"; and Railton, Stephen, ed., "Textual Notes" with 35 facsimile pages of manuscript.

450 _____, ed. Calamus. Boston: L. Maynard, 1897. Collection of Whitman letters to Peter Doyle, 1868-1880.

451 _____, ed. The Wound Dresser: A Series of Letters Written from the Hospitals in Washington During the War of the Rebellion. Boston: Small, Maynard, 1898. Reprinted, New York: Bodley Press, 1949. Letters addressed to Whitman's mother.

452 _____, ed. Notes and Fragments. London and Ontario: Private circulation, 1899.

453 _____, ed. Cosmic Consciousness: A Study in the Evolution of the Human Mind. Philadelphia: Innes, 1901. Reprinted, New York: Dutton, 1923.

454 _____, Thomas B. Harned, and Horace L. Traubel, eds. The Complete Writings of Walt Whitman, 10 vols. New York and London: Putnam's, 1902. Considered the "Standard" Whitman until superseded by Blodgett, Harold W., and Sculley Bradley, eds., The Collected Writings of Walt Whitman, projected 18 vols. New York: New York University Press, 1965-1980's.

455   BUCKINGHAM, Willis J. "Whitman and Dickinson."
      Review of Current Scholarship in American Literary
      Scholarship, 1977. Pp. 65-76.

456   BUELL, Lawrence. "Transcendentalist Catalogue Rhet-
      oric: Vision Versus Form." American Literature,
      40 (1968), 325-339.

457   _____. "Transcendental Egoism in Very and Whit-
      man," in Buell, Literary Transcendentalism: Style
      and Vision in the American Renaissance. Ithaca,
      N.Y.: Cornell University Press, 1973. Pp. 312-
      330.

458   BUGLIARI, Jeanne. "Whitman and Wordsworth: The
      Janus of Nineteenth-Century Idealism." Walt Whit-
      man Review, 19 (1973), 63-67.

459   BUITENHUIS, Peter. "Commentary." Canadian Asso-
      ciation of American Studies, Bulletin, No. 2 (1967),
      19-25. Refers to article by Roger Seamon (1967).

460   BULLETT, Gerald W. Walt Whitman: A Study and a
      Selection. London: Grant Richards, 1924; Philadel-
      phia: Lippincott, 1925.

461   _____. "Walt Whitman," in Brown, A. B., ed.,
      Great Democrats. New York: Nicholson, 1934.
      Pp. 651-662.

462   BUNGE, Nancy Liddell. "Walt Whitman's Influence on
      Hamlin Garland." Walt Whitman Review 23 (1977),
      45-50.

463   BURBANK, R., and John B. Moore, eds. The Litera-
      ture of the American Renaissance. Columbus: Ohio
      State University Press, 1969.

464   BURGESS, Charles E. "Masters and Whitman: A
      Second Look." Walt Whitman Review, 17 (1971),
      25-27.

465   BURGESS, Janna. "Walt Whitman and Elias Hicks."
      Friends' Intelligencer, 101 (1944), 54-55.

466   BURKE, Charles B. "The Open Road, or the Highway

of the Spirit: An Inquiry into Walt Whitman's Ab-
solute Selfhood. " Ph. D. diss. , Cornell, 1901.

467 BURKE, Kenneth. "Acceptance and Rejection. " Southern
Review, 2 (Winter, 1937), 600-632.

468 _____ . "Policy Made Personal: Whitman's Verse
and Prose Salient Traits, " in Hindus, M. , ed. ,
Leaves of Grass: One Hundred Years Later (1955),
pp. 74-108. Discusses Democratic Vistas and Leaves
of Grass.

469 _____ . "Towards Looking Back. " Journal of General Education, 28 (1976), 167-189.

470 BURROUGHS, John. Notes on Walt Whitman as Poet
and Person. New York: American News Company,
1867. Revised edition, New York: Redfield, 1871.
Reprinted, New York: Haskell House, 1971.

471 _____ . Whitman: A Study. Boston: Houghton Mif-
flin, 1896. Volume 10 of the Riverside Edition of
Burroughs' Works. Reprinted, St. Clair Shores,
Mich.: Scholarly Press, 1970.

472 _____ . Birds and Poets. Boston: Houghton Mifflin, 1905. Volume 3 of Works of John Burroughs.
"The Flight of the Eagle: To Walt Whitman, " pp.
207-263.

473 _____ . Field and Study. Boston: Houghton Mifflin,
1919. "Literature, " pp. 221-240.

474 _____ . Accepting the Universe. Boston: Houghton
Mifflin, 1920. "Poet of the Cosmos, " pp. 316-328.

475 _____ . "Leaves of Grass, " in Wann, L. , ed. ,
Century Readings in the English Essays. New York:
Appleton-Century, 1926.

476 _____ . "Walt Whitman, " in Clark, Barrett Harper,
ed. , Great Short Biographies of the World. New
York: McBride, 1928. Pp. 1329-1355.

477 _____ . "Boston Criticism of Whitman, " in Langer,
Susanne K. , ed. , Reflections on Art. Baltimore:
Johns Hopkins Press, 1958. Pp. 229-233.

478   BURTON, Richard.   Literary Leaders of America.
      New York: Scribner's, 1904. Whitman, pp. 264-295.

479   BUSH, Oakleigh R. , ed.   Over the Carnage Rose Pro-
      phetic a Voice: The American Civil War in Prose
      and Verse. Bossum, Netherlands: Paul Brand,
      1965. Includes selections by Whitman and Melville.

480   BUTLER, Eugene Sanders. "When Lilacs Last in the
      Dooryard Bloom'd, " a choral composition. Ph. D.
      diss. , Missouri (Kansas City), 1974. DA, 34 (1974),
      3034A.

481   BUTSCHER, Edward. "Whitman's Attitudes Toward
      Death: The Essential Paradox. " Walt Whitman Re-
      view, 17 (1971), 16-19.

482   BYCHOWSKI, Gustav. "Walt Whitman--A Study in Sub-
      limation, " in Roheim, Géza, ed. , Psychoanalysis and
      the Social Sciences, Vol. III. New York: Interna-
      tional University Press, 1951. Pp. 223-261.

483   BYNNER, Witter, ed. with a Note. "A Hitherto Unpub-
      lished Walt Whitman Letter. " Laughing Horse, 1
      (July, 1923), no page.

484   BYRON, John E. "Significance of T, I, and O in 'Cross-
      ing Brooklyn Ferry.'" Walt Whitman Review, 9
      (1963), 89-90.

485   C. , C. C. "Theosophy in Secular Literature--Walt
      Whitman. " Theosophical Quarterly, 8 (July, 1910),
      28-44.

486   CAHOON, Herbert, Thomas V. Lange, and Charles
      Ryskamp, eds. American Literary Autographs:
      From Washington Irving to Henry James. New York:
      Dover, 1977. Whitman, pp. 52-54.

487   CAIRD, Edward. Essays on Literature (1892). Reprinted,
      Port Washington, N. Y.: Kennikat Press, 1968.

488   CAIRNS, William B. A History of American Literature.
      New York and London: Oxford University Press,
      1912. Whitman, pp. 386-395 et passim.

489 _____. "Walt Whitman." Yale Review, 8 (July, 1919), 734-754.

490 _____. "Swinburne's Opinion of Whitman." American Literature, 3 (May, 1931), 125-136.

491 CALAMUS: An International Whitman Quarterly. Tokyo, Japan. Founded 1969 by Professor William Luther Moore, editor. Published in English by the International Christian University, Tokyo.

492 CALDER, Ellen M. (Mrs. William D. O'Connor). "William D. O'Connor and Walt Whitman." Conservator, 17 (May, 1906), 42.

493 _____. "Personal Recollections of Walt Whitman." Atlantic, 99 (June, 1907), 825-834.

494 CALL, William Timothy. A Plea for Shakespeare and Whitman: Some Findings for Persons Who Like to Do Their Own Thinking. Brooklyn, N.Y.: Privately printed by the author, 1914.

495 CALLOW, James T., and Robert J. Reilly. Guide to American Literature from its Beginnings Through Walt Whitman. New York: Barnes and Noble, 1976. Contains long bibliography.

496 CAMBON, G. "Space, Experiment, and Prophecy," in Cambon, The Inclusive Flame. Bloomington: Indiana University Press, 1963.

497 CAMERON, Kenneth Walter. "Three Ungathered Whitman Manuscripts." Emerson Society Quarterly, 1 (1955), 8-9.

498 _____. "Emerson's Recommendation of Whitman in 1863." Emerson Society Quarterly, 3 (1956), 14-20.

499 _____. "Rough Draft of Whitman's 'By Emerson's Grave.'" Emerson Society Quarterly, 13 (1958), 32-34.

500 _____. "Redpath Writes Whitman on the Transcendentalists." Emerson Society Quarterly, 29 (1962), 21-26.

501 CAMILLUCCI, Marcella. "Walt Whitman." Idea, 8 (February 12, 1956), 1.

502   CAMPBELL, Killis. "Miscellaneous Notes on Whit-
      man. " University of Texas Studies in English, 14
      (1934), 116-122.

503   _____ . "The Evolution of Whitman as Artist. "
      American Literature, 6 (November, 1934), 254-263.

504   CANBY, Henry Seidel. "Walt Whitman, " in American
      Estimates. New York: Harcourt, Brace, 1929.

505   _____ . "Walt Whitman, " in Classic Americans: A
      Study of Eminent American Writers from Irving to
      Whitman. New York: Harcourt, Brace, 1931. Re-
      printed, New York: Russell and Russell, 1939. Pp.
      308-351.

506   _____ . "From Books to Men, " in American Memoir.
      New York: Houghton Mifflin, 1947. Pp. 401-408.

507   _____ . Walt Whitman, An American: A Study in
      Biography. Boston: Houghton Mifflin, 1943. Re-
      printed, Westport, Conn.: Greenwood Press, 1970.

508   _____ . "Who Speaks for New World Democracy? "
      Saturday Review of Literature, 26 (January 16, 1943),
      3-4, 16-18. Reprinted in Memoria del tercer Con-
      greso ... de Lit Iberoamer. 1944. Pp. 195-203.

509   CANNON, Agnes Dicken. "Fervid Atmosphere and
      Typical Events: Autobiography in Drum-Taps. "
      Walt Whitman Review, 20 (1974), 79-96.

510   CANTONI, Louis J. "Walt Whitman, Secular Mystic. "
      Personalist, 36 (August, 1955), 379-384.

511   CAPEK, Abe. "Walt Whitman: A Centennial Re-Eval-
      uation. " Philologica Pragensia, 7 (November, 1955),
      30-45.

512   _____ . "The Evolution of Whitman's 'A Song for
      Occupations.' " Casopis pro Moderni Filologii, 41
      (1959), 29-34.

513   _____ . "Whitman: A Re-evaluation. " American
      Dialogue, 5 (1969), 13-15.

514   _____ , ed. with Introduction. Walt Whitman: Poetry

and Prose. East Berlin: The Seven Seas Publisher,
1958.

515   CAREY, Richard. "Pope and Whitman and God. "
       Walt Whitman Review, 14 (1968), 159-168.

516   CARGILL, Oscar. Intellectual America: Ideas on the
       March. New York: Macmillan, 1941. Whitman,
       passim.

517   . "Walt Whitman and Civil Rights, " in Schulz,
       Max F. , ed. , Essays in American and English Lit-
       erature Presented to Bruce Robert McElderry, Jr.
       Athens: Ohio University Press, 1967. Pp. 48-58.

518   . "Gay Wilson Allen, A Tribute, " in Miller,
       Edwin H. , ed. , The Artistic Legacy (1970), pp. 1-7.

519   CARLILE, Robert Emerson. "Leitmotif and Whitman's
       'When Lilacs Last in the Dooryard Bloom'd. ' " Crit-
       icism, 13 (1971), 329-339.

519a   CARLISLE, Ervin Frederick. "Leaves of Grass: Whit-
       man's Epic Drama of the Soul and I. " Ph. D. diss. ,
       Indiana, 1963. DA, 24 (1964), 3727-3728.

520   . "Walt Whitman: The Drama of Identity. "
       Criticism, 10 (1968), 259-276.

521   . The Uncertain Self: Whitman's Drama of
       Identity. East Lansing, Mich.: State University
       Press, 1973.

522   CARLSON, Eric W. "Whitman's 'Song of Myself, '
       lines 59-65. " Explicator, 18 (November, 1959), item
       13.

523   CARPENTER, Edward. Days with Walt Whitman. Lon-
       don: George Allen, 1906; New York: Macmillan,
       1906.

524   . Some Friends of Walt Whitman: A Study in
       Sex-Psychology. London: George Allen, 1924; New
       York: Atheneum Press, 1924.

525   CARPENTER, Frederic I. Emerson and Asia. Cam-
       bridge, Mass.: Harvard University Press, 1930.
       Whitman, passim.

526 _____. "Whitman's 'Eidolon.'" College English, 3
      (March, 1942), 534-545. Reprinted in Carpenter,
      F. I., American Literature and the Dream. New
      York: Philosophical Library, 1955. Pp. 40-50.

527 CARPENTER, George Rice. Walt Whitman. New York:
      Macmillan, 1909. Reprinted, New York: Haskell
      House, 1967.

528 CARR, Harry L. "The Comparison of Poetry and Paint-
      ing: Whitman's 'Out of the Cradle Endlessly Rocking'
      and Some Paintings of Albert Pinkham Ryder." Ph. D.
      diss., Southern California, 1958. DA, 20 (1959),
      665-666.

529 CARTER, Ann Rutherford. "Songs for the Body Elec-
      tric: A Model for the Poetic Imagination in Emer-
      son, Whitman, and Hart Crane." Ph. D. diss., Case
      Western Reserve, 1978. DA, 39 (1978), 1562A-1563A.

530 CARTER, Everett. The American Idea: The Literary
      Response to American Optimism. Chapel Hill: Uni-
      versity of North Carolina Press, 1977. Whitman,
      pp. 109-133.

531 CARTER, Stephen Leroy. "From the 'Sacred Selfe' to
      the 'Separate Self': A Study of the Mystical Elements
      in Five American Poets Prior to 1900." Ph. D. diss.,
      Texas Tech, 1977. DA, 38 (1978), 4923A. Studies
      Edward Taylor, Edgar Allan Poe, Emerson, Walt
      Whitman, and Emily Dickinson.

532 CARTER, Steve. "The Metaphor of Assimilation and
      'Rise O Days from Your Fathomless Deep.'" Walt
      Whitman Review, 24 (1978), 155-161.

533 CARY, Norman Reed. Christian Criticism in the
      Twentieth Century. Port Washington, N. Y.: Kenni-
      kat Press, 1975. Whitman, passim.

534 CASSERES, Benjamin de. "Enter Walt Whitman."
      Philistine, 25 (November, 1907), 161-172.

535 _____. "Walt Whitman," in Forty Immortals. New
      York: Lawren Publisher, 1926. Pp. 223-232.

536 CATEL, Jean. Walt Whitman: La Naissance du Poète.
      Paris: Les Editions Rieder, 1929.

537 _____. Rythme et langage dans la Première Edition des "Leaves of Grass" (1855). Paris: Les Editions Rieder, 1930.

538 _____. "Whitman's Symbolism, " trans. by Roger Asselineau, in Allen, Gay Wilson, ed., Walt Whitman Abroad (1955), pp. 76-87.

539 _____. "Rythmn and Language in the First Edition of Leaves of Grass," trans. by Roger Asselineau, in Allen, ed., Walt Whitman Abroad (1955), pp. 88-89.

540 _____, ed. with Notes. The Eighteenth Presidency: Voice of Walt Whitman to Each Young Man in the Nation, North, South, East and West. Montpellier, France: Causse, Graille, and Castelnau, 1928. 31 pages not published in Whitman's lifetime. Also printed in Furness, ed., Walt Whitman's Workshop (1928), pp. 85-113. Most recent edition by Grier and Feinburg (1956).

541 CAULDWELL, William. "Walt Whitman as a Young Man." New York Times, January 26, 1901. Reprinted in the Conservator, 20 (July, 1901), 76.

542 CAVITCH, David. "Whitman's Mystery." Studies in Romanticism, 17 (1978), 105-128.

543 CESTRÉ, Charles. "Walt Whitman, Poet of Self." University of California Chronicle, 25 (July, 1923), 318-343.

544 _____. "L'évolution de Walt Whitman." Les Langues Modernes, 51 (February, 1957), 158-160.

545 CHACE, F. M. "A Note on Whitman's Mockingbird." Modern Language Notes, 61 (February, 1946), 93-94.

546 CHADBOURN, Charles C., Jr. "A Note on the Publication of The Good Gray Poet." Books at Brown, 15 (June, 1953), 1-4.

547 CHAFFIN, J. Thomas, Jr. "'Give Me Faces and Streets': Walt Whitman and the City." Walt Whitman Review, 23 (1977), 109-120.

548 CHALFIN, Norma Jean. "Walt Whitman's Philosophy

of History." Ph. D. diss., Southern California, 1975. DA, 36 (1975), 3708A-3709A.

549 CHAMBERLIN, Joseph Edgar. "Walt Whitman," in Waxman, S. M., ed., Nomads and Listeners. New York: Privately printed by the author, 1937. Pp. 118-144.

550 CHANOVER, E. Pierre. "Walt Whitman: A Psychological and Psychoanalytic Bibliography." The Psychoanalytic Review, 59 (1972), 467-474.

551 CHAPMAN, J. A. Papers on Shelley, Wordsworth, and Others. London: Oxford University Press, 1929. Whitman, pp. 115-127.

552 CHAPMAN, John Jay. "Walt Whitman." Chap-Book, 7 (July 15, 1897), 156-159.

553 _____. "Whitman," in Emerson and Other Essays. New York: Scribner's, 1898. Reissued, 1909. Pp. 111-128.

554 _____. "Walt Whitman," in Barzun, Jacques, ed., Selected Writings of John Jay Chapman. New York: Farrar, Straus, and Cudahy, 1959. Pp. 157-164.

555 CHAPNICK, Howard, ed. The Illustrated Leaves of Grass. Introduction by William Carlos Williams. New York: Grosset and Dunlap, 1976.

556 CHARI, V. K. "Americanism Reviewed (1954)," in Allen, Gay Wilson, ed., Walt Whitman Abroad (1955), pp. 261-265.

557 _____. "Whitman and Indian Thought." Western Humanities Review, 13 (Summer, 1959), 291-302.

558 _____. "A Critical Approach to Whitman." Walt Whitman Review, 6 (1960), 54-56.

559 _____. "Structure and Poetic Growth in Leaves of Grass." Walt Whitman Review, 9 (September, 1963), 58-63.

560 _____. Whitman in the Light of Vedantic Mysticism: An Interpretation. Foreword by Gay Wilson Allen. Lincoln: University of Nebraska Press, 1964.

561   . "Whitman and the Best Poets." Emerson
     Society Quarterly, 39 (1965), 34-37.

562   . "Poe and Whitman's Short Poem Style."
     Walt Whitman Review, 13 (1967), 95-97.

563   . "The Limits of Whitman's Symbolism."
     Journal of American Speech, 5 (1971), 173-184.

564   . "Structure of Whitman's Catalogue Poems."
     Walt Whitman Review, 18 (1972), 3-17.

565   . "Whitman and the Language of the Roman-
     tics." Etudes Anglaises, 30 (1977), 314-328.

566   . "Whitman and His Reader." Calamus, 15
     (1977), 23-33

567 CHARNWOOD, G. R. B., First Baron. "Walt Whitman
     and America," in Royal Society of Literature of the
     United Kingdom, London, Vol. I (1920), pp. 103-123.

568 CHASE, Richard V. "Walt Whitman as American
     Spokesman." Commentary, 19 (March, 1955), 260-
     265. Reprinted in Pearce, ed., Walt Whitman: A
     Collection (1962), pp. 155-162.

569   . "Go-Befores and Embryons: A Biographical
     Reprise," in Hindus, ed., Leaves of Grass: One
     Hundred Years After (1955), pp. 32-54.

570   . Walt Whitman Reconsidered. New York:
     William Sloane Associates, 1955.

571   . The Democratic Vista. New York: Double-
     day, 1958. "Comedians All," pp. 104-115. Similar
     to "Walt Whitman as American Spokesman."

572   . "'Ones Self I Sing,'" excerpt from Walt
     Whitman Reconsidered, in Rahv, Philip, ed., Lit-
     erature in America: An Anthology of Literary Crit-
     icism. New York: Meridian, 1957. Pp. 150-167.
     Also in Feidelson, Charles, and Paul Brodtkorb,
     eds., Interpretations of American Literature. New
     York: Oxford University Press, 1959. Pp. 176-185.

573   . Walt Whitman. Minneapolis: University of

Minnesota Press, 1961. University of Minnesota
Pamphlets on American Writers, No. 9.

574 _____. "Walt Whitman Reconsidered, " in Murphy,
Francis, ed., Walt Whitman: A Critical Anthology
(1962), pp. 331-348.

575 _____. "'Out of the Cradle' as a Romance, " in
Lewis, R. W. B., ed., The Presence of Walt Whitman (1962), pp. 52-71.

576 _____. "Walt Whitman, " in Paul, Sherman, ed.,
Six Classic American Writers. Minneapolis: University of Minnesota Press, 1970. Pp. 195-232.

577 _____, ed. with Introduction. Specimen Days. New
York: New American Library, 1961.

578 CHATMAN, Vernon V., III. "Figures of Repetition in
Whitman's 'Songs at Parting.'" Bulletin of New
York Public Library, 69 (February, 1965), 77-82.

579 CHENEY, John Vance. That Dome in Air. Chicago:
McClurg, 1895.

580 CHERRY, Charles L. "Whitman and Language: An
Instance of Semantic Paradox." Walt Whitman Review, 14 (1968), 56-58.

581 CHESIN, Martin F. "The Genesis of the 1855 Leaves
of Grass." Ph.D. diss., Pittsburgh, 1974. DA,
34 (1974), 6632A-6633A.

582 _____. "The Organic Metaphor and the Unity of the
First Edition of Leaves of Grass." Calamus, 15
(1977), 34-50.

583 CHESNICK, Eugene W. "The Amplitude of Time: A
Study of the Time Sense of Walt Whitman." Ph.D.
diss., Washington, 1968. DA, 29 (1969), 3969A-
3970A.

584 _____. "Walt Whitman and the Poetry of the Tril-
lions." Walt Whitman Review, 22 (1976), 14-22.

585 CHESTERTON, Gilbert Keith. "Conventions and the
Hero, " in Collins, D., ed., Lunacy and Letters.
New York: Sheed and Ward, 1958.

586   CHIELENS, Edward E.   "Whitman's Specimen Days and
      the Familiar Essay Genre."   Genre, 8 (1975), 366-
      378.

587   CHITTICK, V. L. O.   "A Footnote to Tales of the
      Sea."   Dalhousie Review, 36 (August, 1956), 275-278.
      Relates to Melville and "Song of Myself."

588   CHRIST, Ronald.   "Walt Whitman: Image and Credo."
      American Quarterly, 17 (Spring, 1965), 92-103.
      Refers to "To a Locomotive in Winter."

589   CHRISTMAN, Henry M., ed.   Walt Whitman's New
      York: From Manhattan to Montauk.   New York:
      Macmillan, 1963.   Collection of Whitman's articles
      published in the Brooklyn Standard, 1861-1862; same
      papers in Holloway, Emory, ed., The Uncollected
      Poetry and Prose of Walt Whitman, Vol. II, 1921.

590   CHUBB, E. W.   "Mr. Thayer Visits Walt Whitman,"
      in Stories of Authors.   New York: Macmillan, 1926.
      Pp. 385-392.

591   CHUKOVSKY, Kornei I.   "What Walt Whitman Means
      to Me."   American Dialog, 5 (1969), 24-26.

592   CHUPACK, Henry.   "Walt Whitman in Camden: The
      Formation of a Literary Circle and the Growth of
      a Poet's Reputation."   Ph.D. diss., New York Uni-
      versity, 1952.

593   _____.   "Walt Whitman and the Camden Circle."
      Proceedings of the New Jersey Historical Society,
      73 (October, 1955), 274-299.

594   CIARDI, John.   "Poet's Progeny?"   Saturday Review,
      43 (June 25, 1960), 35-36.

595   CLARK, George Peirce.   "Solitude: An Early Whitman
      Imitation."   Harvard Library Bulletin, 8 (Spring,
      1954), 213-223.

596   _____.   "'Saerasmid': An Early Promoter of Walt
      Whitman."   American Literature, 27 (May, 1955),
      259-262.

597   CLARK, Grace Delano.   "Walt Whitman in Germany."

Texas Review (Austin), 6 (January, 1921), 123-
137.

598   CLARK, H. A. "The Awakening of the Soul: Whitman
      and Maeterlinck. " Conservator, 11 (June, 1900), 56-
      58.

599   CLARK, Harry Hayden, ed. Major American Poets:
      An Anthology. New York: American Book Company,
      1936. Whitman, pp. 651-732; bibliography, pp. 914-
      919.

600   _____, and Gay Wilson Allen, eds. Literary Crit-
      icism: From Pope to Croce. Detroit: Wayne State
      University Press, 1962. Whitman, pp. 394-412.

601   CLARK, Leadie Mae. "Walt Whitman's Concept of the
      American Common Man. " Ph.D. diss., Illinois
      (Urbana), 1952.

602   _____. Walt Whitman and the American Common
      Man. New York: Philosophical Library, 1955.

603   CLARKE, Katie. "Poets, Orators, Singers: Come. "
      Calamus, 2 (1970), 24-33.

604   CLARKE, William. Walt Whitman. London: Swan
      Sonnenschein; New York: Macmillan, 1892. Re-
      printed, New York: Haskell House, 1970.

605   CLAUDEL, Alice Moser, ed. "Poems as Laurels for
      Walt Whitman. " Walt Whitman Review, 16 (1970),
      81-86. Collection of poems to Whitman.

606   CLIFFORD, William Kingdom. Lectures and Essays,
      2 vols. Ed. by Leslie Stephen and Sir Frederick
      Pollock. London and New York: Macmillan, 1879.
      "Cosmic Emotion, " Vol. II, pp. 252-285.

607   CLUTTON-BROCK, A. "Walt Whitman, " in More Es-
      says on Books. New York: Methuen, 1921.

608   COAD, Oral. S. "A Walt Whitman Manuscript. " Jour-
      nal of the Rutgers University Library, 2 (December,
      1938), 6-10.

609   _____. "Whitman vs Parton. " Journal of the Rut-

gers University Library, 4 (December, 1940), 1-8.

610 _____. "A Whitman Letter." Journal of the Rutgers University Library, 6 (December, 1942), 29.

611 _____. "Whitman as Parent." Journal of the Rutgers University Library, 7 (December, 1943), 31-32.

612 _____. "Seven Whitman Letters." Journal of the Rutgers University Library, 8 (December, 1944), 18-26. To William Sloane Kennedy.

613 COALE, Samuel. "Whitman's War: The March of a Poet." Walt Whitman Review, 21 (1975), 85-101.

614 COBB, Robert Paul. "Society versus Solitude: Studies in Ralph Waldo Emerson, Thoreau, Hawthorne, and Whitman." Ph. D. diss., Michigan, 1955.

615 _____. "Whitman as Hospital Visitor." Emerson Society Quarterly, 22 (1961), 3-5.

616 COBERLY, James H. "Whitman's Children of Adam Poems." Emerson Society Quarterly, 22 (1961), 5-8.

617 COFFEEN, Robert G. "Naming Techniques in Whitman's Leaves of Grass: A Study in Problems of Power." Ph. D. diss., North Carolina, 1969. DA, 30 (1970), 3903A.

618 COFFMAN, Stanley K., Jr. "Whitman's 'Song of the Broad Axe,' Stanza 1, Sec. 1." Explicator, 12 (April, 1954) item 39.

619 _____. "'Crossing Brooklyn Ferry': A Note on the Catalogue Technique in Whitman's Poetry." Modern Philology, 51 (May, 1954), 225-232.

620 _____. "Form and Meaning in Whitman's 'Passage to India.'" PMLA, 70 (June, 1955), 337-349.

621 _____. "The World Dimensional in the Poetry of Leaves of Grass." Emerson Society Quarterly, 22 (1961), 8-10.

622 COHEN, Benjamin Bernard. "'Song of Myself': Entice-
     ment to Faith as Knowledge." American Transcen-
     dental Quarterly, 12 (1971), 49-54.

623 _____, ed. Whitman in Our Season: A Symposium.
     Hartford, Conn.: Transcendental Books, 1971. Also
     published as special Whitman issue of American Tran-
     scendental Quarterly, 12 (1971), 4-98.

624 COHEN, Hennig, ed. The American Culture. Boston:
     Houghton Mifflin, 1968. "The Rainbow and the Grid, "
     by Alan Trachtenberg, pp. 1-17.

625 _____, ed. Landmarks of American Writing. New
     York and London: Basic Books, 1969. "Walt Whit-
     man: 'Song of Myself, '" by James E. Miller, Jr.,
     pp. 144-156.

626 COHEN, Sarah Blacher. "Walt Whitman's Literary
     Criticism." Walt Whitman Review, 18 (1972), 39-
     50.

627 COLE, John Y. "Of Copyright, Men, and a National
     Library." Quarterly Journal of the Library of Con-
     gress, 28 (1971), 114-136. Whitman letter.

628 COLEMAN, Philip Y. "Walt Whitman's Ambiguities of
     'I, '" in Partlow, Robert, ed., Studies in American
     Literature. Edwardsville: Southern Illinois Univer-
     sity, 1969. Pp. 40-59. Published by Papers on
     Language and Literature, 5 supplement, Summer,
     1969.

629 COLEMAN, Rufus A. "Trowbridge and Whitman."
     PMLA, 63 (March, 1948), 262-273.

630 _____. "Further Reminiscences of Walt Whitman."
     Modern Language Notes, 63 (April, 1948), 266-268.

631 _____. "Trowbridge and O'Connor: Unpublished
     Correspondence with Special Reference to Walt Whit-
     man." American Literature, 23 (November, 1951),
     323-331.

632 COLLINS, Christopher. "The Use of Observation: A
     Study of Correspondential Vision in the Writings of
     Emerson, Thoreau, and Whitman." Ph.D. diss.,
     Columbia, 1964. DA, 26 (1965), 352.

633 _____. "Whitman's Open Road and Where It Led."
Nassau Review, 1 (Spring, 1965), 101-110.

634 COLUM, Mary G. M. "Outside Literatures in English:
the Irish and the American," in Colum, From These
Roots. New York: Scribner's, 1937. Pp. 260-311.

635 COLUM, Padraic. "Poetry of Walt Whitman." New
Republic, 19 (June 14, 1919), 213-215.

636 CONGDON, Kirby. "Whitman's Vision." American
Dialogue, 5 (1969), 34-35.

637 CONNER, Frederick William. Cosmic Optimism: A
Study of the Interpretation of Evolution by American
Poets from Emerson to Robinson. Gainesville: Uni-
versity of Florida Press, 1949. "Whitman: High
Tide," pp. 92-127.

638 CONWAY, Moncure Daniel. "Walt Whitman." The
Fortnightly Review, 6 (October 15, 1866), 538-548.

639 _____. Autobiography. Boston: Houghton Mifflin,
1905. Whitman, passim.

640 COOK, Harry James. "The Individualization of a Poet:
The Process of Becoming in Whitman's 'The Sleepers.'" Walt Whitman Review, 21 (1975), 101-110.

641 COOK, Larry W. "The New Critics' Estimate of Walt
Whitman." Walt Whitman Review, 22 (1976), 95-101.

642 COOK, Raymond A. "Emphatic Identification in 'Song
of Myself': A Key to Whitman's Poetry." Walt
Whitman Review, 10 (1964), 3-10.

643 COOKE, Alice Lovelace. "Walt Whitman's Background
in the Life and Thought of His Times." Ph.D. diss.,
Texas (Austin), 1933.

644 _____. Studies in Walt Whitman's Backgrounds.
Austin: University of Texas Press, 1933.

645 _____. "Whitman's Indebtedness to the Scientific
Thought of His Day." University of Texas Studies
in English, 14 (1934), 89-115.

55   Cooke

646 _____. "Whitman's Background in the Industrial
Movements of His Time." University of Texas Studies in English, 15 (1935), 76-91.

647 _____. "American First Editions at the University
of Texas (Austin)." University of Texas Library
Chronicle, 2 (June, 1936), 95-105. Whitman,
passim.

648 _____. "Notes on Whitman's Musical Background."
New England Quarterly, 19 (June, 1946), 224-235.

649 _____. "A Note on Whitman's Symbolism in 'Song
of Myself.'" Modern Language Notes, 65 (April,
1950), 228-232.

650 _____. "The Centennial of Walt Whitman's Leaves
of Grass." University of Texas Library Chronicle,
5 (Spring, 1955), 13-17.

651 _____. "Whitman as a Critic: Democratic Vistas
with Special Reference to Carlyle." Walt Whitman
Newsletter, 4 (June, 1955), 91-95.

652 COOPER, David Dale. "The Paradox of Spirit and In-
stinct: A Comparative Examination of the Psychol-
ogies of Carl G. Jung and Sigmund Freud." Ph.D.
diss., Brown, 1977. DA, 38 (1978), 7330A-7331A.
Includes "There Was a Child Went Forth."

653 CORBETT, Elizabeth. Walt: The Good Gray Poet
Speaks for Himself. New York: Frederick A.
Stokes, 1928.

654 CORMAC, Philip. "Walt Whitman's Diagnosis of Democracy." America, 94 (November 5, 1955), 157-
159.

655 CORY, Robert E. "The Prosody of Walt Whitman."
North Dakota Quarterly, 27 (Summer, 1960), 74-79.

656 COSENTINO, Vincent. "Walt Whitman's Influence on
Thomas Mann, the 'Non Political' Writer," in Goetze,
Albrecht, and Gunther Pflaum, eds., Vorgleichen
und Verandern: Festschrift für Helmut Motekat.
Munchen: Hueber, 1970. Pp. 224-242. In English.

657   COSKREN, Robert. "A Reading of Whitman's 'I Sing
       the Body Electric.'" Walt Whitman Review, 22
       (1976), 125-132.

658   COUSER, G. Thomas. "An Emerson-Whitman Parallel:
       'The American Scholar' and 'A Song for Occupations.'"
       Walt Whitman Review, 22 (1976), 115-118.

659   _____. "Of Time and Identity: Walt Whitman and
       Gertrude Stein as Autobiographers." Texas Studies
       in Literature and Language, 17 (1976), 787-804.

660   COWAN, Michael H. City of the West: Emerson,
       America, and the Urban Metaphor. New Haven:
       Yale University Press, 1967. Whitman, pp. 72,
       210, et passim.

661   COWAN, Thomas D. "Six Poets of the 19th Century:
       Images of the Common Man in a Changing Society."
       Ph.D. diss., St. Louis, 1973. DA, 34 (1974),
       5903A-5904A.

662   COWIE, Alexander. The Rise of the American Novel.
       New York: American Book Company, 1948. Whit-
       man, pp. 306-309. Comments on Franklin Evans,
       a temperance novel published by Whitman in 1842.

663   COWLEY, Malcolm. "Walt Whitman: The Miracle."
       New Republic, 114 (March 18, 1946), 385-388.

664   _____. "Walt Whitman: The Secret." New Re-
       public, 114 (April 8, 1946), 481-484.

665   _____. "Walt Whitman: The Philosopher." New
       Republic, 117 (September 29, 1947), 29-31.

666   _____. "Walt Whitman: The Poet." New Republic,
       117 (October 20, 1947), 27-30.

667   _____. "A Little Anthology: Lyrical Passages
       from Leaves of Grass, Selected with Commentary."
       New Republic, 133 (July 24, 1955), 16-21.

668   _____. "The Guru, the Beatnik, and the Good Gray
       Poet." New Republic, 141 (October 26, 1959), 17-19.

669   _____. "Walt Whitman's Buried Masterpiece."

Saturday Review, 42 (October 31, 1959), 11-13, 32-34.

670 _____. "'Song of Myself' and Indian Philosophy, " in Miller, E. H., ed., A Century of Whitman Criticism (1969), pp. 231-246.

671 _____. "Whitman: The Poet and the Mask, " in Cowley, A Many-Windowed House, ed. by Henry Dan Piper. Carbondale: Southern Illinois University Press, 1970. Pp. 35-75. Expanded version of 1948 article.

672 _____, ed. with Introduction: "Whitman: The Poet and the Mask. " The Complete Poetry and Prose of Walt Whitman. New York: Funk and Wagnalls, 1948. Introduction reprinted as an essay in Murphy, ed., Walt Whitman: A Critical Anthology (1962), pp. 347-352.

673 _____, ed. with Introduction. Walt Whitman's Leaves of Grass: The First (1855) Edition. New York: Viking Press, 1959.

674 _____, ed. with Foreword and Introduction. The Works of Walt Whitman: The Deathbed Edition, 2 vols. New York: Funk and Wagnalls, 1969. Vol. I, The Collected Poetry; Vol. II, The Collected Prose.

675 COX, James M. "Walt Whitman, Mark Twain, and the Civil War. " Sewanee Review, 69 (April-June, 1961), 185-204.

676 COY, Rebecca. "A Study of Whitman's Diction. " University of Texas Studies in English, 16 (July, 1936), 115-124.

677 COYLE, William, ed. The Poet and the President: Whitman's Lincoln Poems. New York: Odyssey Press, 1962. Contains text of four poems and reprinted criticism.

678 CRAWLEY, Thomas Edward. "The Structure of Leaves of Grass. " Ph.D. diss., North Carolina, 1965. DA, 26 (1966), 3948.

679 _____. The Structure of Leaves of Grass. Austin: University of Texas Press, 1970.

680 CREELEY, Robert, ed. with Introduction. Whitman: A Selection of Poems. Baltimore: Penguin Books, 1973.

681 CROCKER, Lionel. "The Rhetorical Influences of Henry Ward Beecher on Whitman." Quarterly Journal of Speech, 18 (February, 1932), 82-87.

682 _____. "Walt Whitman's Interest in Public Speaking." Quarterly Journal of Speech, 26 (December, 1940), 657-667.

683 CROFFUT, W. A. "Poets and Writers," in Croffut, American Procession, 1855-1914: A Personal Chronicle of Famous Men. Boston: Little, Brown, 1931. Pp. 108-113.

684 CRONIN, Frank C. "Modern Sensibility in Stanza 2 of 'Crossing Brooklyn Ferry.'" Walt Whitman Review, 15 (1969), 56-57.

685 CRONKHITE, George Ferris. "Literature as Livelihood: The Attitude of Certain American Writers Toward Literature as a Profession from 1820 to the Civil War." Ph.D. diss., Harvard, 1948.

686 _____. "Notes: Walt Whitman and the Locomotive." American Quarterly, 6 (Summer, 1954), 164-172.

687 CRONYN, G. W. "The Idealism of the Real: Claude Monet and Walt Whitman." Columbia Monthly, May 1908.

688 CROSBY, Ernest. "Walt Whitman's Children of Adam." Philistine, 23 (August, 1906), 65-68.

689 CROWLEY, John W. "Whitman and the Harvard Poets: The Case of George Cabot Lodge." Walt Whitman Review, 19 (1973), 165-168.

690 CUDDY, Lois Arlene. "Explorations of Whitman's 'Eidólons.'" Walt Whitman Review, 19 (1973), 153-157.

691 _____. "Elegy and the American Tradition: Subjective Lyrics on Life and Experience." Ph.D. diss., Brown, 1975. DA, 37 (1976), 273A-274A. Includes Whitman, Melville, and Emerson.

692 _____. "Symbolic Identification of Whitman with
      Hawthorne." American Notes and Queries, 15 (1977),
      71-72.

693 CULBERT, Gary A. "Whitman's Revisions of 'By Blue
      Ontario's Shore.'" Walt Whitman Review, 23 (1977),
      35-45.

694 CUNI, Sandra L. "Matthew Arnold and Walt Whitman:
      Objectionist and Transcendental Orientations in the
      Conflict of Self." Ph.D. diss., Pittsburgh, 1972.
      DA, 33 (1973), 4405A.

695 CUNNINGHAM, Clarence. "A Defense of Walt Whit-
      man's Leaves of Grass." Arena, 33 (January, 1905),
      55-58.

696 CURLE, Richard. Collecting American First Editions:
      Its Pitfalls and Pleasures. Indianapolis: Bobbs-
      Merrill Company, 1930. Whitman, pp. 21-22, 196-
      197, et passim.

697 CURTI, Merle Eugene. "Walt Whitman, Critic of Amer-
      ica." Sewanee Review, 36 (April, 1928), 130-138.

698 DAGGETT, Gwynne H. "Walt Whitman's Poetic Theory."
      Ph.D. diss., North Carolina, 1941.

699 DAHLBERG, Edward. Can These Bones Live? New
      York: Harcourt, Brace, 1941. Revised with a new
      Preface by Herbert Read, and reprinted, New York:
      New Directions, 1960. Whitman, pp. 143-150.

700 DAICHES, David. "Poets After Whitman." Manchester
      Guardian Weekly, 70 (April 22, 1954), 11.

701 _____. "The Philosopher," in Allen, Gay Wilson,
      Mark Van Doren, and David Daiches, contributors,
      Walt Whitman: Man, Poet, Philosopher. Three
      lectures presented under the auspices of Gertrude
      Clarke Whittall Poetry and Literature Fund. Wash-
      ington, D.C.: Library of Congress, 1955. Pp. 34-57.

702 _____. "Guilt and Justice in Shakespeare, Richard-
      son, Dylan Thomas, and Whitman," in Daiches, Lit-
      erary Essays. Edinburgh: Oliver and Boyd, 1956.
      Pp. 62-87.

703 _____. "Walt Whitman: Impressionist Prophet," in Hindus, Milton, ed., Leaves of Grass: One Hundred Years After (1955), pp. 109-122.

704 _____. "Walt Whitman as Innovator," in Bode, Carl, ed., The Young Rebel in American Literature. London: William Heinemann, 1959. Pp. 25-48.

705 _____. "Walt Whitman Today." Walt Whitman Review, 6 (1960), 24-26.

706 _____. "Imagery and Mood in Tennyson and Whitman." English Studies Today, 2 (1961), 217-232.

707 _____. "Lincoln and Whitman." Jahrbuch für Amerikastudien, 11 (1966), 15-28. In English. Reprinted in Daiches, More Literary Essays. Edinburgh: Oliver and Boyd, 1967. Pp. 211-230.

708 DANIEL, L. C. "Two Etchings for Walt Whitman's 'Song of the Open Road.'" Forum, 93 (January, 1935), 32-33.

709 DANIEL, Walter C. "Countee Cullen as Literary Critic." College Language Association Journal, 14 (1972), 281-290.

710 DA PONTE, Durant. "Whitman's 'Young Fellow' Named Da Ponte." Walt Whitman Review, 5 (1959), 16-17.

711 DARROW, Clarence S. "Walt Whitman," in Weinberg, Arthur and Lila, eds., Verdicts Out of Court. New York: Quadrangle, 1963. Pp. 170-185.

712 DART, W. K. "Walt Whitman in New Orleans." Publication of the Louisiana Historical Society, 7 (1915), 97-112.

713 DAS, Manoj. "The Good Gray Poet and the Last Great Rishi." Indian Literature, 12 (1969), 87-91.

714 DAVENPORT, Guy. "Walt Whitman, an American." Parnassus, 5 (1976), 35-48.

715 DAVENPORT, W. E. "Identity of Whitman's Work and Character." Conservator, 13 (February, 1903), 181.

716   DAVIDSON, James. "Whitman's 'Twenty-Eight Young
      Men.'" Walt Whitman Review, 12 (1966), 100-101.

717   DAVIDSON, Loren K. "Walt Whitman's 'Song of My-
      self.'" Ph.D. diss., Duke, 1959. DA, 20 (1960),
      4097-4098.

718   DAVIS, C. T. "Walt Whitman and the Problem of an
      American Tradition." College Language Association
      Journal, 5 (September, 1961), 1-16.

719   DAVIS, D. B. "The Movement to Abolish Capital Pun-
      ishment in America, 1787-1861." American Histor-
      ical Review, 63 (October, 1957), 23-40.

720   DAVIS, Joseph Addison. "Rolling Home: The Open
      Road as Myth and Symbol in American Literature,
      1890-1940." Ph.D. diss., Michigan, 1974. DA,
      35 (1975), 4509A.

721   DAVISON, Richard Allan. "Ambivalent Imagery in
      Whitman's 'Lilacs....'" Walt Whitman Review, 14
      (1968), 51-56.

722   _____. "Mixed Tone in 'Cavalry Crossing a Ford.'"
      Walt Whitman Review, 16 (1970), 114-117.

723   DEAMER, Robert Glen. "The American Dream: A
      Study in the Beliefs, Possibilities, and Problems in
      the American Dream as Dramatized in the Lives and
      Writings of Major American Authors." Ph.D. diss.,
      New Mexico, 1972. DA, 33 (1972), 5717A-5718A.

724   DE FALCO, Joseph M. "The Narrative Shift in Whit-
      man's 'Song of Myself.'" Walt Whitman Review, 9
      (1963), 82-84.

725   _____. "Whitman's Changes in 'Out of the Cradle
      ...' and Poe's 'The Raven.'" Walt Whitman Review,
      16 (1970), 22-27.

726   DE JOUVENEL, Renaud. "Walt Whitman." Lettres
      Françaises, 586 (September 22, 28, 1955), 1, 9.

727   _____. "Walt Whitman." Europe, 33 (November-
      December, 1955), 91-107.

728 DE KOVEN, Bernard, and Sholom J. Kahn. "A 'Sym-
     phonic' Arrangement of Two Whitman Poems." Walt
     Whitman Review, 9 (1963), 37-40.

729 DEL GRECO, Robert David. "Walt Whitman and the
     Epic Impulse." Ph.D. diss., Illinois (Urbana-Cham-
     paign), 1975. DA, 36 (1975), 2819A.

730 _____. "A New Whitman Letter to Talcott Williams."
     Walt Whitman Review, 23 (1977), 52-53.

731 DELL, Floyd. "Walt Whitman, Anti-Socialist." New
     Republic, 3 (June 15, 1915), 85.

732 DELLO JOIO, Norman, ed. The Mystic Trumpeter.
     New York: Schirmer, 1945.

733 DENDINGER, Lloyd. "The Meaning of Poetry." South-
     ern Libertarian Messenger, 1 (1975), 6-10.

734 DE SELINCOURT, Basil. Walt Whitman: A Critical
     Study. London: Martin Secker, 1914. Reprinted,
     New York: Russell and Russell, 1965.

735 DE SELINCOURT, Ernest. Wordsworthian and Other
     Studies. Oxford: Clarendon Press, 1947. Reprinted,
     New York: Russell and Russell, 1964. Whitman,
     pp. 129-153.

736 DETWEILER, Robert. "The Concrete Universal in
     Democratic Vistas." Walt Whitman Review, 9 (1963),
     40-41.

737 DEUTSCHE, Babette. Walt Whitman: Builder for
     America. New York: Julian Messner, 1941. For
     young people.

738 DITSKY, John M. "Whitman-Tennyson Correspondence:
     A Summary and Commentary." Walt Whitman Review,
     18 (1972), 75-82.

739 _____. "'Retrievements Out of the Night': Approach-
     ing Whitman Through the 'Lilacs' Elegy." Calamus,
     7 (1973), 27-37.

740 DOBELL, Bertram, ed. with Introduction. Walt Whit-
     man: The Man and the Poet by James Thomson.
     London: Privately printed by the editor, 1910.

741 DOEPKE, Dale. "Whitman's Theme in 'Cavalry Cross-
     ing a Ford.'" Walt Whitman Review, 18 (1972),
     132-136.

742 DOHERTY, Joseph F. "Whitman's 'Poem of the Mind.'"
     Semiotica, 14 (1975), 345-363. Discusses "There
     Was a Child Went Forth" as a poem of signs or sign
     language.

743 DOMINA, Lyle. "Whitman's 'Lilacs': Process of Self-
     Realization." Emerson Society Quarterly, 58 (1970),
     124-127.

744 DONALDSON, Thomas. Walt Whitman: The Man.
     New York: Harper, 1896.

745 DONOGHUE, Denis. "Walt Whitman," in Donoghue,
     Connoisseurs of Chaos: Ideas of Order in Modern
     American Poetry. New York: Macmillan, 1965.
     Pp. 23-51.

746 DONOSO, Armando. "The Free Spirit of Walt Whit-
     man." Inter-America, 3 (August, 1920), 340-346.
     Whitman in Latin America.

747 DOS PASSOS, John. World in a Glass: A View of Our
     Century Selected from the Novels of John Dos Passos.
     Introduction by Kenneth Lynn. Boston: Houghton
     Mifflin, 1966. Whitman, passim; demonstrates in-
     fluence of Whitman on Dos Passos.

748 DOUDNA, Martin K. "The Atlantic Cable in Whitman's
     'Passage to India.'" Walt Whitman Review, 23
     (1977), 50-52.

749 DOWDEN, Edward. Studies in Literature, 1789-1877.
     London: Kegan Paul, 1878. "The Poetry of Democ-
     racy: Walt Whitman," pp. 468-523.

750 DOWE, Amy Haslam. "A Child's Memories of the
     Whitmans." Unpublished material by the niece of
     Mrs. George Whitman. See article by Edwin Havi-
     land Miller (1967).

751 DOWNEY, Jean, ed. Whitman's Franklin Evans: or,
     The Inebriate, a Tale of the Times. New Haven:
     College and University Press, 1967.

752 DOWNS, Robert Bingham. "Great Democrat," in Downs, Molders of the Modern Mind. New York: Barnes and Noble, 1961. Pp. 303-306.

753 _____. "Poet of Democracy," in Downs, Famous American Books. New York: Macmillan, 1970. Pp. 131-139.

754 DOYLE, Charles Clay. "Poetry and Pastoral: A Dimension of Whitman's 'Lilacs.'" Walt Whitman Review, 15 (1969), 242-245.

755 DOYLE, Glenn E. "A Note on Thomson's Biography of Whitman." Walt Whitman Review, 15 (1969), 122-124. See Thomson, James, Walt Whitman: The Man and the Poet, ed. by Bertram Dobell, 1910.

756 DOYLE, John R., Jr. "The Poetry of Walt Whitman." English Studies in Africa, 3 (March, 1960), 35-47.

757 DOYLE, P. A. "Whitman and Sean O'Faolain." Walt Whitman Review, 16 (1970), 117-119.

758 DRESSMAN, Michael Rowan. "Walt Whitman's Study of the English Language." Ph.D. diss., North Carolina (Chapel Hill), 1974. DA, 36 (1975), 338A.

759 _____. "Walt Whitman, Chaucer, and French Words." Walt Whitman Review, 23 (1977), 77-82.

760 _____. "Names Are Magic: Walt Whitman's Laws of Geographic Nomenclature." Names, 26 (1978), 68-79.

761 _____. "Walt Whitman's Plans for the Perfect Dictionary," in Myerson, ed., Studies (1979), pp. 457-474.

762 DU BOIS, Arthur E. "On Being Born as Whitman Was." University Review, 9 (Winter, 1942), 129-138.

763 _____. "Keeping Whitman's Tally." Modern Language Notes, 67 (June, 1952), 414-417.

764 DU BOIS, William R. "Walt Whitman's Poetry: A Record of Crises in Identity." Ph.D. diss., Illinois (Urbana), 1970. DA, 31 (1971), 6599A-6600A.

765 DUDDING, Griffith. "The Function of Whitman's Im-
     agery in 'Song of Myself,' 1855." Walt Whitman
     Review, 13 (1967), 3-11.

766 DUERKSON, Roland A. "Shelley's 'Defence' and Whit-
     man's 1855 'Preface': A Comparison." Walt Whit-
     man Review, 10 (1964), 51-60.

767 _____. "Markings by Whitman in His Copy of Shel-
     ley's Works." Walt Whitman Review, 14 (1968),
     147-151. Comments on "The Witch of Atlas," and
     "The Sleepers."

768 DUFFEY, Bernard. "Romantic Coherence and Roman-
     tic Incoherence in American Poetry," Parts I and II.
     Canadian Review of American Studies, 7 (1963), 219-
     236; 8 (1964), 453-464.

769 _____. Poetry in America: Expression and Its
     Values in the Times of Bryant, Whitman, and Pound.
     Durham, N.C.: Duke University Press, 1978. Whit-
     man, pp. 61-121 et passim.

770 DUGDALE, Clarence. "Whitman's Knowledge of As-
     tronomy." University of Texas Studies in English,
     16 (1936), 125-137.

771 DUGGAR, Margaret H. "Walt Whitman's Theory of
     His Own Poetry as Revealed in the Prefaces of 1865,
     1872, 1876, and 1888." Ph.D. diss., Indiana, 1971.
     DA, 32 (1972), 6422A-6423A.

772 DUJARDIN, Edouard. "Les Premiers Poètes du Vers
     Libre." Mercure de France, 146 (1921), 577-621.
     In French.

773 DUNCAN, Robert E. "Changing Perspectives in Reading
     Whitman," in Miller, Edwin H., ed., The Artistic
     Legacy (1970), pp. 73-102.

774 DUSSINGER, Gloria R. "The Romantic Concept of the
     Self, Applied to the Works of Emerson, Whitman,
     Hawthorne, and Melville." Ph.D. diss., Lehigh,
     1973. DA, 34 (1974), 5963A.

775 DUTTON, Geoffrey. Walt Whitman. Edinburgh: Oli-
     ver and Boyd; New York: Grove Press, 1961. Writ-
     ers and Critics series.

776   DYER, L. H. "Walt Whitman." Wilshire Magazine,
      November, 1902. Pp. 76-83.

777   DYKES, E. B. "Democracy and Walt Whitman."
      Negro History Bulletin, 6 (May, 1943), 175-177.

778   DYKES, Mattie M. "'A Nondescript Monster' with 'Ter-
      rible Eyes.'" Northwest Missouri State Teachers
      College Studies, 4 (June, 1940), 3-32.

779   DYSON, Verne. "The Whitman Societies." Walt Whit-
      man Bulletin, 1 (April, 1958), 3-7.

780   _____. "Whitman Collections." Walt Whitman Bul-
      letin, 2 (October, 1958), 21-22.

781   _____. Whitmanland: West Hills Memories of the
      Poet and His Ancestors. Brentwood, N.Y.: Pri-
      vately printed by the author, 1960.

782   _____. "Walt Whitman and the Butterfly." Walt
      Whitman Bulletin, 4 (April, 1961), 3-6.

783   _____. "Walt Whitman's Ancestors." Walt Whitman
      Bulletin, 4 (April, 1961), 19-24.

784   EASTMAN, Max. "Walt Whitman: Poet of Democracy."
      Reader's Digest, 42 (June, 1943), 29-33.

785   EBERWEIN, Jane D. "Whitman on Campus," in Spe-
      cial Issue of The Long Islander, July, 1976. Re-
      printed in Walt Whitman Review, 22 supplement
      (1976), 19-20.

786   EBY, Edwin Harold. "Did Whitman Write 'The Good
      Gray Poet'?" Modern Language Quarterly, 11
      (December, 1950), 445-449.

787   _____. A Concordance of Walt Whitman's Leaves
      of Grass, Part I: A through Heart. Seattle: Uni-
      versity of Washington Press, 1951. Reissued, 1959.

788   _____. A Concordance of Walt Whitman's Leaves
      of Grass and Selected Prose Writings, Part II: Com-
      pletes work. Seattle: University of Washington Press,
      1955.

789 _____. "Walt Whitman and the Tree of Life." Walt
        Whitman Review, 7 (1961), 43-51.

790 _____. "Walt Whitman's 'Indirections.'" Walt Whit-
        man Review, 12 (1966), 5-16.

791 ECCLES, Caroline. "An Appreciation of Walt Whitman."
        Quest, 3 (January, 1912), 349-359.

792 ECKLEY, Wilton. "Whitman's 'A Noiseless Patient
        Spider.'" Explicator, 22 (November, 1963), item 20.

793 EDMISTON, S., and L. Cirino. Literary New York:
        A History and a Guide. New York: Houghton Mif-
        flin, 1976.

794 EEKMAN, Thomas. "Walt Whitman's Role in Slavic
        Poetry (Late 19th-Early 20th Century)," in Terras,
        Victor, ed., American Contributions to the Eighth
        International Congress of Slavists. Columbus: Sla-
        vica, 1978. Pp. 166-190.

795 EITNER, Walter H. "Walt Whitman in the Kansas Mag-
        azine." Kansas Quarterly (formerly Kansas Maga-
        zine), 1 (1968), 29-31.

796 _____. "Emily Dickinson's Awareness of Whitman:
        A Reappraisal." Walt Whitman Review, 22 (1976),
        111-115.

797 ELLEDGE, W. P. "Whitman's 'Lilacs' as Romantic
        Narrative." Walt Whitman Review, 12 (1966), 59-67.

798 ELLIOT, Charles N. Walt Whitman as Man, Poet, and
        Friend. Boston: Richard G. Badger, 1915.

799 ELLIOTT, George Ray. "Browning's Whitmanism."
        Sewanee Review, 37 (April, 1929), 164-171. Re-
        printed in Elliott, Cycle of Modern Poetry. Prince-
        ton, N.J.: Princeton University Press, 1929. Pp.
        83-90.

800 ELLIS, Havelock. The New Spirit. London: Walter
        Scott, 1890. Reprinted, New York: Random House
        Modern Library, 1930. Whitman, pp. 89-132.

801 _____. The Dance of Life. Boston: Houghton

Mifflin, 1923. Discussion of natural rhythms in life.

802 ELMESSIRI, Abdelwahab M. "The Critical Writings of Wordsworth and Whitman: A Study of the Historical and Anti-Historical Imaginations." Ph.D. diss., Rutgers, 1969. DA, 30 (1970), 3904A-3905A.

803 EMMANUEL, Lenny. "Whitman's Fusion of Science and Poetry." Walt Whitman Review, 17 (1971), 73-82.

804 ENGEL, Wilson F., III. "Two Biblical Echoes in 'Crossing Brooklyn Ferry.'" Walt Whitman Review, 23 (1977), 88-90.

805 ENGLEKIRK, John E. "Notes on Whitman in Spanish America." Hispanic Review, 6 (1938), 133-138.

806 EPSTEIN, Perle. Individuals All: Profiles of Americans Who Defied the Establishment. New York: Crowell-Collier, 1972. Includes Thoreau and Whitman.

807 ERKKILA, Betsy Jacqueline. "Walt Whitman and the French Tradition." Ph.D. diss., California (Berkeley), 1976. DA, 38 (1977), 774A.

808 _____. "Walt Whitman and Jules Laforgue." Walt Whitman Review, 24 (1978), 71-77.

809 ERNEST, Joseph M., Jr. "Whittier and Whitman: Uncongenial Personalities." Bulletin of the Friends Historical Society, 42 (August, 1953), 85-89.

810 _____. "Holmes to Whittier Re Whitman." Walt Whitman Newsletter, 4 (March, 1958), 76-77.

811 ERSKINE, John. "Whitman's Prosody." Studies in Philology, 20 (July, 1923), 336-344.

812 _____. The Start of the Road. New York: Frederick A. Stokes, 1938. Novel based on the life of Walt Whitman.

813 FABRE, Michel. "Walt Whitman and the Rebel Poets:

A Note on Whitman's Reputation Among Radical Writers During the Depression. " Walt Whitman Review,
12 (1966), 88-93.

814 FALK, Robert P. "Walt Whitman and German Thought."
      Journal of English and Germanic Philology, 40 (July,
      1941), 315-330.

815 _____. "Shakespeare's Place in Walt Whitman's
      America." Shakespeare Association Bulletin, 17
      (April, 1942), 86-96.

816 FANER, Robert D. "Operatic Music and the Poetry of
      Walt Whitman." Ph. D. diss., Pennsylvania, 1947.

817 _____. Walt Whitman and the Opera. Philadelphia:
      University of Pennsylvania Press, 1951. Reprinted,
      Carbondale: Southern Illinois University Press, 1972.

818 _____. "The Use of Primary Source Materials in
      Whitman Study." Emerson Society Quarterly, 22
      (1961), 10-12.

819 _____. "Whitman on Records." Walt Whitman Re-
      view, 8 (1962), 33-38.

820 FARZAN, Massud. "Whitman and Sufism: Towards a
      'Persian Lesson.'" American Literature, 47 (1976),
      572-582.

821 FASEL, Ida. "Whitman's 'The World Below the Brine.'"
      Explicator, 25 (1966), item 7.

822 _____. "Whitman and Milton." Walt Whitman Re-
      view, 13 (1967), 79-87.

823 _____. "'Song of Myself' as Prayer." Walt Whit-
      man Review, 17 (1971), 19-22.

824 _____. "Whitman and Marvell's 'The Garden.'"
      Walt Whitman Review, 20 (1974), 114-115.

825 FAUSSET, Hugh l'Anson. Walt Whitman: Poet of De-
      mocracy. New Haven: Yale University Press, 1942.

826 _____. "Whitman's Mysticism," in Fausset, Poets
      and Pundits. New Haven: Yale University Press,
      1947. Pp. 31-51.

827 FAWCETT, James Waldo. "One Hundred Critics Gauge Walt Whitman's Fame." New York Times Book Review, June 10, 1923.

828 FEIDELSON, Charles, Jr. Symbolism and American Literature. Chicago: University of Chicago Press, 1953. "Whitman as Symbolist," pp. 16-27, et passim. Reprinted in Pearce, ed., Whitman: A Collection (1962), pp. 80-88.

829 FEIN, Richard J. "'When Lilacs ... ' and Lamentations." Walt Whitman Review, 15 (1969), 115-117.

830 _____. "Whitman and the Emancipated Self." Centennial Review, 20 (1976), 36-49.

831 FEINBERG, Charles E. "A Whitman Collector Destroys a Whitman Myth." Papers of the Bibliographic Society of America, 52 (1958), 73-92. On young Whitman's alleged impracticality.

832 _____. "Percy Ives, Detroit, and Walt Whitman." Detroit Historical Society Bulletin, 16 (February, 1960), 4-11.

833 _____. "Walt Whitman and His Doctors." Archives of Internal Medicine, 114 (1964), 834-842.

834 _____. "Walt Whitman: Yesterday, Today, and Tomorrow." Nassau Review, 1 (Spring, 1965), 1-18.

835 FEINBERG, Susan G. "Whitman's 'Out of the Cradle....'" Explicator, 37 (1978), item 35.

836 FELHEIM, Marvin. "The Problem of Structure in Some Poems by Whitman," in Ludwig, R. M., ed., Aspects of American Poetry. Columbus: Ohio State University Press, 1962. Pp. 79-97.

837 FENDER, Stephen. "Ezra Pound and the Words off the Page: Historical Allusions in Some American Long Poems." Yearbook of English Studies, 8 (1978), 95-108. Includes Whitman, Hart Crane, Williams.

838 FERGUSON, John De Lancey. "Walt Whitman," in American Literature in Spain. New York: Columbia University Press, 1916. Pp. 170-201.

839   FERLAZZO, Paul J. "Walt Whitman's Poetry: The
      Liberation of the Body." Ph. D. diss., Oklahoma,
      1970. <u>DA</u>, 31 (1971), 3545A.

840   _____ . "Anne Gilchrist, Critic of Walt Whitman."
      South Dakota Review, 10 (1972), 63-79.

841   _____ . "Encounter: Whitman and His Reader."
      Walt Whitman Review, 18 (1972), 138-140.

842   _____ . "Sex for Whitman--The Body Mystic."
      Calamus, 9 (1974), 29-40.

843   _____ . "Dylan Thomas and Walt Whitman: Birth,
      Death, and Time." Walt Whitman Review, 23 (1977),
      136-141.

844   FERM, E. B. "The Democracy of Walt Whitman."
      Mother Earth, 1 (January-February, 1907), 11-12.

845   FIEDLER, Leslie A. An End to Innocence. Boston:
      Beacon Press, 1955. "Images of Walt Whitman,"
      pp. 152-173. Reprinted in Hindus, ed., Leaves of
      Grass: One Hundred Years After (1955), pp. 55-73.
      Also reprinted in Fiedler, Collected Essays (1971),
      Vol. I, pp. 152-173.

846   _____ . "Walt Whitman: Portrait of the Artist as
      a Middle-Aged Hero," in Fiedler, No! In Thunder:
      Essays on Myth and Literature. Boston: Beacon
      Press, 1960; London: Eyre and Spottiswoode, 1963.
      Pp. 61-75. Reprinted in Fiedler, Collected Essays
      (1971), Vol. I, pp. 281-296.

847   _____ . The Return of the Vanishing American. New
      York: Stein and Day, 1968.

848   _____ . The Collected Essays of Leslie Fiedler,
      2 vols. New York: Stein and Day, 1971.

849   _____ , ed. The Art of the Essay. New York:
      Thomas Y. Crowell, 1958. "Whitman, American
      Baby," by Ward B. Lewis, pp. 584-587.

850   _____ , ed. with Introduction. Whitman: Selections
      from Leaves of Grass. New York: Dell, 1959. In-
      troduction similar to essay in An End to Innocence.

851 FIELDS, Ronald Milburn. "Four Concepts of an Or-
     ganic Principle: Horatio Greenough, Henry David
     Thoreau, Walt Whitman, and Louis Sullivan." Ph.D.
     diss., Ohio, 1968. DA, 29 (1969), 3929A.

852 FINKEL, William Leo. "Whitman and the Calendar."
     Word Study, 25 (February, 1950), 29-52.

853 _____. "Walt Whitman's Manuscript Notes on Ora-
     tory." American Literature, 22 (March, 1950), 29-
     52.

854 _____. "Sources of Walt Whitman's Manuscript
     Notes on Physique." American Literature, 22 (No-
     vember, 1950), 308-331.

855 _____, ed. "Charles Kent's 'Most Affectionate and
     Overflowing Tribute to Whitman's Great Gifts.'"
     Walt Whitman Review, 11 (1965), 3-19. Reprint
     of an 1868 review.

856 FINKELSTEIN, Sidney. "Whitman's Mannahatta."
     American Dialog, 5 (1969), 18-23. Illustrated.

857 FIRKINS, O. W. "Walt Whitman." Weekly Review,
     1 (May 31, 1919), 56-58.

858 FISHER, Marvin, and W. J. Buckingham. "Whitman
     and Dickinson." Review of Current Scholarship in
     American Literary Scholarship, 1975, 1976. Pp. 83-
     102, 61-78.

859 FITCH, George H. "Walt Whitman, the Prophet in His
     Shirt-Sleeves," in Fitch, Great Spiritual Writers of
     America. San Francisco: Elder, 1916. Pp. 12-20.

860 FLECK, Richard F. "A Note on Whitman in Ireland."
     Walt Whitman Review, 21 (1975), 160-162.

861 FLEISHER, Frederic. "Walt Whitman's Swedish Recep-
     tion." Walt Whitman Newsletter, 3 (June, Septem-
     ber, and December, 1957), 19-22, 44-47, and 58-62.

862 FLETCHER, Edward G. "Walt Whitman's Beginnings."
     Freeman, 3 (May 4, 1921), 188.

863 _____. "Walt Whitman." North American Review,
     219 (March, 1924), 355-366.

864   _____. "'Pioneers! O Pioneers!'" American Lit-
       erature, 19 (November, 1947), 259-261.

865   FLETCHER, John Gould. "Review of Newton Arvin's
       Whitman." Poetry, 53 (February, 1939), 273-279.
       Of value as a review and critical study.

866   FLEWELLING, Ralph T. "Personalism," in Runes,
       Dagobert D., ed., Twentieth Century Philosophy.
       New York: Philosophical Library, 1943. Reprinted,
       Westport, Conn.: Greenwood Press, 1968. Pp.
       323-341.

867   FLINT, R. W. "The Living Whitman." Partisan Re-
       view, 22 (Summer, 1955), 391-399.

868   FLOAN, Howard. The South in Northern Eyes: 1831-
       1861. Austin: University of Texas Press, 1958.
       Whitman, pp. 148-168.

869   FOERSTER, Norman. "Whitman as a Poet of Nature."
       PMLA, 31 (December, 1916), 736-758.

870   _____. "Whitman and the Cult of Confusion." North
       American Review, 213 (June, 1921), 799-812.

871   _____. Nature in American Literature. New York:
       Macmillan, 1923. Reprinted, New York: Russell
       and Russell, 1958. Whitman, pp. 176-220.

872   _____. American Criticism: A Study in Literary
       Theory from Poe to the Present. Boston: Houghton
       Mifflin, 1928. Whitman, pp. 157-222.

873   _____, and Robert P. Falk, eds. Eight American
       Writers: An Anthology. New York: Norton, 1963.
       "Walt Whitman," by James E. Miller, Jr., pp. 971-
       1168.

874   FOLEY, Patrick Kevin. American Authors: 1795-1895.
       Boston: Publisher's Printing Company, 1897.

875   FOLSOM, L. Edwin. "Approaches and Removals: W.
       S. Merwin's Encounter with Whitman's America."
       Shenandoah, 29 (1978), 57-73.

876   FORD, Thomas W. "Significance of Whitman's Revisions

in 'Excelsior.'" Walt Whitman Review, 5 (1959), 60-72.

877 _____. "Invitation from a Thrush: Frost Versus Whitman." Walt Whitman Review, 22 (1976), 166-167.

878 _____. "Whitman's 'Excelsior': The Poem as Microcosm." Texas Studies in Literature and Language, 17 (1976), 777-785.

879 FORREST, John K. "Walt Whitman's Naturalism." Ph.D. diss., Washington, 1942.

880 FORREY, Robert. "Whitman to Wolfe." Mainstream, 13 (October, 1960), 19-27.

881 _____. "Whitman and the Freudians." Mainstream, 14 (January, 1961), 45-52.

882 FOSTER, Steven. "Bergson's 'Intuition' and Whitman's 'Song of Myself.'" Texas Studies in Literature and Language, 6 (August, 1964), 376-387.

883 FRANCIS, Gloria A., and Artem Lozynsky, eds. Whitman at Auction, 1899-1972. Introduction by Charles E. Feinberg. Detroit: Gale Research, 1978.

884 FRANCIS, K. H. "Walt Whitman's French." Modern Language Review, 51 (October, 1956), 493-506.

885 FRANCIS, Sculley. "Walt Whitman." Andean Quarterly, 2 (January, 1943), 52-61.

886 FRANCO, Luis. Walt Whitman. Buenos Aires: Poseidon Press, 1945. In Spanish; has not been translated.

887 FRANK, Waldo. "With a Voice as Big as America." New York Times Book Review, July 3, 1955. Pp. 1, 13. Also in New York Times, "Opinions and Perspectives," July 3, 1955. Pp. 70-76.

888 FREDERICK, J. G. "Are the Beatniks Offsprings of Walt?" Walt Whitman Review, 4 (April, 1961), 10-12.

889 FREEDMAN, Florence Bernstein. "Walt Whitman and

Heinrich Zschokke: A Further Note." American
Literature, 15 (May, 1943), 181-182. Refers to a
German writer, 1771-1848, author of Hours of De-
votion.

890 _____. "Walt Whitman Looks at the Schools."
Ph.D. diss., Columbia (Education), 1948.

891 _____. "A Motion Picture 'First' for Whitman:
O'Connor's 'The Carpenter.'" Walt Whitman Review,
9 (1963), 31-33. Refers to William Douglas O'Connor, best known as the author of The Good Gray Poet
(1866). Film, based on a story published in 1892,
released and reviewed July 10, 1910.

892 _____. "Whitman's Leaves and O'Connor's Harring-
ton: An 1860 Review." Walt Whitman Review, 9
(1963), 63-65. Abolitionist novel, published in 1860.

893 _____. "Caricature in Picture and Verse: Walt
Whitman in Vanity Fair, 1860." Walt Whitman Review, 10 (March, 1964), 18-19, 23.

894 _____. "New Light on An Old Quarrel: Walt Whitman and William Douglas O'Connor, 1872." Walt
Whitman Review, 11 (1965), 27-52.

895 _____. "Walt Whitman and the Chicago Fire." Walt
Whitman Review, 12 (1966), 43-44.

896 _____. "A Whitman Letter to Josiah Child, June
1879." Walt Whitman Review, 16 (1970), 55-57.

897 _____. "A Sociologist Views a Poet." Walt Whitman Review, 16 (1970), 99-104.

898 _____. "Emerson Giving Joy: Summer of 1855."
Walt Whitman Review, 21 (1975), 162-163.

899 _____, ed. with Introduction. Walt Whitman Looks
at the Schools. New York: Kings Crown Press,
1950. Whitman's articles on education in the Brooklyn
Evening Star and Daily Eagle, 1845-1848.

900 FREEDMAN, William A. "Whitman and Morality in the
Democratic Republican." Walt Whitman Review, 7
(1961), 53-65.

901 _____. "Whitman's 'The World Below the Brine.'" Explicator, 23 (January, 1965), item 39.

902 FREILIGRATH, Ferdinand. "Walt Whitman" (originally published in Germany, 1868, 1877), in Allen, Gay Wilson, ed., Walt Whitman Abroad (1955), pp. 3-7. Translated from the German by Horst Frenz.

903 FRENCH, Roberts W. "Reading Whitman: 'Cavalry Crossing a Ford.'" English Review, 27 (1976), 16-19.

904 _____. "Whitman in Crises: A Reading of 'Scented Herbage of My Breast.'" Walt Whitman Review, 24 (1978), 29-32.

905 _____. "Symbolic Values in 'The Dalliance of the Eagles.'" Walt Whitman Review, 24 (1978), 124-128.

906 FREND, Grace Gilchrist. "Walt Whitman as I Remember Him." Bookman (London), 22 (July, 1927), 203. See also Grace Gilchrist.

907 FRENZ, Horst. "American Literature and World Literature." Comparative Literature Newsletter, 2 (February, 1944), 4-6.

908 _____. "Karl Knortz, Interpreter of American Literature and Culture." American-German Review, 13 (December, 1946), 27-30. German-American translator of Whitman with T. W. Rolleston, published in 1889.

909 _____. "Walt Whitman's Letters to Karl Knortz." American Literature, 20 (May, 1948), 155-163.

910 _____. Whitman and Rolleston: A Correspondence. Bloomington: Indiana University Press, 1951. Humanities Series, No. 26.

911 FREY, Ellen Frances. Catalogue of the Whitman Collection in the Duke University Library. Durham, N. C.: Duke University Press, 1945. Reprinted, Port Washington, N. Y.: Kennikat Press, 1965. Reprint volume includes Wells, Caroline, and Alfred F. Goldsmith, A Bibliography of Walt Whitman (1922).

912 FREYRE, Gilberto. "Camerado Whitman" (1948), in

Allen, ed., Walt Whitman Abroad (1955), pp. 223-
234. Translated from French by Benjamin M. Woodbridge, Jr.

913 FRIDHOLM, Roland V. "Pindar from Paumanok," in
Allen, ed., Walt Whitman Abroad (1955), pp. 127-
136. Translated by Evie Allison Allen.

914 FRIEDMAN, John S. "A Whitman Primer: Solipsism
and Identity." American Quarterly, 27 (1975), 443-
460.

915 FRIEDMAN, Stanley. "Whitman and Laugharne." Anglo-
Welsh Review, 18 (1969), 81-82. Relates Whitman
to Dylan Thomas' "Poem in October."

916 FRIEND, Robert. "The Quest for Rondure: A Comparison of Two Passages to India." Hebrew University Studies in Literature (Jerusalem), 1 (1973), 76-
85.

917 FROST, Ronald George. "William Blake as a Possible
Influence on Walt Whitman." M.A. Thesis, Texas
(Arlington), 1970.

918 FRUMP, Timothy. "A Whitman Manuscript." Notes
and Queries, 166 (March 24, 1934), 206.

919 FULGHUM, Walter B., Jr. "Whitman's Debt to Joseph
Gostwick." American Literature, 12 (January, 1941),
491-496. Refers to Gostwick's German Literature,
1854.

920 _____. "Quaker Influences on Whitman's Religious
Thought." Ph.D. diss., Northwestern, 1943.

921 FUNNELL, Bertha H. Walt Whitman on Long Island.
Port Washington, N.Y.: Kennikat Press, 1971.

922 FURNESS, Clifton Joseph. "Walt Whitman Looks at
Boston." New England Quarterly, 1 (1928), 353-370.

923 _____. "Walt Whitman's Politics." American
Mercury, 16 (April, 1929), 459-466.

924 _____. "Walt Whitman's Estimate of Shakespeare."
Harvard Studies and Notes in Philology and Literature,

14 (1932), 1-33. Also printed as pamphlet, New York: Haskell House, 1965. Reissued, 1972. Facsimile.

925 _____ . "Winwar's American Giant: Walt Whitman and His Times." American Literature, 13 (January, 1942), 423-432. Review article; interesting as an essay.

926 _____ . "Walt Whitman and Reincarnation." The Forerunner, 3 (August, 1942), 9-20.

927 _____ , ed. with Introduction. Walt Whitman's Workshop: A Collection of Unpublished Manuscripts. Cambridge: Harvard University Press, 1928. Reprinted, New York: Russell and Russell, 1964.

928 _____ , ed. with Notes. Leaves of Grass: 1855 Edition. New York: Facsimile Text Society, 1939.

929 FUSSELL, Edwin S. "Leaves of Grass and Brownson." American Literature, 31 (March, 1959), 77-78. Refers to Orestes Brownson.

930 _____ . The Frontier: American Literature and the American West. Princeton, N.J.: Princeton University Press, 1965. "Walt Whitman's Leaves of Grass," pp. 397-441.

931 FUSSELL, Paul, Jr. "Whitman's Curious Warble: Reminiscence and Reconciliation," in Lewis, R. W. B., ed., The Presence of Walt Whitman (1962), pp. 28-51. Discusses "Out of the Cradle...."

932 GABRIEL, José. Walt Whitman: La Voz Democrática de America. Montevideo, Uruguay: Claudio García y Cía, 1944. In Spanish; has not been translated.

933 GABRIEL, Ralph H. The Course of American Democratic Thought. New York: Ronald Press, 1940. "Whitman and the Civil War," pp. 123-131.

934 GALINSKY, Hans. "The Overseas Writer and the Literary Language of the Mother Country: American and British English as Viewed by American Writers from Whitman through Wilder." Langue et littérature, 6 (1962), 437-438.

935 GAMBERALE, Luigi. "The Life and Work of Walt
     Whitman." Conservator, 15 (September, 1904),
     103-106.

936 GARCÍA-LORCA, Federico. "Ode to Walt Whitman,"
     trans. by Ben Belitt. Poetry, 85 (January, 1955),
     187-192.

937 GARGANO, James W. "Technique in 'Crossing Brooklyn
     Ferry': The Everlasting Moment." Journal of Eng-
     lish and Germanic Philology, 62 (April, 1963), 262-
     269.

938 GARLAND, Hamlin. "Walt Whitman, Old and Poor,"
     in Roadside Meetings. New York: Macmillan, 1930.
     Pp. 127-143.

939 GARRISON, C. G. "Walt Whitman, Christian Science,
     and Vedanta." Conservator, 15 (February, 1904),
     182-185.

940 GARRISON, Joseph Marion, Jr. "John Burrough's Re-
     view of the 1867 Leaves of Grass." Walt Whitman
     Review, 6 (1960), 45-48. Reprint from 1867.

941 _____. "John Burroughs as a Literary Critic: A
     Study Emphasizing His Treatment of Emerson, Whit-
     man, Thoreau, Carlyle, and Arnold." Ph. D. diss.,
     Duke, 1962. DA, 23 (1963), 3372-3373.

942 GAY, William. Walt Whitman: His Relation to Science
     and Philosophy. Melbourne, Australia: Firth and
     McCutcheon, 1895.

943 GAY, Zhenya, illustrator. "There Was a Child Went
     Forth." Children's edition. New York: Golden
     Press, 1943.

944 GEFFEN, Arthur. "Walt Whitman and Jules Michelet--
     One More Time." American Literature, 45 (1973),
     107-114. Influence on "Passage to India."

945 GEISMAR, Maxwell. "The World of Walt Whitman."
     Nation, 180 (March 26, 1955), 265-267.

946 _____, ed. The Whitman Reader. New York:
     Pocket Books, 1955.

947 GELPI, Albert. "Walt Whitman: The Self as Circumference," in The Tenth Muse: The Psyche of the American Poet. Cambridge: Harvard University Press, 1975. Pp. 153-216.

948 GERSTER, Patrick G. "Aesthetic Individualism: Key to the Alienation of the American Intellectual--Studies in Ralph Waldo Emerson, Henry David Thoreau, and Walt Whitman." Ph.D. diss., Minnesota (History), 1970. DA, 31 (1971), 4673A.

949 GHOSE, Sisirkumar. "Chari, Whitman, and the Vedantic Self: A Note." Calamus, 4 (December, 1970), 9-20.

950 GIBBONS, Robert F. "Ocean's Poem: A Study of Marine Symbolism in Leaves of Grass." Ph.D. diss., Tulane, 1958. DA, 19 (1959), 2344-2345.

951 GIBSON, Morgan. "Whitman and the Tender and Junior Buddha." Eigo Seinen (The Rising Generation: Tokyo), 122 (1976), 264-268.

952 GILCHRIST, Anne. "An Englishwoman's Estimate of Walt Whitman." The Radical (Boston), 7 (1870), 345-359. Abridged version reprinted in Gilchrist, Herbert H., ed., Anne Gilchrist: Her Life and Writings. New York: Doubleday; London: Unwin, 1887. Pp. 287-307.

953 GILCHRIST, Grace (daughter of Anne Gilchrist). "Chats with Walt Whitman." Temple Bar Magazine, 113 (February, 1898), 200-212. See also Frend.

954 GILENSON, Boris. "Whitman in Russia." Soviet Literature, 5 (1969), 176-181.

955 GIRGUS, Sam B. "Culture and Post-Culture in Walt Whitman." Centennial Review, 18 (1974), 392-410.

956 GLICKSBERG, Charles I. "Walt Whitman and the Civil War." Ph.D. diss., Pennsylvania, 1932.

957 _____. "Walt Whitman in the Civil War." Revue Anglo-Américaine, 9 (April, 1932), 327-328.

958 _____. "Walt Whitman and Heinrich Zschokke."

Notes and Queries, 166 (June 2, 1934), 382-384.
See article by Florence B. Freedman (1943).

959   . "Walt Whitman in 1862." American Literature, 6 (November, 1934), 264-282.

960   . "A Whitman Discovery." Colophon, 1 (August, 1935), 227-233.

961   . "A Walt Whitman Parody." American Literature, 6 (January, 1935), 436-437.

962   . "A Friend of Walt Whitman." American
Book Collector, 6 (March, 1935), 91-94.

963   . "Whitman and Bryant." Fantasy, 5 (1935),
2.

964   . "Walt Whitman, the Journalist." Americana,
30 (July, 1935), 474-490. Three articles sent to
Brooklyn City News, 1860, 1862.

965   . "Walt Whitman in New Jersey: Some Unpublished Manuscripts." New Jersey Historical Society Proceedings, 55 (January, 1937), 42-46.

966   . "Walt Whitman and Bayard Taylor." Notes
and Queries, 1973 (July 3, 1937), 5-7. Taylor's
"John Godgrey's Fortunes," based on the character
of Whitman.

967   . "Walt Whitman and 'January Searle.'"
American Notes and Queries, 6 (July, 1946), 51-53.

968   . "Walt Whitman Parodies Provoked by the
Third Edition of Leaves of Grass." American Notes
and Queries, 7 (March, 1948), 163-168.

969   , ed. Walt Whitman and the Civil War: A
Collection of Original Articles and Manuscripts.
Philadelphia: University of Pennsylvania Press,
1933. Reprinted, New York: Barnes, 1963.

970 GODDARD, Harold C. Alphabet of the Imagination.
Atlantic Highlands, N.J.: Humanities Press, 1974.
Posthumous publication of previously unpublished es-
says; Goddard died in 1950.

971 GOEDE, William J. "Swinburne and the Whitmaniacs."
Victorian Newsletter, 33 (1968), 16-21.

972 GOHDES, Clarence F. "Whitman and Emerson."
Sewanee Review, 37 (January, 1929), 79-93.

973 _____. "The 1876 English Subscription for Whitman."
Modern Language Notes, 50 (April, 1935), 257-258.

974 _____. "A Note on Whitman's Use of the Bible as
a Model." Modern Language Quarterly, 2 (March,
1941), 105-108.

975 _____. "Nationalism and Cosmopolitanism in Whitman's Leaves of Grass." Comparative Literature,
2 (1950), 472-479. Reprinted in Walt Whitman Review, 5 (1959), 3-7.

976 _____. "Democracy in Free Verse," in Quinn, Arthur Hobson, ed., The Literature of the American
People: An Historical and Critical Survey. New
York: Appleton-Century-Crofts, 1915. Reissued,
1951. Pp. 598-621.

977 _____. "A Comment on Section 5 of Whitman's
'Song of Myself.'" Modern Language Notes, 69
(December, 1954), 583-586.

978 _____. "Section 50 of Whitman's 'Song of Myself.'"
Modern Language Notes, 75 (December, 1960), 654-
656.

979 _____. "Whitman and the 'Good Old Cause.'" American Literature, 34 (November, 1962), 400-403.

980 _____. "Whitman as 'One of the Roughs.'" Walt
Whitman Review, 8 (1962), 18.

981 _____, ed. Essays on American Literature in Honor
of Jay B. Hubbell. Durham, N.C.: Duke University
Press, 1967.

982 _____, and P. F. Baum, eds. Letters of William
M. Rossetti Concerning Whitman, Blake, and Shelley.
Durham, N.C.: Duke University Press, 1934. Letters to Anne Gilchrist and her son Herbert H. Gilchrist.

983   _____, and Rollo G. Silver, eds. Faint Clews and
           Indirections: Manuscripts of Walt Whitman and His
           Family. Durham, N. C.: Duke University Press,
           1949. Selected from the Trent Collection at Duke
           University.

983a GOING, William T. "O'Neill's Ah, Wilderness." Ex-
           plicator, 29 (1970), item 28. Relates play to Whit-
           man.

984   GOLDBERG, Bernard. "Patriotic Allusions in Sections
           15 and 33 of 'Song of Myself.'" Walt Whitman Re-
           view, 21 (1975), 58-66.

985   GOLDEN, Arthur. "An Uncollected Whitman Article."
           Bulletin New York Public Library, 64 (July, 1960),
           353-360.

986   _____. "A Note on a Whitman Holograph Poem."
           Papers of the Bibliographic Society of America, 55
           (1961), 233-236.

987   _____. "A Glimpse into the Workshop: A Critical
           Evaluation and Diplomatic Transcription of the 'Blue
           Book,' Walt Whitman's Annotated Copy of the 1860
           Edition of Leaves of Grass," Parts I and II. Ph.D.
           diss., New York University, 1962. DA, 24 (1963),
           743.

988   _____. "New Light on Leaves of Grass: Whitman's
           Annotated Copy of the 1860 (Third) Edition." Bulle-
           tin of the New York Public Library, 69 (March,
           1965), 283-306. Reprinted with revisions in Golden,
           ed., Walt Whitman: A Collection (1974), pp. 111-
           135.

989   _____. "Three Letters of 1882." Walt Whitman
           Review, 15 (1969), 59-60.

990   _____. "Review of Edwin H. Miller's Walt Whit-
           man's Poetry: A Psychological Journey (1968),"
           Literature and Psychology, 19 (1969), 61-65.

991   _____. "A Reply [To Stephen A. Black]." Litera-
           ture and Psychology, 20 (1970), 83-92.

992   _____. "Passage to Less Than India: Structure and

Meaning in Whitman's 'Passage to India.'"   PMLA,
88 (1973), 1095-1103.

993 _____ . "Whitman Day by Day, 1876-1891: A Review." Walt Whitman Review, 24 (1978), 84-89.

994 _____ , ed. with Textual Analysis in Volume II.
Walt Whitman's Blue Book: The 1860-1861 Leaves
of Grass, Containing His Manuscript Additions and
Revisions, 2 vols. New York: New York Public
Library, 1968. Volume I, Facsimile of the Unique
Copy in the Oscar Lion Collection of the New York
Public Library.

995 _____ , ed. with Introduction and Notes. Walt Whit-
man: A Collection of Criticism. New York: Mc-
Graw-Hill, 1974. Reprints nine essays in criticism;
Contemporary Studies in Literature Series.

996 GOLDFARB, Clare R. "The Poet's Role in 'Passage
to India.'" Walt Whitman Review, 8 (1962), 75-79.

997 GOLDFARB, Russell M. and Clare R. Spiritualism
and Nineteenth-Century Letters. Rutherford, N.J.:
Fairleigh Dickinson University Press, 1978. Whitman, passim.

998 GOLEMBA, Henry. "Charles Ives' Whitman." American Transcendental Quarterly, 29 (1976), 36-39.

999 GONZÁLES, Louis. "Whitman's Hispanic Fame." Ph.D.
diss., Columbia, 1959. DA, 21 (1960), 195-196.

1000 GONZÁLES-PADILLA, Maria Enriqueta. "Walt Whitman." Abside, 30 (1966), 127-151.

1001 GOODALE, David. "Some of Walt Whitman's Borrow-
ings." American Literature, 10 (May, 1938), 202-
213.

1002 _____ . "Walt Whitman's 'Banner at Day-Break,'
1860." Huntington Library Quarterly, 26 (November,
1962), 105-110.

1003 _____ . "'Wood Odors.'" Walt Whitman Review,
8 (1962), 17.

1004 GOODHEART, Eugene. "Walt Whitman: Democracy and

the Self," in Goodheart, The Cult of the Ego: The
Self in Modern Literature. Chicago: University of
Chicago Press, 1968. Pp. 133-160.

1005 GOODMAN, Ellen S. "'Lilacs' and the Pastoral Elegy
Reconsidered." Books at Brown, 24 (1971), 119-133.

1006 GOODMAN, Randolph. I, Walt Whitman. A Play.
Brooklyn, N.Y.: Library Association of Brooklyn
College, 1955.

1007 GOODSON, William Lester. "A Critical Study of the
1856 Leaves of Grass." Ph.D. diss., Tulsa, 1968.
DA, 29 (1969), 2211A.

1008 _____. "Whitman and the Problem of Evil." Walt
Whitman Review, 16 (1970), 45-50.

1009 _____. "The Second Leaves of Grass (1856), A
Re-valuation," in Zimmerman and Weathers, eds.,
Papers (1970), pp. 26-34.

1010 GORDON, Randolph Ian. "Whitman as a Franciscan
Within the Modern Universal Construct." Walt Whitman Review, 22 (1976), 36-42.

1011 GOSSE, Sir Edmund W. "Whitman Centenary." Living
Age, 302 (July 5, 1919), 41-43.

1012 _____. "Walt Whitman," in Gosse, Leaves and
Fruit. London: William Heinemann, 1927. Pp.
203-211. Reprinted in Gosse, Selected Modern Eng-
lish Essays. London: William Heinemann, 1928.
Pp. 77-92. Also reprinted in Hastings, William
Thompson, ed., Contemporary Essays. Boston:
Houghton Mifflin, 1928. Pp. 158-173.

1013 GOULD, Elizabeth Porter, ed. Gems from Walt Whitman. Philadelphia: David McKay, 1889.

1014 _____. Anne Gilchrist and Walt Whitman. Philadelphia: David McKay, 1900.

1015 GRAHAM, Mary-Emma. "Politics in Black and White:
A View of Walt Whitman's Career as a Political
Journalist." College Language Association Journal,
17 (1973), 263-270.

1016 GRANT, Barry Keith. "The Word En-Masse: Language and Form in American Literature, 1800-1860." Ph.D. diss., New York (Buffalo), 1975. DA, 36 (1975), 1504A.

1017 _____. "Whitman and Eisenstein." Literature/Film Quarterly, 4 (1976), 264-270. Soviet director-producer of motion pictures; died in 1948.

1018 GRANT, Douglas. Walt Whitman and His English Admirers: An Inaugural Lecture. Leeds, England: Leeds University Press, 1962. 24-page pamphlet.

1019 _____. Purpose and Place. London and New York: Macmillan, 1965. Three essays on Whitman, pp. 64-91.

1020 GRANT, Rena V. "The Newly Discovered Whitman Manuscript Collection." Walt Whitman Bulletin, 4 (January, 1961), 13-14.

1021 _____. "The Livezey-Whitman Manuscripts." Walt Whitman Review, 7 (1961), 3-14.

1022 _____, ed. "'Wood Odors.'" Harper's Magazine, 221 (December, 1960), 43. Newly discovered poem by Whitman; see also article by David Goodale (1962).

1023 GRAZIA, Emilio de. "More on Whitman's Twenty-eight Young Men." Walt Whitman Review, 21 (1975), 158-160.

1024 GREASLEY, Philip Alan. "American Vernacular Poetry: Studies in Whitman, Sandburg, Anderson, Masters, and Lindsay." Ph.D. diss., Michigan State, 1975. DA, 36 (1976), 8058A-8059A.

GREBANIER, Frances Winwar see WINWAR, Frances.

1025 GREGG, Larry. "Kornei Chukovsky's Whitman." Walt Whitman Review, 20 (1974), 50-60. Discussion of Chukovsky's My Whitman, published in Moscow, 1966.

1026 GREEN, David Bonnell. "Charles Ollier: An Early English Admirer of Walt Whitman." Walt Whitman Newsletter, 4 (December, 1958), 106-108.

1027 GREEN, Martin B. "Twain and Whitman: The Problem

of 'American' Literature, " in Green, Re-Appraisals:
Some Commonsense Readings in American Literature.
New York: Norton, 1966. Pp. 113-143.

1028 GREENBERG, Wendy. "Hugo and Whitman: Poets of
     Totality. " Walt Whitman Review, 24 (1978), 32-36.

1029 GRIER, Edward F. "Walt Whitman's Democratic Ideal-
     ism. " Ph.D. diss., Pennsylvania, 1949.

1030 _____. "Walt Whitman, the Galaxy, and Democratic
     Vistas. " American Literature, 23 (November, 1951),
     332-350.

1031 _____. "Whitman's Attack on the Temperance Move-
     ment." Walt Whitman Newsletter, 4 (March, 1958),
     78.

1032 _____. "Whitman and Contemporary Verse. " Walt
     Whitman Review, 6 (1960), 26-27.

1033 _____. "Whitman. " Review of current scholarship
     in American Literary Scholarship, 1964 through 1968.
     Pp. 43-49, 45-56, 40-47, 48-55, 50-65.

1034 _____. "Whitman's Earliest Known Notebook. "
     PMLA, 83 (1969), 1453-1456.

1035 _____. "Whitman's Sexuality. " Walt Whitman Re-
     view, 22 (1976), 163-166.

1036 _____, and Charles Feinberg, eds. The Eighteenth
     Presidency: A Critical Text. Lawrence: University
     Kansas Press, 1956. See also Jean Catel (1928).

1037 GRIFFIN, Robert J. "Notes on Structural Devices in
     Whitman's Poetry. " Tennessee Studies in Literature,
     6 (1961), 15-24.

1038 _____. "Whitman's 'Song of Myself.' " Explicator,
     21 (October, 1962), item 16.

1039 _____. "The Inter-connectedness of 'Our Old Feuil-
     lage. ' " Walt Whitman Review, 8 (1962), 8-12.

1040 _____. "Whitman's 'This Compost.' " Explicator,
     21 (April, 1963), item 68.

1041 GRIFFITH, Clark. "Sex and Death: The Significance of Whitman's Calamus Themes." Philological Quarterly, 39 (January, 1960), 18-38.

1042 GRIPPI, Charles S. "The Literary Reputation of Walt Whitman in Italy." Ph. D. diss., New York University, 1970. DA, 32 (1971), 2090A.

1043 GROSS, E. B. "'Lesson of the Two Symbols': An Undiscovered Whitman Poem." Walt Whitman Review, 12 (December, 1966), 77-80. Originally in the Subterranean, July 15, 1843.

1044 GROSS, Harvey S. "Nineteenth-Century Precursors," in Gross, Sound and Form in Modern American Poetry. Ann Arbor: University of Michigan Press, 1964. Pp. 79-99.

1045 GROSS, Theodore L. "Walt Whitman: The Putative Hero," in Gross, The Heroic Ideal in American Literature. Riverside, N.J.: Free Press, 1971. Pp. 51-67.

1046 GROSSKURTH, Phyllis. The Woeful Victorian: A Biography of John Addington Symonds. New York: Holt, Rinehart, and Winston, 1965. Whitman, pp. 151-155 et passim.

1047 GROVER, Edwin Osgood. "'The First Words of Warm Approval.'" Walt Whitman Review, 5 (June, 1959), 30-33.

1048 GUMMERE, Francis Bacon. Democracy and Poetry. Boston: Houghton Mifflin, 1911. "Whitman and Taine," pp. 96-148.

1049 GUMMERE, R. M. "Walt Whitman and His Reaction to the Classics," in Harvard Studies in Classical Philology, ed. Committee of Classical Instructors. Cambridge: Harvard University Press, 1948-1953. Vol. 60, pp. 263-289.

1050 GUPTA, Rameshwar K. "Whitman, the Poet of Cosmic Dynamism." Banasthali Patrika (India), 4 (1968), 95-103.

1051 _____. "Indian Response to Walt Whitman." Revue de Littérature Comparée, 47 (1973), 58-70.

1052 _____, trans. from Bengali with Notes. "Walt Whitman, " by Rabindranath Tagore, published originally
in 1891. Walt Whitman Review, 19 (1973), 3-11.

1053 GUTHRIE, William N. Walt Whitman: The Camden
Sage. Cincinnati: Robert Clark, 1897.

1054 GUTTRY, Lottie L. "Walt Whitman and the Woman
Reader. " Walt Whitman Review, 22 (1976), 102-110.

1055 HACKMAN, Martha. "Whitman, Jeffers, and Freedom. "
Prairie Schooner, 20 (Fall, 1946), 182-184.

1056 HAGENBÜCHLE, Roland. "Whitman's Unfinished Quest
for an American Identity. " English Literary History,
40 (1973), 428-478.

1057 HALKIN, Simon. "A Song of Joys (1860 poem). " Bit-
zaron, The Hebrew Monthly of America, 22 (1950),
92-100.

1058 HALPER, Albert. "The Soldier Who Wanted to See
Whitman. " Prairie Schooner, 22 (March, 1948), 82-
91. Fictional narrative.

1059 HALL, Vernon. "Walt Whitman, " in Hall, A Short
History of Literary Criticism. New York: New
York University Press, 1963. Pp. 95-98.

1060 HAMILTON, Clayton. "Walt Whitman as a Religious
Seer. " Forum (London), 42 (July, 1909), 80-85.

1061 HAMILTON, David. "Music Section. " Nation, 220
(1975), 478. Comments on "Lilacs, " a cantata by
Roger Sessions; Delius' "Sea Drift"; and Hindemith's
"A Requiem for Those We Love. "

1062 HAMLIN, Fred. "Land of Liberty, " in Hamlin, Land
of Liberty. New York: Crowell, 1947.

1063 HAMSUN, Knut. "Primitive Poet: Walt Whitman, "
published in Copenhagen, 1889, in Allen, ed., Walt
Whitman Abroad (1955), pp. 112-123. Translated
by Evie Allison Allen.

1064 HANNA, Suhailibn-Salim. "Gibran and Whitman: Their

Literary Dialogue. " Literature East and West, 12 (1968), 174-198.

1065 HANSEN, Chadwick C. "Walt Whitman's 'Song of Myself': Democratic Epic, " in Hendrick, George, ed. , American Renaissance (1961), pp. 77-88.

1066 HANSON, Russell Galen. "Reflections on Whitman's Role as Tragic Poet of the American Civil War. " Walt Whitman Review, 14 (1968), 50-54.

1067 _____ . "Whitman as Social Theorist: Worker in Poetics and Politics. " Walt Whitman Review, 16 (1970), 41-45.

1068 _____ . "A Critical Reflection on Whitman's 'The Base of All Metaphysics.'" Walt Whitman Review, 18 (1972), 67-70.

1069 _____ . "Anxiety as Human Predicament: Whitman's 'Calamus' No. 9." Walt Whitman Review, 21 (1975), 73-75.

1070 HARDING, Brian R. "Transcendental Symbolism in the Works of Emerson, Thoreau, and Whitman. " Ph.D. diss. , Brown, 1971. DA, 32 (1972), 5789A.

1071 HARDING, Walter R. "A Sheaf of Whitman Letters. " Studies in Bibliography (University of Virginia), 5 (1952-1953), 203-210. 14 letters relating to Whitman's public affairs.

1072 _____ . "A Glimpse of Walt Whitman. " Walt Whitman Newsletter, 3 (March, 1957), 7.

1073 HARKNESS, David J. , and R. Gerald McMurty. Lincoln's Favorite Poets. Knoxville: University of Tennessee Press, 1959. Whitman, pp. 82-86 et passim.

1074 HARNED, Thomas B. "Walt Whitman in the Present Crisis of Our Democracy." Conservator, 16 (January, 1906), 167-168.

1075 _____ . "Slanderers of Whitman. " Conservator, 18 (December, 1907), 151-154.

1076 _____ . Memoirs of Thomas B. Harned, Walt Whit-

man's Friend and Literary Executor, edited by Peter
Van Egmond.   Hartford, Conn.:   Transcendental
Books, 1972.

1077 _____, ed.   Letters Written by Walt Whitman to
His Mother from 1866 to 1872.   New York and
London: Putnam's, 1902.

1078 _____, ed.   The Letters of Anne Gilchrist and Walt
Whitman.   Garden City, N.Y.:   Doubleday, Doran,
1918.

1079 HARRIS, Frank.   "Walt Whitman," in Contemporary
Portraits, 3rd.   Series.   New York: Brentano's,
1915.   Pp. 211-233.

1080 _____.   My Life and Loves, 5 vols.   Originally
published in Germany, 1923-1927.   New edition,
edited by John F. Gallagher, 5 vols. in 1, reprinted,
New York: Grove Press, 1963.   Whitman, passim.

1081 HARRIS, L. H.   "Walt Whitman as Artist and Teacher."
South Atlantic Quarterly, 20 (April, 1921), 120-136.

1082 HARRIS, Marion.   "Nature and Materials: Fundamentals
in Whitman's Epistemology."   Walt Whitman Review,
9 (December 1963), 85-88.

1083 HARRISON, Joseph B.   "Modernity and Walt Whitman."
Frontier and Midland, 14 (January, 1934), 101-109.

1084 HARRISON, Phillipa P.   "'Eidōlons':   An Entrance-
Song."   Walt Whitman Review, 17 (1971), 35-45.

1085 HARRISON, Richard Clarence.   "Walt Whitman and
Shakespeare."   PMLA, 44 (December, 1929), 1201-
1238.

1086 HARRISON, Stanley R.   "Sacrilege of Preference in
Whitman and Sartre."   Walt Whitman Review, 15
(1969), 51-54.

1087 HARTLEY, L. Conrad.   The Spirit of Walt Whitman:
A Psychological Study in Blank Verse.   Manchester,
England: Cornish, 1908.

1088 HARTLEY, Marion.   "Whitman and Cézanne," in Adventures in the Arts. New York: Boni and Liveright, 1921. Pp. 30-36.

1089 HARTMANN, Sadakichi. Conversations with Walt Whitman. New York: E. P. Coby, 1895.

1090 _____. "Salut au Monde: A Friend Remembers Whitman." Southwest Review, 12 (July, 1927), 262-267.

1091 HARTT, G. M. "Whitman: An Inspiration to Democracy." Conservator, 19 (August, 1908), 87-88.

1092 HARVEY, Nancy Lenz. "Whitman's Use of 'Arms' in Leaves of Grass." Walt Whitman Review, 18 (1972), 136-138. Arms as in embrace; also as in war.

1093 HASTINGS, William Thompson. "Jean Catel's Interpretation of Walt Whitman." Annotator (Purdue), 3 (May, 1954), 5-9.

1094 HAY, Stephen H. "Rabindranath Tagore in America." American Quarterly, 14 (Fall, 1962), 439-463. Emerson, Thoreau, Whitman; modern interest in the Indian poet.

1095 HAYS, Will. Walt Whitman: The Prophet of the New Era. London: Daniel, 1920.

1096 _____. "The Birth of a Bible." Texas Review, 8 (October, 1923), 21-31. Genesis of Leaves of Grass.

1097 HAYMAN, Ronald. Arguing with Walt Whitman. London: Covent Garden Press, 1971.

1098 HAZARD, Lucy. "The Golden Age of Transcendentalism," in Hazard, The Frontier in American Literature. New York: Crowell, 1927. Reprinted, New York: Frederick Ungar, 1967. Pp. 147-180. Whitman, passim.

1099 HAZEN, James. "Whitman and [Gerard Manley] Hopkins." American Transcendental Quarterly, 12 (1971), 41-48.

1100 HEAVILL, Sister Mary Kathleen, R.S.M. "A Whitmanian Look at Whitman." Walt Whitman Review, 10 (1964), 17-18.

1101 HEDGES, Elaine R., and William L., eds. Land and
     Imagination: The Rural Dream in America. Ro-
     chelle Park, N.J.: Hayden, 1980. Includes work
     by Emerson, Thoreau, and Whitman.

1102 HENCH, Atcheson L. "Walt Whitman Recollected."
     American Notes and Queries, 1 (October, 1962), 22.
     Whitman and Folger McKinsey.

1103 _____. "Walt Whitman and Folger McKinsey."
     American Notes and Queries, 8 (October, 1969), 53.

1104 HENDERSON, Mrs. Alice Corbin. "Walt Whitman."
     Poetry, 14 (May, 1919), 89-94.

1105 HENDRICK, George. "Walt Whitman and Sadakichi
     Hartmann." Emerson Society Quarterly, 11 (1958),
     50-52.

1106 _____. "Whitman's Copy of the Bhagavad Gita."
     Walt Whitman Review, 5 (1959), 12-14.

1107 _____. "Prose Criticism Accompanying 'I Happify
     Myself.'" Walt Whitman Bulletin, 2 (July, 1959),
     11-13.

1108 _____. "Mrs. Davis' Claim Against the Whitman
     Estate." Walt Whitman Bulletin, 4 (October, 1960),
     6-7.

1109 _____. "Whitman and Sir Edwin Arnold." Western
     Humanities Review, 14 (1960), 83-89.

1110 _____. "Newspaper Squibs About Whitman." Walt
     Whitman Bulletin, 4 (April, 1961), 7-9.

1111 _____. "Unpublished Notes on Whitman in William
     Sloane Kennedy's Diary." American Literature, 34
     (May, 1962), 279-285.

1112 _____, ed. American Renaissance: The History
     and Literature of an Era. Berlin and Frankfurt:
     Diesterweg, 1961. A collection of critical essays;
     in English. "Walt Whitman's 'Song of Myself': Dem-
     ocratic Epic," by Chadwick C. Hansen, pp. 77-88.

1113 HENSLER, Donna L. "The Voice of the Grass Poem,

'I': Whitman's 'Song of Myself.' " Walt Whitman
Review, 15 (1969), 26-32.

1114 HERANNEY, David Lucien. "Style and Structure in
Walt Whitman's Drum-Taps and Sequel. " Ph. D.
diss. , New York University, 1974. DA, 35 (1975),
4430A.

1115 HERNDON, Jerry A. "Parallels in Melville and Whitman. " Walt Whitman Review, 24 (1978), 95-108.

1116 _____. "Hopkins and Whitman. " Walt Whitman
Review, 24 (1978), 161-162.

1117 HERVEY, J. L. "The Growth of the Whitman 'Legend.' "
Dial, 59 (June 24, 1915), 12-14.

1118 HESS, John. "Reception of Whitman in the German
Democratic Republic. " Walt Whitman Review, 22
(1976), 30-35.

1119 HESSE, Hermann. "Walt Whitman, " in Hesse, My Be-
lief, trans. from German by Denver Lindley and
Ralph Manheim. New York: Farrar, Straus, and
Giroux, 1974.

1120 HESSELTINE, William B. Civil War Prisons--A Study
in War Psychology. Columbus: Ohio University
Press, 1930. Whitman, passim.

1121 HESSER, Dale. "The Religion of Walt Whitman. "
Ph. D. diss. , Kansas, no date.

1122 HIBLER, David J. "Drum-Taps and [Melville's] Battle-
pieces. " Personalist, 50 (1969), 130-147.

1123 HICKEY, Sister Ellen Mary, S. N. D. "Shadows in Whitman. " Calamus, 4 (December, 1970), 21-33.

1124 HICKS, Granville. The Great Tradition: An Interpretation of America Since the Civil War. New York:
Macmillan, 1933. "Heritage, " pp. 1-31.

1125 HIER, F. P. , Jr. "The End of a Literary Mystery. "
American Mercury, 1 (April, 1924), 471-478.

1126 HIGGINSON, Thomas Wentworth. "Walt Whitman, " in

Higginson, Contemporaries. Boston: Houghton Mifflin, 1899. Pp. 72-84.

1127 HIGHET, Gilbert. The Powers of Poetry. New York:
Oxford University Press, 1960. "Whitman: The
Fourth of July, " pp. 106-113. Refers to "A Boston
Ballad, " untitled in 1855 edition.

1128 HIND, C. L. "Walt Whitman, " in Hind, Authors and
I. London: John Lane, 1921. Pp. 312-317.

1129 HINDEMITH, Paul, composer. "'When Lilacs Last in
the Dooryard Bloom'd': A Requiem 'For Those We
Love.'" New York: Associated Music Publisher,
1948. Recorded by the New York Philharmonic with
Paul Hindemith conducting. Columbia Odyssey Record, 1963.

1130 HINDUS, Milton. "Centenary of Leaves of Grass, " in
Hindus, ed., One Hundred Years (1955), pp. 3-21.

1131 _____. "Review of Allen's Walt Whitman Abroad
(1955)." Kenyon Review, 19 (Winter, 1957), 156-168.

1132 _____. "Whitman and Poe: A Note." Walt Whitman Newsletter, 3 (March, 1957), 5-6.

1133 _____. "Whitman's Influence at Present." Walt
Whitman Review, 6 (1960), 27-29.

1134 _____. "Dostoyevsky's Religion and Whitman's."
Walt Whitman Review, 6 (1960), 66-69.

1135 _____. "Literary Echoes in Whitman's 'Passage to
India.'" Walt Whitman Review, 7 (1961), 52-53.

1136 _____. "The Goliad Massacre in 'Song of Myself.'"
Walt Whitman Review, 7 (1961), 77-78.

1137 _____. "Notes Toward the Definition of a Typical
Poetic Line in Whitman." Walt Whitman Review,
9 (1963), 75-81.

1138 _____, ed. Leaves of Grass: One Hundred Years
After. Stanford, Calif.: Stanford University Press,
1955.

1139 _____, ed. Walt Whitman: The Critical Heritage.
     New York and London: Barnes and Noble, 1971.

1140 HINTZ, H. W. "Walt Whitman," in Hintz, Quaker In-
     fluence in American Literature. Westwood, N.J.:
     Fleming H. Revell, 1940. Pp. 59-75. Reprinted
     as "Quakerism of Walt Whitman," in Hintz, H. W.,
     and B. D. N. Grebanier, eds., Modern American
     Vistas. New York: Dryden Press, 1940. Pp. 449-
     456.

1141 HINZ, Evelyn J. "Whitman's 'Lilacs': The Power of
     Elegy." Bucknell Review, 20 (1972), 35-54.

1142 HIRSCH, David H. "American Dionysian Poetry and
     Modern Poetics." Sewanee Review, 83 (1975), 334-
     347. Review of eight recent books on American
     poetry; Whitman passim.

1143 HITCHCOCK, Bert. "Walt Whitman: The Pedagogue as
     Poet." Walt Whitman Review, 20 (1974), 140-146.

1144 HOBSBAUM, Philip. "Eliot, Whitman, and American
     Tradition." Journal of American Speech, 3 (1969),
     239-264.

1145 HOELTJE, Hubert H. "Whitman's Letter to Robert
     Carter." American Literature, 25 (November, 1953),
     360-362. Request for a notice in the American En-
     cyclopedia.

1146 HOFFMAN, Frederick John. "Emerson, Whitman, and
     the Silhouette of Sweeney," in Hoffman, The Twenties.
     New York: Viking Press, 1955. Pp. 123-131.

1147 HOFFMAN, Michael J. "Whitman's Preface: Every
     Man His Own Priest," in Hoffman, The Subversive
     Vision. Port Washington, N.Y.: Kennikat Press,
     1972. Pp. 58-68.

1148 _____. "Miller's Debt to Whitman, Emerson,
     Thoreau, et al: Henry Miller and the Apocalypse
     of Transcendentalism." Lost Generation Journal,
     4 (1976-1977), 18-21.

1149 HOGAN, Robert. "The Amorous Whale: A Study in
     the Symbolism in D. H. Lawrence." Modern Fiction

Studies, 5 (Spring, 1959), 39-46. Whitman, passim.

1150 HOLCOMB, Esther Lolita. "Whitman and Sandburg."
English Journal, 17 (September, 1928), 549-555.

1151 HOLDER, Alex. "On the Structure of Henry James'
Metaphor." English Studies, 41 (October, 1960),
290-297.

1152 HOLLINGSWORTH, Marian. "Americanism in Franklin
Evans." Walt Whitman Review, 8 (1962), 88-89.

1153 HOLLIS, C. Carroll. "Whitman's 'Ellen Eyre.'"
Walt Whitman Newsletter, 2 (September, 1956), 24-
26. Refers to a woman who loved Whitman.

1154 _____. "Names in Leaves of Grass." Names, 5
(September, 1957), 129-156.

1155 _____. "Whitman and the American Idiom." Quarterly Journal of Speech, 43 (December, 1957), 408-
420.

1156 _____. "Whitman's Word Game." Walt Whitman
Newsletter, 4 (March, 1958), 74-76.

1157 _____. "Whitman and William Swinton: A Co-
operative Friendship." American Literature, 30
(January, 1959), 425-449.

1158 _____. "Whitman on 'Periphrastic' Literature."
Fresco, 10 (Winter, 1960), 5-13.

1159 _____. "The Oratorical Stance and Whitman's
Early Poetry," in Zimmerman and Weathers, eds.,
Papers (1970), pp. 56-79.

1160 HOLLOWAY, Emory. "Walt Whitman in New Orleans."
Yale Review, 5 (October, 1915), 166-183.

1161 _____. "Early Writings of Walt Whitman." Nation,
101 (October 14, 1915), 463.

1162 _____. "Some Recently Discovered Poems by Walt
Whitman." Dial, 60 (April 13, 1916), 369-370.

1163 _____. "Early Poems of Walt Whitman." Nation, 102 (February 10, 1916), 15; 103 (December 21, 1916), 5-6.

1164 _____. "Walt Whitman's History of Brooklyn, Just Found." New York Times, September 17, 1916. P. 1.

1165 _____. "Walt Whitman's First Free Verse." Nation, 105 (December 27, 1917), 717.

1166 _____. "Walt Whitman's Love Affair?" Dial, 69 (November, 1920), 473-483.

1167 _____. "Childhood Traits in Whitman." Dial, 72 (February, 1922), 169-177.

1168 _____. "Whitman as Critic of America." Studies in Philology, 20 (July, 1923), 345-369.

1169 _____. "More Light on Whitman." American Mercury, 2 (February, 1924), 183-189. Whitman for the Brooklyn Evening Star in 1845-1846.

1170 _____. "A Whitman Manuscript." American Mercury, 3 (December, 1924), 475-480. Small notebook of pre-Leaves of Grass.

1171 _____. "Whitman's Embryonic Verse." Southwest Review, 10 (July, 1925), 28-40.

1172 _____. "The Walt Whitman Exhibition." Bulletin of New York Public Library, 29 (November, 1925), 763-766.

1173 _____. Whitman: An Interpretation in Narrative. New York and London: Knopf, 1926. Reprinted, New York: Biblo and Tannen, 1969. New edition includes a new preface.

1174 _____. "Some New Whitman Letters." American Mercury, 16 (February, 1929), 183-188.

1175 _____. "Whitman as His Own Press Agent." American Mercury, 18 (December, 1929), 482-488. Reprinted in Spivak, L. E., and Charles Angoff, eds., American Mercury Reader. New York: Blakiston, 1944. Pp. 82-90.

1176   . "Whitman on the War's Finale." The Colophon: A Book Collector's Quarterly, 1 (February,
1930), part 1, no page.

1177   . "Whitman as Journalist." Saturday Review
of Literature, 8 (April 23, 1932), 679-680.

1178   . "Walt Whitman's Visit to the Shakers, with
Whitman's Notebook Containing His Description and
Observation of the Shaker Group at Mt. Lebanon."
Colophon, 4 (March, 1933), part 13.

1179   . "Notes from a Whitman Student's Scrapbook."
American Scholar, 2 (May, 1933), 269-278.

1180   . "Whitman's Message for Today." American
Mercury, 62 (February, 1946), 202-206.

1181   . "Whitman's Last Words." American Literature, 24 (November, 1952), 367-369.

1182   . "Whitman Pursued." American Literature,
27 (March, 1955), 1-11.

1183   . "A Whitman Source." Walt Whitman Newsletter, 2 (April, 1956), 23-24. Refers to the sea
fight in "Song of Myself."

1184   . "More Temperance Tales by Whitman."
American Literature, 27 (January, 1956), 577-578.

1185   . Free and Lonesome Heart: The Secret of
Walt Whitman. New York: Vantage Press, 1960.
Whitman's bisexuality and paternity.

1186   . "Whitman and Band Music." Walt Whitman
Review, 6 (1960), 51-52.

1187   , ed. The Uncollected Poetry and Prose of
Walt Whitman, 2 vols. Garden City, N.Y.: Double-
day, Page, 1921; London: William Heinemann, 1922.
Reprinted, New York: Peter Smith, 1932.

1188   , ed. Whitman's Leaves of Grass, inclusive
edition. Garden City, N.Y.: Doubleday, Page, 1925.

1189   , ed. Pictures: An Unpublished Poem of Walt

Whitman. New York: The June House; London:
Faber and Gwyer, Ltd., 1928.

1190 _____, ed. Franklin Evans; or, The Inebriate: A
Tale of the Times. New York: Random House,
1929.

1191 _____, ed. Complete Poetry and Selected Prose
and Letters. London and New York: The Nonesuch
Press, 1938. Reprinted, New York: Haskell House,
1971.

1192 _____, ed. Leaves of Grass: The Collected Poems.
Garden City, N.Y.: Doubleday, Doran, 1942.

1193 _____, and Henry S. Saunders. "Whitman," in
Trent, William P., et al., eds., Cambridge History
of American Literature, 4 vols. New York: Macmillan, 1917-1921. Reprinted in one-volume edition,
New York: Macmillan, 1944. Part II, pp. 258-274.

1194 _____, and Vernolian Schwarz, eds. I Sit and Look
Out: Editorials from the Brooklyn Daily Times.
New York: Columbia University Press, 1932. Re-
printed, New York: AMS Press, 1966.

1195 _____, and Ralph Adimari, eds., with Introduction
and Notes. New York Dissected: A Sheaf of Recently Discovered Newspaper Articles. New York:
Rufus Rockwell Wilson, 1936.

1196 HOLMES, Oliver Wendell. "Walt Whitman," in Holmes,
Over the Tea Cups. Boston: Houghton Mifflin, 1892.
Reprinted in Brown, Clarence A., ed., The Achieve-
ment of American Criticism. New York: Ronald
Press, 1954. Pp. 367-368.

1197 HOLROYD, Stuart. "Walt Whitman's Healthy-Mindedness," in Holroyd, Emergence from Chaos. Boston:
Houghton Mifflin, 1957. Pp. 95-112.

1198 HOLTZ, Nancy Ann. "The Great Measures of Time:
A Study of Cosmic Order in Nineteenth-Century
American Thought." Ph.D. diss., Washington, 1977.
DA, 38 (1977), 3500A-3501A.

1199 HONIG, Edwin. "American Poetry and the Rationalistic

Critic." Virginia Quarterly Review, 36 (Summer, 1960), 416-429.

1200 HOOPLE, Robin P. "Leaves of Grass (1860) as Opinion: A Study of Whitman's Understanding of the Major Problems of 1860 American Culture as Reflected in the Third Edition of Leaves of Grass." Ph.D. diss., Minnesota, 1965. DA, 27 (1966), 1319A-1320A.

1201 _____. "Chants Democratic and Native American: A Neglected Sequence in the Growth of Leaves of Grass." American Literature, 42 (1970), 181-196.

1202 _____. "Walt Whitman and the City of Friends." American Transcendental Quarterly, 18 (1973), 45-51.

1203 HORTON, Rod W. and Herbert W. Edwards. Backgrounds of American Literary Thought. New York: Meredith, 1967. Whitman, passim. Contains good bibliographies on various philosophical modes.

1204 HOSEK, Chaviva. "The Rhetoric of Whitman's 1855 'Song of Myself.'" Centennial Review, 20 (1976), 263-277.

1205 HOWARD, Leon. "Walt Whitman's Evangel of Democracy." Ph.D. diss., Johns Hopkins, 1929.

1206 _____. "Walt Whitman and the American Language." American Scholar, 5 (August, 1930), 444-451.

1207 _____. "For a Critique of Whitman's Transcendentalism." Modern Language Notes, 47 (February, 1932), 79-85.

1208 _____. Literature and the American Tradition. Garden City, N.Y.: Doubleday, 1960. Melville and Whitman, pp. 168-183.

1209 HOWARTH, Herbert. "Whitman Among the Irish." London Magazine, 7 (January, 1960), 48-55. Includes Yeats, AE, and Joyce.

1210 _____. "Whitman and the Irish Writers." Comparative Literature, 12 (1960), 479-488.

1211 _____. "Whitman and the English Writers," in

Zimmerman and Weathers, eds., Papers (1970), pp. 6-25.

1212 HOWE, Irving. "Walt Whitman: 'Garrulous to the Very Last.'" New Republic, 132 (March 28, 1955), 17-21. Reprinted in Howe, A World More Attractive. New York: Horizon Press, 1963. Pp. 131-143.

1213 _____. "Walt Whitman," in Howe, Modern Literary Criticism. Boston: Beacon Press, 1958. Pp. 419-429.

1214 HOWE, M. A. DeWolfe. "The Spell of Whitman." Atlantic, 98 (December, 1906), 849-855.

1215 HOWELL, A. C. "Walt Whitman, Singer of the American Spirit." English Language and Literature (Korea), 4 (October, 1957), 265-278.

1216 HOWELLS, William Dean. Literary Friends and Acquaintances (1900), ed. David F. Hiatt and Edwin H. Cady. Bloomington: Indiana University Press, 1968. Whitman, pp. 68-76.

1217 HRUBESKY, Donald W. "Robinson Jeffers: An Inverted Whitman." Ph.D. diss., Kansas State, 1970. DA, 32 (1971), 3253A.

1218 HUBACH, Robert R. "Walt Whitman in Kansas." Kansas Historical Quarterly, 10 (May, 1941), 150-155.

1219 _____. "Three Uncollected St. Louis Interviews of Walt Whitman." American Literature, 14 (May, 1942), 141-147.

1220 _____. "Walt Whitman and the West." Ph.D. diss., Indiana, 1943.

1221 _____. "A Kansas City Newspaper Greets Walt Whitman." Notes and Queries, 185 (December 18, 1943), 365-366.

1222 _____. "Walt Whitman Visits St. Louis, 1879." Missouri Historical Review, 37 (July, 1943), 386-393.

Hubach

1223 _____ . "Walt Whitman and Taliessin." American Literature, 18 (January, 1947), 329-331. Also spelled Taliesin; a bard of sixth-century Welsh legend.

1224 _____ . "An Uncollected Whitman Letter (November 30, 1890)." Duke University Library Notes, 23 (January, 1950), 13.

1225 _____ . "Western Newspaper Accounts of Whitman's 1879 Trip to the West." Walt Whitman Review, 18 (1972), 56-62.

1226 HUBBELL, Jay B. "DeTocqueville and Whitman." Nation, 109 (November 22, 1919), 655.

1227 _____ . Who Are the Major American Writers? Durham, N.C.: Duke University Press, 1972. Whitman, pp. 65-70.

1228 HUDSON, Vaughan. "Melville's Battle-Pieces and Whitman's Drum-Taps: A Comparison." Walt Whitman Review, 19 (1973), 81-92.

1229 HUFFSTICKLER, Star. "Walt Whitman as a Precursor of Frederick Jackson Turner." Walt Whitman Review, 8 (1962), 3-8.

1230 HUGHES, Charles. "Impact of Evil on the Poetry of Walt Whitman." Walt Whitman Review, 15 (1969), 237-242.

1231 HUGHES, James Michos. "The Dialectic of Death in Poe, Dickinson, Emerson, and Whitman." Ph.D. diss., Pennsylvania, 1969. DA, 31 (1970), 1280A.

1232 HUGHES, Langston. "The Ceaseless Rings of Walt Whitman." American Dialogue, 5 (1969), 8-9.

1233 HUGHSON, Lois. "In Search of the True America: Dos Passos' Debt to Whitman in U.S.A." Modern Fiction Studies, 19 (1973), 179-192.

1234 HUGÔT, François. "Poets to Come," trans. from French by Nan Braymer. American Dialogue, 5 (1969), 27-28.

1235 HULT, G. E. "Whitman Once More." University of

North Dakota Quarterly Journal, 9 (July, 1919),
309-331.

1236 HUME, R. A. "Wine with Walt." South Atlantic Quarterly, 41 (October, 1942), 437-440.

1237 _____. "Walt Whitman and the Peace." College
English, 6 (March, 1945), 313-319. Reprinted in
Loomis, Roger Sherman, and Donald Lemen Clark,
eds., Modern English Readings. New York: Holt,
Rinehart, and Winston, 1946. Pp. 469-475.

1238 HUMPHREYS, Charles A. Field, Camp, Hospital, and
Prison in the Civil War. Boston: George H. Ellis,
1918. Whitman, passim.

1239 HUNEKER, James Gibbons. "Visit to Walt Whitman,"
in Huneker, Ivory Apes and Peacocks. New York:
Scribner's, 1915. Pp. 22-31. Reprinted in Huneker,
Essays, ed. posthumously by H. L. Mencken. New
York: Scribner's, 1929. Pp. 416-423. Huneker
died in 1921.

1240 HUNGERFORD, Edward. "Walt Whitman and His Chart
of Bumps." American Literature, 2 (January, 1931),
350-384.

1241 HUNT, Joel A. "Mann [Thomas] and Whitman: Hu-
maniores Litterae." Comparative Literature, 14
(Summer, 1962), 266-271.

1242 _____. "Thomas Mann and André Spire: The Wal-
purgisnacht Chapter." Modern Language Notes, 87
(April, 1972), 502-505. On Whitman's influence.

1243 HUNT, Russell A. "Whitman's Poetics and the Unity
of 'Calamus.'" American Literature, 46 (1975),
482-494.

1244 HUNTLEY, Frank L. "Walt Whitman and the Death of
President John F. Kennedy." East-West Review
(Japan), 1 (1964), 79-85.

1245 HUNZICKER, Karen Dell. "Whitman the Teacher: The
Poet in a Democratic Society." Ph.D. diss., Yale,
1977. DA, 39 (1978), 1569A-1570A.

1246 HURWITZ, Harold M. "Whitman, Tagore, and 'Passage to India.'" Walt Whitman Review, 13 (1967), 56-60.

1247 HYNES, Samuel. "Whitman, Pound, and the Prose Tradition," in Lewis, R. W. B., ed., The Presence of Walt Whitman (1962), pp. 110-136.

1248 IDZERDA, Stanley J. "Walt Whitman, Politician." New York History, 37 (April, 1956), 171-184.

1249 IFKOVIC, Edward. "'I Took a Jaunt': Dickens' American Notes and Whitman's Franklin Evans." Walt Whitman Review, 14 (1968), 171-174.

1250 IGNATOW, David. Say Pardon: A Book of Poems. Middletown, Conn.: Wesleyan University Press, 1961. "Walt Whitman in the Civil War Hospitals."

1251 IGNOFFO, Matthew F., Jr. "The American Dream and Its Culmination in Walt Whitman." Ph.D. diss., Loyola (Chicago), 1971. DA, 33 (1972), 1171A.

1252 _____ . What the War Did to Whitman: A Brief Study of the Effects of the Civil War on the Mind of Walt Whitman. New York: Vantage Press, 1975. 54-page pamphlet.

1253 INDEX TO EARLY AMERICAN PERIODICAL LITERATURE, 1728-1870. Whitman, Part III. New York: Pamphlet Distributing Company, 1941. Sponsored by New York University Libraries with WPA aid.

1254 INGERSOLL, Robert Green. Liberty in Literature: Testimonial to Walt Whitman. New York: Truthseeker Company, 1890.

1255 IRWIN, F. J. "The Religion of Walt Whitman." Truthseeker Magazine, March 11, 1905. P. 147.

1256 IRWIN, Mabel MacCoy. Whitman, The Poet-Liberator of Woman. New York: Privately printed by the author, 1905.

1257 ISAACS, Neil D. "The Auto-erotic Metaphor in Joyce,

Sterne, Lawrence, Stevens, and Whitman." <u>Litera-</u>
<u>ture and Psychology</u>, 15 (1965), 92-106.

1258 IVANETICH, Aloysus. "<u>Leaves of Grass</u>, Its Purport:
Evolution of the Cumulative." <u>Calamus</u>, 6 (1972),
3-21.

1259 _____. "Gentlemen, Your Facts Are Useful."
<u>Calamus</u>, 10 (1975), 2-17.

1260 JACKSON, Holbrook. <u>Dreamers of Dreams: The Rise</u>
<u>and Fall of Nineteenth-Century Idealism.</u> London:
Faber and Faber, 1948. Whitman, pp. 253-280.

1261 JACOBSON, Anna. "Walt Whitman in Germany Since
1914." <u>Germanic Review</u>, 1 (April, 1926), 132-141.

1262 JAÉN, Didier Tisdel. "Borges y Whitman." <u>Hispania</u>,
50 (1967), 49-53. In Spanish.

1263 _____, ed. and translated from Spanish. <u>Homage to</u>
<u>Walt Whitman: A Collection of Poems to Walt Whit-</u>
<u>man</u>, by various authors. Foreword by Jorge Luis
Borges. University: University of Alabama Press,
1969.

1264 JAFFE, Harold. "Richard Maurice Bucke's Walt Whitman: Edited with an Introduction and Variant Readings." Ph.D. diss., New York University, 1967.
<u>DA</u>, 29 (1968), 899A.

1265 _____. "Edwin Markham on Whitman." <u>Markham</u>
<u>Review</u>, 2 (1968), 1.

1266 _____. "Bucke's Walt Whitman: A Collaboration."
<u>Walt Whitman Review</u>, 15 (1969), 190-194.

1267 _____. "Richard Maurice Bucke's <u>Walt Whitman</u>."
<u>Serif</u>, 7 (1970), 3-10.

1268 _____. "Richard Maurice Bucke and Walt Whitman."
<u>Canadian Review of American Studies</u>, 2 (1971), 37-
47.

1269 JAMES, Henry, "Mr. Walt Whitman," a review of Whitman's <u>Drum-Taps</u>, originally in the <u>Nation</u>, Novem-

ber 16, 1865. Reprinted in James, Views and Re-
views. Introduction by LeRoy Phillips. Boston:
Ball, 1908. Pp. 101-110. Has been frequently re-
printed, as in the following: Richardson, Lyon, ed.
Henry James: Representative Selections. New York:
American Book Company, 1941. Pp. 3-8. Zabel,
Morton D., ed. The Portable Henry James. New
York: Viking Press, 1951. Pp. 426-433. Condon,
Richard A., and Burton O. Kurth, eds. Writing
From Experience. New York: Harper, 1970. Pp.
219-225.

1270 JAMES, William. "The Religion of Healthy-Mindedness,"
in Kiell, Norman, ed., Psychological Studies (1964),
pp. 244-253.

1271 JANNACCONE, Pasquale (Italian economist, 1872-1959).
La Poesía di Walt Whitman e l'Evoluzione delle
Forme Ritmiche. Torino, Italy, 1898. Trans.
from Italian in part by William Struthers and published as "The Poetry of Walt Whitman," in the
Conservator, 11 (1900), 21, 38, 53, 120, 135; and
12 (1901), 7. La Poesia the first scientific study
of Whitman's poetical method.

1272 _____. "L'Ultima Invocazione." La Stampa (Torino
newspaper), August 28, 1952. P. 6. Discusses
poems of death, including the Carol in "Lilacs" and
"The Last Invocation" by Whitman, whom he calls
the greatest poet of death. Article has not been
translated or reprinted to my knowledge. See article by Raffaniello (1968).

1273 JARRELL, Randall. "Walt Whitman: He Had His
Nerve." Kenyon Review, 14 (Winter, 1952), 63-79.

1274 _____. "Some Lines from Whitman." Perspectives,
USA, 2 (Winter, 1953), 61-77. Same as 1952 article.
Has been frequently reprinted under both titles, as
in the following: Jarrell, Poetry and the Age. New
York: Knopf, 1953. Pp. 101-120. Fiedler, L. A.,
ed. The Art of the Essay. New York: Crowell,
1958. Pp. 587-598. Kazin, Alfred, ed. The Open
Form. New York: Harcourt, Brace, and World,
1961. Pp. 87-100. Second edition, 1965, pp. 109-
123. Third edition, 1970, pp. 295-308. Mazzaro,
Jerome, ed. Modern American Poetry: Essays in

Criticism.   New York: David McKay, 1970.   Pp.
1-17.

1275 JARRETT, David and Mary.   "American Literature to
1900," in Redmund, James, et al., eds.   Year's
Work in English Studies, Vol. 55 (1974).   New York:
Humanities Press, 1976.   Pp. 482-504.   Emerson,
Whitman, et al., passim.

1276 JEFFARES, A. Norman.   "Whitman: The Barbaric
Yawp," in Bode, Carl, ed., The Great Experiment
in American Literature.   New York: Praeger, 1961.
Pp. 29-49.

1277 _____, ed. with Introduction.   Selected Poems and
Prose.   London: Oxford University Press, 1966.

1278 JELLEMA, R. H.   "Victorian Critics and the Orientation of American Literature with Special Reference
to the Reception of Walt Whitman and Henry James."
Ph.D. diss., Edinburgh, 1962-1963.

1279 JELLICORSE, John Lee.   "Poet as Persuader: A Rhetorical Explication of the Life and Works of Walt
Whitman."   Ph.D. diss., Northwestern (Speech),
1967.   DA, 28 (1968), 3799-3800.

1280 _____.   "Whitman and Modern Literary Criticism."
American Transcendental Quarterly, 12 (1971), 4-11.

1281 JENSEN, Johannes V.   "Walt Whitman (Copenhagen,
1919)," trans. from Danish by Evie Allison Allen,
in Allen, Gay Wilson, ed., Walt Whitman Abroad
(1955), pp. 123-127.

1282 JENSEN, Millie D.   "Whitman and Hegel: The Curious
Triplicate Process."   Walt Whitman Review, 10
(1964), 27-34.

1283 JERROLD, Laurence.   "Mr. Chapman on Whitman: An
English Reply."   Chap-Book, 7 (September 1, 1897),
274-275.

1284 JOHNSON, C. W. M.   "Whitman's 'Out of the Cradle....'"
Explicator, 5 (May, 1947), item 52.

1285 JOHNSON, David J.   "The Effect of Suspension Dots,

Parentheses, and Italics on Lyricism of 'Song of
Myself.'" Walt Whitman Review, 21 (1975), 47-58.

1286 JOHNSON, Linck C. "The Design of Walt Whitman's
      Specimen Days." Walt Whitman Review, 21 (1975),
      3-14.

1287 JOHNSON, Jane. "Whitman's Changing Attitude Toward
      Emerson." PMLA, 73 (September, 1958), 452.

1288 JOHNSON, J. H., ed. "'Rise Lurid Stars': An Earl-
      ier Version." Century Magazine, 59 (February, 1911),
      532. Facsimile copy with an introduction.

1289 JOHNSON, Mark Andrew. "American Visions, Ameri-
      can Forms: A Study of Four Long Poems." Ph.D.
      diss., Ohio, 1977. DA, 38 (1978), 4828A. Studies
      Joel Barlow's The Columbiad (1807); Whitman's Leaves
      of Grass; Hart Crane's The Bridge (1930); and Allen
      Ginsberg's The Fall of America (1972).

1290 JOHNSON, Maurice O. "Walt Whitman as a Critic of
      Literature." University of Nebraska Studies in Lan-
      guage, Literature, and Criticism, 16 (1938), 1-73.
      Reprinted, New York: Haskell House, 1970.

1291 JOHNSON, Ronald. "Letters to Walt Whitman." Poetry,
      108 (June, 1966), 152-161. Reprinted in Johnson,
      Valley of the Many-Colored Grasses. New York:
      Norton, 1969. Series of poems to Whitman.

1292 JOHNSTON, A. C. "Personal Memories of Walt Whit-
      man." Bookman, 46 (December, 1917), 402-413.

1293 JOHNSTON, Bertha. "Walt Whitman and the American
      Teacher." Conservator, 20 (July, August, Septem-
      ber, 1909), 70, 85, 102.

1294 JOHNSTON, John H. "Half-Hours with Whitman."
      Everywhere, 21 (January, 1908), 212-214.

1295 _____. "Walt Whitman--The Poet of Nature."
      Fortnightly Review, 93 (June 1, 1910), 1123-1136.

1296 _____, and J. W. Wallace. Visits to Walt Whitman
      in 1890-1891 by Two Lancashire Friends. London:
      George Allen and Unwin, 1917; New York: Dodd,

Mead, 1918. Reprinted, New York: Haskell House,
1970.

1297 JOHNSTON, Kenneth G., and John O. Rees, Jr. "Whitman and the Foo-Foos: An Experiment in Language."
Walt Whitman Review, 17 (1971), 3-10.

1298 JONES, Dan P. "Walt Whitman's Perception of Time."
Ph.D. diss., Texas (Austin), 1966. DA, 27 (1967),
3050A.

1299 JONES, Howard Mumford. The Theory of American
Literature. Ithaca, N.Y.: Cornell University Press,
1948.

1300 _____. "The Cosmic Optimism of Walt Whitman,"
in Jones, Belief and Disbelief in American Literature.
Chicago: University of Chicago Press, 1967.

1301 JONES, Joseph. "Whitman's 'When Lilacs Last in the
Dooryard Bloom'd.'" Explicator, 9 (April, 1951),
item 42.

1302 _____. "New Acquisitions: Rare Book Collections--
I, Walt Whitman." Library Chronicle of the University of Texas, 6 (Spring, 1958), 44-46.

1303 _____. "Carlyle, Whitman, and the Democratic Dilemma." English Studies in Africa, 3 (September,
1960), 179-197.

1304 _____. "Emerson and Whitman 'Down Under': Their
Reception in Australia and New Zealand." Emerson
Society Quarterly, 42 (1966), 35-46.

1305 _____. Radical Cousins: Nineteenth-Century America and Australia. St. Lucia, Australia: University
of Queensland Press, 1976.

1306 JONES, P. Mansell. "Whitman and Verhaeren." Abery-
stwyth Studies (University College of Wales, Abery-
stwyth, Wales), 2 (1914), 71-106. Refers to a Bel-
gian poet, 1855-1916, said to be influenced by Whitman.

1307 _____. "Whitman in France." Modern Language
Review, 10 (January, 1915), 1-27.

1308 _____ . "The Influence of Walt Whitman on the Origin of the 'Vers Libre.'" Modern Language Review, 11 (April, 1916), 186-194.

1309 _____ . "On the Track of an Influence in 1913." Comparative Literature Studies, 6-7 (1942), 20-22. Whitman in France before World War I.

1310 _____ . "Whitman and the Origins of the 'vers-libre.'" French Studies (Oxford, England), 2 (April, 1948), 129-139.

1311 _____ . "Whitman and the Symbolists," in Jones, The Background of Modern French Poetry. Cambridge, England: Cambridge University Press, 1951. Pp. 69-88.

1312 JORDY, William H. "Henry Adams and Walt Whitman." South Atlantic Quarterly, 40 (April, 1941), 132-145.

1313 JOSEPHSON, Matthew. "Those Who Stayed," in Josephson, Portrait of the Artist as American. New York: Harcourt, Brace, 1930. Pp. 139-198.

1314 JUDINE, Sister M., I.H.N. "Whitman and Dickinson: Implications for School Programs," in Leary, ed., The Teacher and American Literature (1965), pp. 128-133.

1315 JUSTIN, Jeffrey A. "Unknown Land Poetry: Walt Whitman, Robert Bly, and Gary Snyder." Ph.D. diss., Michigan, 1973. DA, 35 (1974), 457A-458A.

1316 KADIR, Kjelal. "Neruda and Whitman: Short-Circuiting the Body Electric." Pacific Coast Philology, 8 (1973), 16-22.

1317 KAGAN, Norman. "The Return of the Emperor Jones." Negro History Bulletin, 34 (1972), 160-162.

1318 KAGLE, Steven Earl. "Temporal Structure in Leaves of Grass." Illinois Quarterly, 33 (1971), 42-49.

1319 _____ . "Time as a Dimension in Whitman." American Transcendental Quarterly, 12 (1971), 55-60.

1320 KAHN, Sholom J. "Walt Whitman in Hebrew." Scopus,
      6 (March, 1952), 6-7.

1321 _____. "Whitman's Sense of Evil: Criticisms," in
      Allen, ed., Walt Whitman Abroad (1955), pp. 236-
      254.

1322 _____. "The American Backgrounds of Whitman's
      Sense of Evil." Scripta Hierosolymitana (Studies in
      English Language and Literature: Jerusalem), 2
      (1955), 82-118.

1323 _____. "Whitman's 'Black Lucifer': Some Possible
      Sources." PMLA, 71 (December, 1956), 932-944.

1324 _____. "Towards a Popular Edition of Whitman's
      'Complete Poems.'" Walt Whitman Review, 5 (1959),
      23-26.

1325 _____. "Eliot's 'Polyphiloprogenitive': Another
      Whitman Link." Walt Whitman Review, 5 (1959),
      52-54. Term is used in "Mr. Eliot's Sunday Morn-
      ing Service" (1920).

1326 _____. "Stephen Crane and Whitman: A Possible
      Source for 'Maggie.'" Walt Whitman Review, 7
      (1961), 71-77.

1327 _____. "Whitman's Allegorical Lyricism." Scripta
      ..., 17 (1966), 209-225.

1328 _____. "Whitman's 'New Wood.'" Walt Whitman
      Review, 15 (1969), 201-214.

1329 _____. "Whitman's 'Overstaid Fraction' Again."
      Walt Whitman Review, 20 (1974), 67-73.

1330 KAHN, Sy M. "Two Poetic Perspectives on the Deaths
      of Presidents: Whitman and Ferlinghetti." Ameri-
      cana-Austriaca, 3 (1974), 59-66. Magazine edited
      by Klaus Lanzinger. Stuttgart, Germany: Wilhelm
      Braumuller, 1974.

1331 KALITA, Dwight. "Walt Whitman: Ecstatic Sea-Voy-
      ager." Walt Whitman Review, 21 (1975), 14-22.

1332 _____. "Whitman and the Correspondent Breeze."
      Walt Whitman Review, 21 (1975), 125-130.

1333 KALLEN, Horace M. "Of Love, Death, and Walt Whitman." Walt Whitman Review, 15 (1969), 171-180.

1334 KALLSEN, Theodore J. "Leaves of Grass: A Study of Structure." Ph.D. diss., Iowa, 1949.

1335 _____. "The 'World' of 'When Lilacs Last in the Dooryard Bloom'd.'" West Virginia University Philological Papers, 8 (October, 1951), 59-65.

1336 _____. "'Song of Myself': Logical Unity Through Analogy." West Virginia University Bulletin, 9 (June, 1953), 33-40.

1337 _____. "The Improbabilities in Section 11 of 'Song of Myself.'" Walt Whitman Review, 13 (1967), 87-92.

1338 KAMEI, Shunsuke. "Walt Whitman and Takeo Arishima." Walt Whitman Bulletin, 3 (October, 1960), 8-12.

1339 _____. "Takeo Arishima's Two-Day Lecture on Whitman and His Suicide." Walt Whitman Bulletin, 4 (January, 1961), 3-7.

1340 _____. "Emerson, Whitman, and the Japanese in the Meiji Era (1868-1912)." Emerson Society Quarterly, 29 (1962), 28-32.

1341 KANES, Martin. "Whitman, Gide, and Bazalgette: An International Encounter." Comparative Literature, 14 (Fall, 1962), 341-355.

1342 KANJO, Eugene R. "Spokes of Light: Whitman's Vision of Being." Ph.D. diss., Claremont, 1967. DA, 29 (1968), 605A-606A.

1343 _____. "Time and Eternity in 'Crossing Brooklyn Ferry.'" Walt Whitman Review, 18 (1972), 82-90.

1344 KAPLAN, Harold. "Whitman: 'Song of the Answerer,'" in Kaplan, Democracy, Humanism, and American Literature. Chicago: University of Chicago Press, 1972. Pp. 198-224.

1345 KAPLAN, J. "The Real Life," in Aaron, Daniel, ed., Studies in Biography. Cambridge: Harvard University Press, 1978. Pp. 1-8.

1346 KARSNER, David. Horace Traubel: His Life and
     Work. New York: Arens, 1919.

1347 KATZ, Jonathan. Gay American History. New York:
     Crowell, 1977. Whitman, pp. 337-365, 449-508.

1348 KATZ, Joseph. "Whitman, Crane, and the Odious Com-
     parison." Notes and Queries, 14 (1967), 66-67.
     Reprints 1885 review of Crane's Black Riders by
     Isaac Hull Platt.

1349 _____. "Theodore Dreiser: Enter Chicago, Hope,
     and Walt Whitman." Walt Whitman Review, 14
     (1968), 169-171.

1350 KAZIN, Alfred. "The Great American Poet." New
     York Review of Books, 15 (1970), 42-46.

1351 _____. "Democracy According to Whitman." Com-
     mentary, 61 (June, 1976), 52-58.

1352 _____, ed. The Open Form. New York: Harcourt,
     Brace, and World, 1961. Whitman, by Randall Jar-
     rell, pp. 87-100.

1353 KEATING, L. C. "Francis Vielé-Griffin and America."
     Symposium, 14 (Winter, 1960), 276-281.

1354 KEHLER, Joel R. "A Typological Reading of 'Passage
     to India.'" Emerson Society Quarterly, 23 (1977),
     123-129.

1355 KELLER, Dean H. "Walt Whitman in England: A
     Footnote." Walt Whitman Review, 15 (1969), 54-55.

1356 KELLER, Elizabeth Leavitt. "Walt Whitman: The Last
     Phase." Putnam's Magazine, 6 (June, 1909), 331-
     337.

1357 _____. Walt Whitman in Mickle Street. New York:
     Mitchell Kennerly, 1921. Reprinted, New York:
     Haskell House, 1971.

1358 KELLEY, W. V. "The Deification of 'One of the
     Roughs.'" Homiletic Review, 42 (September, 1901),
     202-208.

1359 KELLNER, Robert Scott. "Whitman, Melville, and the
      Civil War: A Sharing of Mood and Metaphor." Amer-
      ican Notes and Queries, 13 (1975), 102-105.

1360 KELLY, Erna Emmighausen. "Whitman and Words-
      worth: Childhood Experience and the Future Poet."
      Walt Whitman Review, 23 (1977), 59-68.

1361 KENNEDY, William Sloane. "The Friendship of Whit-
      man and Emerson." Poet-Lore, 7 (February, 1895),
      71-74.

1362 _____. Reminiscences of Walt Whitman. Boston
      and London: Alexander Gardner, 1896.

1363 _____. "The Style of Leaves of Grass," in Kennedy,
      Reminiscences (1896), pp. 149-190. Listed separately
      because this article is of particular interest to a stu-
      dent of Whitman.

1364 _____. "On the Trail of the Good Gray Poet."
      Conservator, 17 (February, 1907), 82-85.

1365 _____. The Fight of a Book for the World: A
      Companion Volume to Leaves of Grass. West Yar-
      mouth, Mass.: The Stonecraft Press, 1926.

1366 _____. An Autolycus Pack, or What You Will.
      West Yarmouth, Mass.: The Stonecraft Press, 1927.
      Contains an article, 11 columns, "Walt Whitman's
      Indebtedness to Emerson," pp. 45-51.

1367 _____, ed. Walt Whitman's Diary in Canada. Bos-
      ton: Small, Maynard, 1904.

1368 KENNER, Hugh. "Review of Allen's The Solitary Singer
      (1955)." Poetry, 87 (December, 1955), 183-189.

1369 _____. "Whitman's Multitudes," in Kenner, Gnomon.
      New York: McDowell, Obolensky, 1958. Pp. 67-79.

1370 KENT, Rockwell, illustrator. Leaves of Grass. New
      York: Heritage Press, 1936. Contains 100 drawings.

1371 KIDNEY, Jennifer. "An American Prelude: Nostalgia
      and the Sense of Death in American Poetry." Ph.D.
      diss., Yale, 1974. DA, 36 (1975), 275A.

1372 KIELL, Norman, ed. Psychological Studies of Famous
     Americans: The Civil War Era. New York: Twayne,
     1964. Whitman, pp. 226-299.

1373 KIELY, Mary F. "'I Was Looking a Long While....'"
     American Book Collector, 21 (1971), 11-13. On the
     1860 Leaves of Grass.

1374 KILBY, James A. "Walt Whitman's 'Trippers and
     Askers.'" American Notes and Queries, 4 (Novem-
     ber, 1965), 37-39.

1375 KILEY, John F. "Whitman as Player." Nassau Re-
     view, 1 (Spring, 1965), 80. An original poem.

1376 KILLINGSWORTH, Myrth Jimmie. "Another Source for
     Whitman's Use of 'Electric.'" Walt Whitman Re-
     view, 23 (1977), 129-132.

1377 KIMBALL, William J. "'O Captain! My Captain! Un-
     typical Walt Whitman." Literary Criticism (Mysore,
     India, University), 6 (1965), 44-47.

1378 KINKEAD-WEEKES, M. "Walt Whitman passes the
     ful-stop by ...," in Lee, Brian S., ed., An English
     Miscellany: Presented to W. S. Mackie. Capetown,
     South Africa: Oxford University Press, 1977.

1379 KINNAIRD, John. "Whitman: The Paradox of Identity."
     Partisan Review, 25 (1958), 380-405. Reprinted in
     revised form in Pearce, ed., Walt Whitman: A Col-
     lection (1962), pp. 24-36.

1380 KINNELL, Galway. "Whitman's Indicative Words."
     American Poetry Magazine, 2 (1973), 9-11. Re-
     printed in Railton, ed., Walt Whitman's Autograph
     Revision (1974), pp. 53-55.

1381 KIRKLAND, Winifred Margaretta. "Americanization and
     Walt Whitman." Dial, 66 (May 31, 1919), 537-539.
     Expanded version printed in Kirkland, View Vertical.
     Boston: Houghton Mifflin, 1920. Pp. 236-243.

1382 KNAPP, Adeline. "A Whitman Coincidence." Critic,
     44 (May, 1907), 467-468. Walt Whitman and Jules
     Michelet, identical passages in Whitman's "The Man-
     of-War-Bird" and Michelet's The Bird. See also
     article by Gay Wilson Allen (1937).

1383 KNIEGER, Bernard. "The Compassion of Walt Whit-
      man. " Chicago Jewish Forum, 21 (Winter, 1962-
      1963), 144-147.

1384 KNOWLTON, Edgar C., Jr. "Whitman's 'Aliaska' and
      'Bajadore' Identified. " Walt Whitman Review, 22
      (1976), 84-86.

1385 KNOX, George A., and Harry Lawton. The Whitman-
      Hartmann Controversy, Including "Conversations with
      Walt Whitman (1895), " and Other Essays. Bern:
      Herbert Lang; Frankfurt: Munchen, 1976.

1386 KOCH, Richard Earl. "Walt Whitman, T. S. Eliot, and
      the Dilemma of Modern Consciousness. " Ph. D.
      diss., Michigan State, 1974. DA, 36 (1975), 319A.

1387 KOLB, Deborah S. "Walt Whitman and the South. "
      Walt Whitman Review, 22 (1976), 3-14.

1388 KOLINSKY, Muriel. "'Me Tarzan, You Jane?': Whit-
      man's Attitudes Toward Women from a Women's Lib-
      eration Point of View. " Walt Whitman Review, 23
      (1977), 155-165.

1389 KOLLERER, Charles T. "The Valved Voice: A Stylis-
      tic Analysis of Whitman's 1855 Leaves of Grass. "
      Ph. D. diss., California (Berkeley), 1973. DA, 35
      (1974), 3687A.

1390 KOMROFF, Manuel. Walt Whitman: The Singer and
      the Chains. New York: Privately printed by the
      author, 1966. Pamphlet.

1391 KORNBLATT, Joyce. "Whitman's Vision of the Past
      in 'The Sleepers.'" Walt Whitman Review, 16 (1970),
      86-89.

1392 KOSTER, Donald. Transcendentalism in America.
      Boston: Twayne, 1975. Whitman, pp. 57-63.

1393 KOUWENHOVEN, John A., ed. Leaves of Grass and
      Selected Prose. New York: Random House, 1950.
      Modern Library edition. See also ANGELO, Valenti,
      Modern Library edition, 1936.

1394 KOVEN, Bernard de, and Sholom J. Kahn. "A 'Symphonic' Arrangement of Two Whitman Poems." <u>Walt</u> <u>Whitman Review</u>, 9 (1963), 37-40.

1395 KOZLOFF, Max. "Walt Whitman and American Art," in Miller, E. H., ed., <u>The Artistic Legacy</u> (1970), pp. 29-53.

1396 KRAMER, Aaron. "The Prophetic Tradition in American Poetry, 1835-1900." Ph.D. diss., New York University, 1967. <u>DA</u>, 27 (1967), 3461A.

1397 _____. The Prophetic Tradition in American Poetry, 1835-1900. Rutherford, N.J.: Fairleigh Dickinson University Press, 1968. Whitman, pp. 31-33 et passim.

1398 KRAMER, Maurice. "Review of Stephen Black's Whitman's Journeys into Chaos (1975)." <u>Literature and</u> <u>Psychology</u>, 26 (1976), 124-130.

1399 KRAPF, Norbert. "Whitman's 'Calamus': Adam from the Garden to the City." <u>Walt Whitman Review</u>, 19 (1973), 162-164.

1400 KRAUSE, Sydney J. "Whitman, Music, and 'Proud Music of the Storm.'" <u>PMLA</u>, 72 (September, 1957), 705-721.

1401 _____. "Whitman's Yawping Bird as Comic Defense." <u>Bulletin of New York Public Library</u>, 68 (June, 1964), 347-360.

1402 _____, ed. Essays on Determinism in American <u>Literature</u>. Kent, Ohio: Kent State University Press, 1964. Whitman, passim; see "The Devil Is White," by Edward Stone, pp. 55-66.

1403 KRAUTH, Leland. "Whitman and His Readers: The Comradeship Theme." <u>Walt Whitman Review</u>, 20 (1974), 147-151.

1404 KREUTER, Kent Kirby. "The Literary Response to Science, Technology, and Industrialism: Studies in the Thought of Nathaniel Hawthorne, Melville, Whitman, and Twain." Ph.D. diss., Wisconsin, History, 1963. <u>DA</u>, 24 (1964), 2446.

1405 KRIM, Seymour. "Review of Gay Wilson Allen's The
      Solitary Singer." Hudson Review, 9 (Spring, 1956),
      134-140.

1406 KROGVIG, Kjell. "Approach to Whitman Through Werge-
      land, " trans. by Sigrid Moe, in Allen, ed., Walt
      Whitman Abroad (1955), pp. 137-143.

1407 KROLL, Barbara. "The 'Confession' in 'Crossing
      Brooklyn Ferry' and the Jewish Day of Atonement
      Prayers." Walt Whitman Review, 23 (1977), 125-
      129.

1408 KROLL, Ernest, et al., eds. Walt Whitman: A Cen-
      tennial Celebration. Beloit, Wis.: Beloit Poetry
      Journal, 1954. A collection of verse.

1409 KUEBRICH, David. "Whitman's New Theism." Emer-
      son Society Quarterly, 24 (1978), 229-241.

1410 KUHN, John G. "Whitman's Artistry: 'The Reproduce
      All in My Own Forms.'" Walt Whitman Review, 8
      (1962), 51-63.

1411 KUMAR, Shiv K., ed. Leaves of Grass. New Delhi:
      Eurasia Publishing House, 1963.

1412 KUMMINGS, Donald D. "Whitman's Voice in 'Song of
      Myself': From Private to Public." Walt Whitman
      Review, 17 (1971), 10-15.

1413 _____. "The Poetry of Democracies: Tocqueville's
      Aristocratic View." Comparative Literature Studies,
      11 (1974), 306-319.

1414 _____. "A Note on the Americanness of Walt Whit-
      man." Calamus, 10 (1975), 18-27.

1415 _____. "Walt Whitman's Vernacular Poetics." Ca-
      nadian Review of American Studies, 7 (1976), 119-131.

1416 _____. "The Vernacular Hero in Whitman's 'Song
      of Myself.'" Walt Whitman Review, 23 (1977), 23-
      34.

1417 KWIAT, Joseph J. "Robert Henri and the Emerson-

Whitman Tradition." PMLA, 71 (September, 1956),
617-636. Reprinted in Kwiat, Joseph J., and Mary
C. Turpie, eds., Studies in American Culture: Dominant Ideas and Images. Minneapolis: University of
Minnesota Press, 1960. Pp. 153-170.

1418 LA BELLE, Jenijoy. "'Out of the Cradle Endlessly
Rocking': Whitman, Eliot, and Theodore Roethke."
Walt Whitman Review, 22 (1976), 75-84.

1419 LABIANCE, Dominick A., and William J. Reeves.
"'A March in the Ranks Hard-Prest, and the Road
Unknown': A Chemical Analysis." American Notes
and Queries, 15 (1977), 110-111.

1420 LACKEY, Robert Samuel A. "The Argument of 'Song
of Myself' (1860 edition): An Archetypal and Rhetorical Analysis." Ph.D. diss., Tulsa, 1975. DA,
36 (1975), 1505A.

1421 LAFOURCADE, Georges. "Swinburne and Walt Whitman." Modern Language Review, 22 (January, 1927),
84-86. Also printed in Revue Anglo-Américaine, 8
(October, 1931), 49-50.

1422 LALOR, Eugene T. "The Literary Bohemians of New
York City in the Mid-Nineteenth Century." Ph.D.
diss., St. John's (Queens, N.Y.), 1977. DA, 38
(1977), 264A.

1423 LANDAUER, Bella. Leaves of Music by Walt Whitman.
New York: Privately printed, 1937.

1424 LANDGREN, Marchal E. "George C. Cox: Whitman's
Photographer." Walt Whitman Review, 9 (1963), 11-
15.

1425 LANG, Cecil Y. "A Further Note on Swinburne and
Whitman." Modern Language Notes, 64 (March,
1949), 176-177. See also article by Lafourcade.

1426 LANIER, Sidney. "Walt Whitman: The Dandy-Upside-
Down," in Anderson, Charles R., ed., The Centen-
nial Edition of Sidney Lanier, 10 vols. Baltimore:
Johns Hopkins Press, 1945. Reprinted in Leary,
Lewis G., ed., American Literary Essays (1960),
pp. 116-117.

1427 LANUX, Pierre de. Young France and New America.
     New York: Macmillan, 1917. Whitman, passim.

1428 LA PORTE, P. M. "Cézanne and Whitman." Maga-
     zine of Art, 37 (September, 1944), 223-227. See
     also article by Marion Hartley.

1429 LARBAUD, Valéry. "Development of the Poet" (Paris,
     1918), trans. by Roger M. Asselineau, in Allen, ed.,
     Walt Whitman Abroad (1955), pp. 61-75.

1430 LA RUE, Robert. "Whitman's Sea: Large Enough for
     Moby Dick?" Walt Whitman Review, 7 (1966), 51-
     59.

1431 LASSER, Michael L. "Sex and Sentimentality in Whit-
     man's Poetry." Emerson Society Quarterly, 43
     (1966), 94-97.

1432 LAUTER, Paul. "Walt Whitman: Love and Comrade."
     American Imago, 16 (Winter, 1959), 407-435. Re-
     printed in Kiell, ed., Psychological Studies (1964),
     pp. 271-300. Also reprinted in Ruitenbeek, H. M.,
     ed., The Literary Imagination: Psychoanalysis and
     the Genius of the World. Chicago: Quadrangle,
     1965.

1433 LAUBENTHAL, Penne J. "Prometheus, Prophet and
     Priest: An Interpretation of García Lorca's Poet in
     New York in Relationship to Walt Whitman's Leaves
     of Grass." Ph.D. diss., George Peabody College
     for Teachers, 1971. DA, 33 (1972), 1732A.

1434 LAW, Richard A. "The Respiration Motif in 'Song of
     Myself.'" Walt Whitman Review, 10 (1964), 92-97.

1435 LAWRENCE, D. H. "Whitman," in Studies in Classic
     American Literature. New York: Thomas Seltzer,
     1923. Reprinted, New York: Doubleday, Anchor,
     1953. Pp. 241-264. "Whitman," has been frequently
     reprinted, as in the following: Wilson, Edmund, ed.,
     The Shock of Recognition (1943), pp. 1061-1077.
     Beck, Anthony, ed., Selected Literary Criticism.
     New York: Viking Press, 1956, Pp. 392-407. Ar-
     nold, Armin, ed., with a Preface by Harry T. Moore,
     The Symbolic Meaning. New York: Viking Press,
     1962. Pp. 229-240. Murphy, Francis, ed., Walt
     Whitman: A Critical Anthology (1962), pp. 196-205.

1436 _____. "Democracy," in Phoenix: The Posthumous
Papers, ed. E. D. McDonald. New York: Viking
Press, 1936. Pp. 699-718. Lawrence died in 1930.

1437 LAW-ROBERTSON, Harry. Walt Whitman in Deutsch-
land. Giessen: W. Schnitz, 1935. Reprinted, Ams-
terdam: Swets and Zeitlinger, 1968.

1438 LEACH, N. R. "Edith Wharton's Interest in Walt Whitman." Yale University Library Gazette, 33 (October,
1958), 63-66.

1439 LEARY, Lewis Gaston, compiler. Articles on American Literature: 1900-1950. Durham, N.C.: Duke
University Press, 1954. Whitman, pp. 303-316.

1440 _____, comp. Articles on American Literature:
1950-1967. Durham, N.C.: Duke University Press,
1968. Whitman, pp. 550-572.

1441 _____. "Kate Chopin and Walt Whitman." Walt
Whitman Review, 16 (1970), 120-121. "Out of the
Cradle ..." and The Awakening.

1442 _____. American Literature: Study and Research
Guide. New York: St. Martin's Press, 1976.
Whitman, pp. 132-134.

1443 _____, ed. American Literary Essays. New York:
Crowell, 1960. "Walt Whitman," by Sidney Lanier,
pp. 116-117.

1444 _____, ed. The Teacher and American Literature.
Champaign, Ill.: National Council of Teachers of
English, 1965. "Recent Scholarship on Whitman and
Dickinson," by Edmund Reiss, pp. 115-127; and
"Whitman and Dickinson: Implications for School
Programs," by Sister M. Judine, I.H.N., pp. 128-
133.

1445 LE CLAIR, Thomas. "Prufrock and the Open Road."
Walt Whitman Review, 17 (1971), 123-126.

1446 LEDBETTER, J. T. "Whitman's Power in the Short
Poem: A Discussion of 'Whispers of Heavenly Death.'"
Walt Whitman Review, 21 (1975), 155-158.

1447 LEE, G. S. "Order for the Next Poet." Putnam's
     Magazine, 1 (March, 1907), 697-703; 2 (April, 1907),
     99-107.

1448 LEGGETT, B. J. "The Structure of 'On Journeys
     Through the States.'" Walt Whitman Review, 14
     (1968), 58-59.

1449 LEGLER, Henry Eduard. Walt Whitman: Yesterday
     and Today. Chicago: Brothers of the Book, 1916.

1450 LEHMBERG, P. S. "'That Vast Something': A Note
     on Whitman and the American West." Studies in
     Humanities, 6 (1978), 50-53.

1451 LEIGHTON, Walker. "Whitman's Note of Democracy."
     Arena, 28 (July, 1902), 61-65.

1452 LE MASTER, J. R. "Some Traditional Poems from
     Leaves of Grass." Walt Whitman Review, 13 (1967),
     44-51.

1453 _____. "Jesse Stuart's 'Album of Destiny'--in Whit-
     man's Eternal Flow." Illinois Quarterly, 36 (1973),
     38-48.

1454 LENHART, Charmenz S. "Walt Whitman and Music in
     Leaves of Grass," in Lenhart, Musical Influence on
     American Poetry. Athens: University of Georgia
     Press, 1956. Pp. 161-209.

1455 LEONARD, David Charles. "Lamarchian Evolution in
     Whitman's 'Song of Myself.'" Walt Whitman Review,
     24 (1978), 21-28.

1456 LEONARD, M. H. "Walt Whitman to His Followers."
     South Atlantic Quarterly, 16 (July, 1917), 222-226.

1457 LERNER, Arthur. "Psychoanalytical Orientation of
     Three American Poets: Poe, Whitman, and Aiken."
     Ph.D. diss., Southern California, 1967. DA, 29
     (1968), 1229A.

1458 _____. Psychoanalytical Orientation of Three Amer-
     ican Poets: Poe, Whitman, and Aiken. Rutherford,
     N.J.: Fairleigh Dickinson University Press, 1970.

1459 LESSING, Otto Eduard. "Whitman and His German
      Critics." Journal of English and Germanic Philology,
      9 (January, 1910), 85-98.

1460 _____. "Walt Whitman's Message." Open Court,
      33 (August, 1919), 449-462.

1461 _____. "Walt Whitman and His German Critics
      Prior to 1910." American Collector, 3 (October,
      1926), 7-15.

1462 LE WINTER, Oswald. "Whitman's 'Lilacs.'" Walt
      Whitman Review, 10 (1964), 10-14.

1463 LEWIS, R. W. B. "The Danger of Innocence: Adam
      as Hero in American Literature." Yale Review, 29
      (Spring, 1950), 473-490.

1464 _____. The American Adam: Innocence, Tragedy,
      and Tradition in the Nineteenth Century. Chicago:
      University of Chicago Press, 1955. Reprinted,
      Chicago: Phoenix Books, 1958. "The New Adam:
      Holmes and Whitman," pp. 28-53.

1465 _____. "The Aspiring Clown," in Scholes, Robert,
      ed., Learners and Discerners: A Newer Criticism.
      Charlottesville: University Press of Virginia, 1964.
      Pp. 63-108. Discusses theme of aspiring clown in
      Whitman, Hart Crane, Stevens, Nathanael West, et al.

1466 _____, ed. The Presence of Walt Whitman: Se-
      lected Papers from the English Institute. New York:
      Columbia University Press, 1962.

1467 _____, ed. "Walt Whitman," in Miller, Perry, ed.
      Major Writers of America, 2 vols. New York:
      Harcourt, Brace, and World, 1962. Vol. I, pp. 969-
      1119. "Introduction," pp. 969-986, reprinted as
      "Walt Whitman: Always Going Out and Coming In,"
      in Lewis, Trials of the Word: Essays in American
      Literature and the Humanistic Tradition. New Haven:
      Yale University Press, 1965. Pp. 3-35.

1468 LEWIS, Sylvia. "Impressions of Emily Dickinson," in
      Slatoff, Walter J., ed., With Respect to Readers:
      Dimensions of Literary Response. Ithaca, N.Y.:
      Cornell University Press, 1970. Pp. 191-207. Com-
      pares to Whitman.

1469 LEWIS, Ward B. "Walt Whitman: American Baby, "
     in Fiedler, ed. , The Art of the Essay (1958), pp.
     584-587.

1470 _____. "Walt Whitman: Johannes Schlaf's New
     Being ('Neuer Mensch'). " Calamus, 6 (1972), 22-34.
     Also published in Revue de Littérature Comparée,
     47 (1973), 596-611.

1471 _____. "Message from America: The Verse of
     Walt Whitman as Interpreted by German Authors in
     Exile. " German Life and Literature, 29 (1976), 215-
     227.

1472 LEWISOHN, Ludwig. "Whitman. " This Quarter, 4
     (July-September, 1931), 75-87.

1473 _____. Expressionism in America (1932). Revised
     and reissued as The Story of American Literature.
     New York: Harper, 1937. Reprinted, New York:
     Random House Modern Library, 1939.

1474 LIEBER, Todd Michael. "The Continuing Encounter:
     Studies of the American Romantic Hero. " Ph. D.
     diss. , Case Western Reserve, 1969. DA, 30 (1970),
     3911A.

1475 _____. Endless Experiments. Columbus: Ohio
     State University Press, 1973. "Walt Whitman: The
     Paradox of Cosmic Selfhood, " pp. 75-112.

1476 LIEBERMAN, Elias. "Walt Whitman, " in Mason,
     Gabriel Richard, ed. , Great American Liberals.
     Boston: Starr King Press, 1956. Pp. 83-95.

1477 LIN, Maurice Yaofu. "Children of Adam: Ginsberg,
     Ferlinghetti, and Snyder in the Emerson-Whitman
     Tradition. " Ph. D. diss. , Minnesota, 1972. DA,
     34 (1973), 781A.

1478 LINDFORS, Bernth. "Whitman's 'When I Heard the
     Learn'd Astronomer. ' " Walt Whitman Review, 10
     (1964), 19-21.

1479 LINDSAY, Vachel. "Walt Whitman. " New Republic,
     37 (December 5, 1923), 3-5.

1480 LITTLE, William A. "Walt Whitman and the

Nibelungenlied." PMLA, 80 (December, 1965),
562-570.

1481 LIVINGSTON, James L. "Walt Whitman's Epistle to
the Americans." American Literature, 40 (1969),
542-544. New Testament influence in "A Song of
the Rolling Earth."

1482 _____. "With Whitman and Hegel Around the Camp-
fire." Walt Whitman Review, 15 (1969), 120-122.

1483 LOCKE, E. W. Three Years in Camp and Hospital.
Boston: George D. Russell, 1870. Similar to Whitman's accounts.

1484 LOMBARD, Charles M. "Whitman on French Romanticism." Walt Whitman Review, 12 (1966), 41-43.

1485 _____. "Whitman and (Victor) Hugo." Walt Whitman Review, 19 (1973), 19-25.

1486 LONG, Haniel. Walt Whitman and the Springs of Courage. Sante Fe, N.M.: Writers' Editions, 1938.
Reprinted Port Washington, N.Y.: Kennikat Press,
1977.

1487 LONG-ISLANDER. "Annual Walt Whitman Page," ed.
by various critics. Newspaper established by Whitman, May 29, 1838; sold one year later, May, 1839.

1488 LORCH, Fred W. "Henry David Thoreau and the Organic Principle in Poetry." Ph.D. diss., Iowa,
1936. Whitman, passim.

1489 _____. "Thoreau and the Organic Principle in Poetry." PMLA, 53 (March, 1938), 286-302. Whitman, passim.

1490 LOVEJOY, Arthur O. The Great Chain of Being: A
Study of the History of an Idea. Cambridge: Harvard University Press, 1936. Emerson-Whitman
ideas, passim.

1491 LOVELL, John, Jr. "Appreciating Whitman: 'Passage
to India.'" Modern Language Quarterly, 21 (June,
1960), 131-141.

1492 LOVING, Jerome M. "Civil War Letters of George

Washington Whitman from North Carolina." North
Carolina Historical Review, 50 (1973), 73-92.

1493 _____. "Civil War Letters of George Washington
Whitman." Ph.D. diss., Duke, 1974. DA, 34
(1974), 5979A-5980A.

1494 _____. "'A Brooklyn Soldier, and a Noble One':
A Brooklyn Daily Union Article by Whitman." Walt
Whitman Review, 20 (1974), 27-30. Refers to Whit-
man's brother, George Washington Whitman.

1495 _____. "'Our Veterans Mustering Out'--Another
Newspaper Article by Whitman About His Soldier
Brother." Yale University Library Gazette, 49
(1974), 217-224.

1496 _____. "The Estate of George Washington Whitman:
An Horatio Alger Story in Walt Whitman's Family."
Missouri Historical Society Bulletin, 31 (1975), 105-
110.

1497 _____. "Walt Whitman: Is He Persecuted?" in
White, ed., "The Bi-centennial Walt Whitman: Essays
from The Long-Islander," June 24, 1976. Reprinted
in Walt Whitman Review, 22 supplement (1976), 25-
26. Refers to a TV program on Whitman.

1498 _____. "Whitman and Harlan: New Evidence."
American Literature, 48 (1976), 219-222. Refers to
James Harlan, Secretary of the Interior, who dis-
missed Whitman in June, 1865.

1499 _____. Walt Whitman's Champion: William Douglas
O'Connor. College Station, Texas: A & M University Press, 1977. Includes a reprint of six of O'Connor's writings on Whitman, including The Good Gray
Poet (1866), and "Emerson and Whitman" (1882).
Also contains a bibliography of O'Connor, pp. 243-
245.

1500 _____. "Genesis of The Good Gray Poet." Texas
Studies in Literature and Language, 19 (1977), 227-
233.

1501 _____, ed. Civil War Letters of George Washington
Whitman. Foreword by Gay Wilson Allen. Durham,
N.C.: Duke University Press, 1975.

1502 LOVING, Pierre. "Towards Walt Whitman." Double
Dealer (New Orleans), 4 (September, 1922), 139-142.

1503 LOWELL, Amy. "Walt Whitman and the New Poetry."
Yale Review, 16 (April, 1927), 502-519. Reprinted
in Lowell, Poetry and Poets: Essays. Boston:
Houghton Mifflin, 1930. Article and book published
posthumously; Lowell died in 1925.

1504 LOWENFELS, Walter. "Walt Whitman's Civil War."
Walt Whitman Review, 6 (1960), 52-53.

1505 _____. "Whitman on Bruno." Walt Whitman Review,
9 (1963), 42-43. Refers to Giordano Bruno; see listing above.

1506 _____. "The Eternal Meanings." American Dialogue,
5 (1969), 5-7.

1507 _____, ed. with Introduction. The Tenderest Lover:
The Erotic Poetry of Walt Whitman. New York:
Delacorte Press, 1970. A Collection, illustrated by
J. K. Lambert.

1508 _____, and Nan Braymer, eds. Walt Whitman's
Civil War. New York: Knopf, 1961. Notebooks,
letters, newspaper articles; illustrated with 16 pages
of Civil War drawings by Winslow Homer.

1509 LOWES, John Livingston. Convention and Revolt in
Poetry. Boston: Houghton Mifflin, 1919. Whitman,
passim.

1510 LOZYNSKY, Artem. "Irresponsible Reprint: Bucke's
Walt Whitman." Walt Whitman Review, 18 (1972),
104-106.

1511 _____. "Whitman's Complete Poems and Prose:
'Bible' or 'Volume.'" Walt Whitman Review, 19
(1973), 28-30. Examines variations in three print-
ings of R. M. Bucke's "An Impromptu Criticism."

1512 _____. "A Lost Whitman Letter to Bucke." Walt
Whitman Review, 19 (1973), 168-169.

1513 _____. "Walt Whitman in Canada." American Book
Collector, 23 (1973), 21-23.

1514 _____. "'Us Three Meaning America': Whitman's
Literary Executors." Papers of the Bibliographic
Society of America, 68 (1974), 442-444.

1515 _____. "The Letters of Dr. Richard Maurice Bucke
to Walt Whitman: Edited with a Critical Introduction
and Historical Annotations." Ph. D. diss., Wayne
State, 1974. DA, 35 (1975), 7913A.

1516 _____. "Whitman the Man and Hawthorne the Artist:
An English Evaluation." Nathaniel Hawthorne Journal, 5 (1975), 270-271.

1517 _____. "Whitman's Death Bed: Two Nurses' Re-
ports." American Literature, 47 (1975), 270-273.

1518 _____. "Whitman and Man's Moral Nature." Walt
Whitman Review, 21 (1975), 36-37. Refers to work
by Richard M. Bucke (1879).

1519 _____. "Walt Whitman on Marriage." Notes and
Queries, 22 (1975), 120-121.

1520 _____. "S. Weir Mitchell on Whitman: An Unpublished Letter." American Notes and Queries, 13
(1975), 120-121.

1521 _____. "Dr. Richard Maurice Bucke: A Religious
Disciple of Whitman," in Myerson, ed., Studies:
1977 (1978), pp. 387-404.

1522 _____. "What's in a Title? Whitman's 'Calamus'
and Bucke's Calamus," in Myerson, ed., Studies
(1979), pp. 475-488.

1523 _____, ed. The Letters of Dr. Richard Maurice
Bucke, to Walt Whitman. Detroit: Wayne State Uni-
versity Press, 1977. Available through University
Microfilms.

1524 _____, ed. Richard Maurice Bucke, Medical Mystic:
Letters of Dr. Bucke to Walt Whitman and His
Friends. Foreword by Gay Wilson Allen. Detroit:
Wayne State University Press, 1977.

1525 _____, and Gloria A. Francis, eds. Whitman at
Auction, 1899-1972. Introduction by Charles E.

Feinberg. Detroit: Gale Research, 1978. Also
listed under FRANCIS, Gloria A.

1526 LUCAS, Edward Verrall. "Carpenters' Sons," in All
of a Piece: New Essays. New York: Lippincott,
1937. Pp. 55-60. Discusses Leaves of Grass.

1527 LUCAS, F. L. "Enfant terrible: Enfant gâté," in Authors Dead and Living. London: Chatto and Windus,
1926; New York: Macmillan, 1926. Pp. 115-123.

1528 LUECK, Beth Lynne. "Whitman's 'Mystic Deliria.'"
Walt Whitman Review, 24 (1978), 77-84.

1528a LYND, Robert. "Whitman: Man and Poet," in Lynd,
Books and Writers. New York: Dent, 1952. Pp. 1-7.

1529 LYNEN, John F. The Design of the Present: Essays
on Time and Form in American Literature. New
Haven: Yale University Press, 1969. "The Poetry
of the Present and the Form of the Moment: Walt
Whitman," pp. 273-339.

1530 MABBOTT, Thomas Ollive. "Walt Whitman and the
Aristidean." American Mercury, 2 (June, 1924),
205-207. Refers to Whitman's four contributions
(short stories), in the magazine edited by Thomas
Dunn English, 1845.

1531 _____. "Notes on Walt Whitman's Franklin Evans."
Notes and Queries, 149 (December 12, 1925), 419-
420.

1532 _____. "Early Quotations and Allusions of Walt
Whitman." Notes and Queries, 150 (March 6, 1926),
169-170.

1533 _____. "Some Account of Sojourner Truth." American Collector, 4 (April, 1927), 18-20. Reprints a
letter to Whitman.

1534 _____. "Whitman's Lines on Duluth." American
Literature, 3 (November, 1931), 316-317.

1535 _____. "William Winter's Serious Parody of Walt
Whitman." American Literature, 5 (March, 1933),
63-66.

1536 _____ . "Walt Whitman and William Motherwell."
Notes and Queries, 168 (May 4, 1935), 314.

1537 _____ . "Walt Whitman's Use of 'Libertad.'" Notes
and Queries, 174 (May 21, 1938), 367-368.

1538 _____ . "Walt Whitman and the Brooklyn Freeman."
Notes and Queries, 183 (September 26, 1942), 186-
187.

1539 _____ . "Whitman: Notes on Emerson." Notes and
Queries, 185 (February 26, 1944), 14.

1540 _____ . "Whitman's 'Song of Myself,' Sec. 24, line
19." Explicator, 5 (April, 1947), item 43.

1541 _____ . "Walt Whitman and Catullus." Notes and
Queries, 196 (November 10, 1951), 500.

1542 _____ . "Whitman's 'Song of Myself.'" Explicator,
11 (March, 1953), item 34.

1543 _____ . "Walt Whitman Edits the Sunday Times,
July, 1842-June, 1843." American Literature, 39
(March, 1967), 99-102.

1544 _____ , and Rollo G. Silver. "Mr. Whitman Recon-
siders." Colophon, 3 (February, 1932), part 9.

1545 _____ , ed. with Introduction. The Half-Breed and
Other Stories. New York: Columbia University
Press, 1927. Four short stories published in the
Aristidean Magazine, 1845.

1546 _____ , and Rollo G. Silver, eds. with Introduction
and Notes. A Child's Reminiscence. Seattle: University of Washington Press, 1930. 44 pages.

1547 _____ , and Rollo G. Silver, eds. "Walt Whitman's
'Tis but Ten Years Since.'" American Literature,
15 (March, 1943), 51-62. Reprints articles in the
New York Weekly Gazette (1874), not in later writings.

1548 _____ , and Rollo G. Silver, eds. Walt Whitman's
'Tis But Ten Years Since. Durham, N.C.: Duke
University Press, 1943. Pamphlet.

1549 MABIE, Hamilton W. "American Life in Whitman's
Poetry." Outlook, 75 (September 5, 1903), 67-78.
Reprinted in Mabie, Backgrounds of Literature.
New York: Macmillan, 1912. Pp. 195-243. Ex-
panded.

1550 McALEER, John J. "Whitman and Goethe: More on
the 'Van Rensellaer' Letter." Walt Whitman Review,
8 (1962), 83-85.

1551 McCAIN, Rea. "Walt Whitman in Italy: A Bibliography." Bulletin of Bibliography, 17 (January-April,
May-August, 1941), 66-67, 92-93. Annotated.

1552 _____. "Walt Whitman in Italy." Italica, 20 (March,
1943), 4-16.

1553 MacCARTHY, Desmond. "Walt Whitman," in MacCarthy, Memories. Forewords by Raymond Mortimer
and Cyril Connolly. New York: Oxford University
Press, 1953. Pp. 132-136.

1554 McCARTHY, Harold T. "Henry Miller's Democratic
Vistas." American Quarterly, 23 (1971), 221-235.

1555 McCARTHY, Justin. Reminiscences, 2 vols. New
York: Harper, 1899. Whitman, Vol. I, pp. 225-228.

1556 McCLARY, B. H. "Burroughs to Whitman on Emerson." Emerson Society Quarterly, 43 (1966), 67-68.

1557 McCORMICK, Edgar L. "Walt Whitman, Santayana's
Poet of Barbarism." Serif, 5 (1968), 24-28.

1558 McCORMICK, James P. "Walt Whitman in Japan."
Walt Whitman Newsletter, 3 (March, 1957), 11-13.

1559 McCULLAGH, James C. "'Proud Music of the Storm':
A Study in Dynamics." Walt Whitman Review, 21
(1975), 66-73.

1560 McCUSKER, Honor. "Leaves of Grass: First Editions
and Manuscripts in the Whitman Collection." More
Books, 13 (May, 1938), 179-192.

1561 McDERMOTT, John Francis. "Whitman and the Par-
tons: Glimpses from the Diary of Thomas Butler

Gunn, 1856-1860." American Literature, 29 (November, 1957), 316-319.

1562 MacDONALD, Donald, ed. Parodies. New York: Random House, 1960. Whitman, pp. 143-146 et passim.

1563 McDOWELL, Michael M. "American Attitudes Towards Death, 1825-1865." Ph.D. diss., Brandeis, 1978. DA, 38 (1978), 7335A.

1564 McELDERRY, Bruce R., Jr. "Hamlin Garland's View of Whitman." Personalist, 36 (August, 1955), 369-378.

1565 _____. "The Inception of 'Passage to India.'" PMLA, 71 (September, 1956), 837-839.

1566 _____. "Poetry and Religion: A Parallel in Whitman and Arnold." Walt Whitman Review, 8 (1962), 80-83.

1567 _____. "Robert Penn Warren and Whitman." Walt Whitman Review, 8 (1962), 91.

1568 _____. "Personae in Whitman (1855-1860)." American Transcendental Quarterly, 12 (1971), 25-32.

1569 McGHEE, Richard D. "Concepts of Time in Whitman's Poetry." Walt Whitman Review, 15 (1969), 76-85.

1570 _____. "Leaves of Grass and Cultural Development." Walt Whitman Review, 16 (1970), 3-14.

1571 McGLINCHIE, Claire. "Three Indigenous Americans: Whitman, Eakins, Gilbert," in Proceedings of the Sixth International Congress of Aesthetics. Uppsala, Sweden: University of Uppsala Press, 1972. Pp. 709-713.

1572 McILWRAITH, J. N. "A Dialogue in Hades: Omar Khayyám and Walt Whitman." Atlantic, 89 (June, 1902), 808-812.

1573 MACKALL, L. L. "Whitman and Bucke: Notes for Bibliophiles." New York Herald Tribune Books, 12 (April 12, 1936), 23.

1574 McKEITHAN, Daniel M. Whitman's "Song of Myself,"
Sec. 34, and Its Background. Essays and Studies
on American Language and Literature, Monograph
No. 18. Uppsala, Sweden: Lundequistska bokh,
1969. Refers to the Texas Battle section.

1575 _____. "Two Avian Images in Marvell and Whitman."
Walt Whitman Review, 17 (1971), 101-113.

1576 McKENZIE, Gordon M. "Is Whitman the Hippies' Guru?"
University-College Quarterly, 16 (1971), 14-19.

1577 MacLACHLAN, C. H. "Walt Whitman as a Country
Editor." Grassroots Editor, 1 (January, 1960),
15-16.

1578 McLEOD, Alan L. "Walt Whitman in Australia."
Walt Whitman Review, 7 (1961), 23-35.

1579 _____. "Jan Christian Smuts' Walt Whitman."
Calamus, 5 (April, 1972), 1-9.

1580 _____, ed. Walt Whitman in Australia and New
Zealand: A Record of His Reception. Lock Haven,
Pa., and Sydney, Australia: Wentworth Press, 1964.
Mimeographed, 17 lectures, some by William Gay,
and essays from 1892 to 1907.

1581 _____, ed. "Nineteen Letters Exchanged by Whitman
and Bernard O'Dowd in 1890-1891," in Walt Whitman
in Australia (1964).

1582 McMARTIN, Gaines Noble. "A Perspective on Unity
in the Poems of Bryant, Longfellow, Emerson, and
Whitman: The Use of Analogy and Example in Metaphor." Ph.D. diss., California (Los Angeles), 1975.
DA, 36 (1976), 4494A.

1583 McMULLIN, Stanley E. "Walt Whitman's Influence in
Canada." Dalhousie Review, 49 (1969), 361-368.

1584 _____. "Review of Walt Whitman Correspondence,
Vols. 4 and 5." Dalhousie Review, 50 (1970), 135-
137.

1585 _____. "Whitman and the Canadian Press, 1872-1919:
A Brief Survey." Walt Whitman Review, 20 (1974),
132-140.

1586 McMURRAY, Patricia E. "Whitman's Personae."
      Ph.D. diss., Pennsylvania, 1971. DA, 32 (1972),
      4622A.

1587 McNALLY, James. "Varieties of Alliteration in Whit-
      man." Walt Whitman Review, 13 (1967), 28-32.

1588 MacPHAIL, Andrew. Essays in Puritanism. London:
      T. Fisher, Unwin; Boston: Houghton Mifflin, 1905.
      "Walter Whitman," pp. 168-206.

1589 McPHERSON, Hugo. "Whitman, Howells, and the Amer-
      ican Scholars." University of Toronto Quarterly,
      30 (October, 1960), 101-105.

1590 McSWEENEY, Kerry. "Melville, Dickinson, Whitman,
      and Psychoanalytic Criticism." Critical Quarterly,
      19 (1977), 71-82.

1591 McWILLIAMS, John P., Jr. "'Drum Taps' and Battle-
      Pieces: The Blossom of War." American Quarterly,
      23 (1971), 181-201.

1592 McWILLIAMS, Wilson Carey. The Idea of Fraternity
      in American Literature. Berkeley: University of
      California Press, 1973. Whitman, passim.

1593 MACY, John Albert. The Spirit of American Litera-
      ture. New York: Boni and Liveright, 1908; Garden
      City, N.Y.: Doubleday, 1913. Whitman, pp. 210-
      247.

1594 _____. The Critical Game. Garden City, N.Y.:
      Doubleday, 1922. "Biographies of Whitman," pp.
      203-211.

1595 _____, ed. American Writers on American Litera-
      ture. New York: Horace Liveright, 1931. "Whit-
      man," by James Oppenheim, pp. 258-273.

1596 MADIGAN, Francis V., Jr. "A Mirror of Shelley in
      Whitman." Greyfriar, 11 (1970), 3-19.

1597 MADSEN, Varden. "William Dean Howells' Formal
      Poetics and His Appraisals of Whitman and Emily
      Dickinson." Walt Whitman Review, 23 (1977), 103-
      109.

1598 MAGEE, John D. "Whitman's Cosmofloat." Walt Whitman Review, 10 (1964), 43-46. Recurrent concept of "float."

1599 _____. "'Crossing Brooklyn Ferry': A Hundred Years Hence." Walt Whitman Review, 15 (1969), 38-43.

1600 MAGOWAN, Robin. "The Horse of the Gods: Possession in 'Song of Myself.'" Walt Whitman Review, 15 (1969), 67-76.

1601 MAINI, Darshan Singh. "Walt Whitman and Puran Singh: A Study in Affinities," in Maini, ed., Variations on American Literature. New Delhi: U.S. Education Foundation in India, 1968.

1602 MAJAR, Minor W. "A New Interpretation of Whitman's Calamus Poems." Walt Whitman Review, 13 (1967), 51-54.

1603 MAJOR, Clarence. "Close to the Ground." American Dialogue, 5 (1969), 35.

1604 MALBONE, Raymond G. "Organic Language in 'Patrolling Barnegat.'" Walt Whitman Review, 13 (1967), 125-127.

1605 MALE, Roy R. "Whitman's Radical Utterance." Emerson Society Quarterly, 60 (1970), 73-75.

1606 _____. "Whitman's Mechanical Muse," in Zimmerman and Weathers, eds., Papers (1970), pp. 35-43.

1607 MALIN, Stephen D. "'A Boston Ballad' and the Boston Riot." Walt Whitman Review, 9 (1963), 51-57.

1608 MALONE, Walter Kark. "Parallels to Hindu and Taoist Thought in Walt Whitman." Ph.D. diss., Temple, 1964. DA, 25 (1965), 4689-4690.

1609 MANCA, Marie A. "Harmony and the Poet: Six Studies in the Creative Ordering of Reality." Ph.D. diss., Yale, 1970. DA, 32 (1971), 2647A.

1610 MANN, Charles W., Jr. "Review of the Illustrated Specimen Days." Library Journal, 96 (1971), 3761.

Refers to Whitman, Specimen Days. Boston: God-
ine, 1971.

1611 MANN, Klaus (son of Thomas Mann). "The Present
Greatness of Walt Whitman." Decision, 1 (April,
1941), 14-30.

1612 _____. André Gide and the Modern Spirit. New
York: Creative Age Press, 1944.

1613 MANN, Thomas. "Letter to Hans Reisiger" (Frankfurt,
1922), trans. Horst Frenz, in Allen, ed., Walt Whitman Abroad (1955), p. 16.

1614 MARCELL, David W. "The Two Whitmans and Democ-
racy in America," in Browne, Ray B., Larry N.
Landrum, and William Bottorff, eds., Challenge in
American Culture. Bowling Green, Ohio: Bowling
Green University Press, 1971. Pp. 178-189.

1615 MARCUS, Mordecai. "Walt Whitman and Emily Dickinson." Personalist, 43 (October, 1962), 497-514.

1616 MARINACCI, Barbara. O Wondrous Singer! An Introduction to Walt Whitman. New York: Dodd, Mead,
1970. For a young audience.

1617 MARR, David Marshall. "'The Infinitude of the Pri-
vate Man': Essays on Emerson, Whitman, William
James, Blackmur, and Heller." Ph.D. diss.,
Washington State, 1978. DA, 39 (1978), 2941A-2942A.

1618 MARSDEN, James Douglas. "Modern Echoes of Transcendentalism: Kesey, Snyder, and Other Counter-
cultural Authors." Ph.D. diss., Brown, 1977. DA,
38 (1978), 4830A-4831A. Influence of Emerson,
Whitman, Thoreau on certain modern poets.

1619 MARTI, José. "Martí, in His Own Words, 'I, Walt
Whitman.'" Bulletin of Pan American Union, 2
(May, 1945), 270-272.

1620 _____. The America of José Martí. Trans. with
Introduction by José de Onís. New York: Privately
printed, 1954. Essays on Whitman, Emerson, et al.

1621 _____. "Poet Walt Whitman, April 19, 1887," trans.

Arnold Chapman, in Allen, ed., Walt Whitman
Abroad (1955), pp. 201-213.

1622 MARTIN, Edward A. "Whitman's 'A Boston Ballad
(1854).'" Walt Whitman Review, 11 (1965), 61-69.

1623 MARTIN, Geraldine E. "Whitman and His Reader:
The Evolution of a Poetic." Ph.D. diss., Notre
Dame, 1976. DA, 36 (1976), 7423A-7424A.

1624 MARTIN, Jay. Harvests of Change. Englewood Cliffs,
N.J.: Prentice-Hall, 1967. Whitman, pp. 279-285.

1625 MARTIN, Robert K. "Whitman's 'The Sleepers,' lines
33-35." Explicator, 33 (1974), item 13.

1626 _____. "Whitman's Song of Myself': Homosexual
Dream and Vision." Partisan Review, 42 (1975),
80-96.

1627 MARTIN, Willard E., Jr. "Whitmaniana from the
Boston Journal." Walt Whitman Review, 23 (1977),
90-92.

1628 MARTZ, Louis L. The Poem of the Mind. New York:
Oxford University Press, 1966. Whitman, pp. 82-90.

1629 MARX, Leo. "The Vernacular Tradition in American
Literature: Walt Whitman and Mark Twain." Die
Neueren Sprachen, (1958), 46-57. Reprinted in
Kwiat, Joseph J., and Mary C. Turpie, eds. Stud-
ies in American Culture: Dominant Ideas and Images.
Minneapolis: University of Minnesota Press, 1960.
Pp. 109-122.

1630 _____. "Democratic Vistas: Notes for a Discussion."
Emerson Society Quarterly, 22 (1961), 12-15.

1631 _____, ed. with Introduction. The Americanness of
Walt Whitman. Boston: Heath, 1960. A collection
of critical essays.

1632 MASON, John Byrum. "Walt Whitman's Catalogues:
Rhetorical Means for Two Journeys in 'Song of Myself.'" American Literature, 45 (1973), 34-49.

1633 _____. "Walt Whitman's Reader: A Study of Whit-

man's Aesthetics and Methods of Reader Engage-
ment." Ph.D. diss., Oregon, 1976. DA, 37 (1976),
3627A.

1634 MASTERS, Edgar Lee. Whitman. New York: Scribner's, 1937.

1635 MATHEW, V. John. "Self in 'Song of Myself': A Defense of Whitman's Egoism." Walt Whitman Review,
15 (1969), 102-107.

1636 MATHEWS, Godfrey W. Walt Whitman. Liverpool:
Daily Post, 1921.

1637 MATHEWS, Joseph C. "Walt Whitman's Reading of
Dante." University of Texas Studies in English, 19
(1939), 177-179.

1638 MATLE, John H. "The Body Acclaimed." Walt Whitman Review, 16 (1970), 110-114. Based on 1892
"I Sing the Body Electric."

1639 _____. "Walt Whitman's Drum-Taps and Sequel:
A New Appraisal." Ph.D. diss., Wayne State,
1970. DA, 31 (1971), 6063A-64A.

1640 MATSUHARA, Iwao. "Walt Whitman in Japan: From
the First Introduction to the Present." Thought Cur-
ents in English Literature (Tokyo), 29 (January,
1957), 5-42.

1641 MATTHIESSEN, Francis Otto. American Renaissance:
Art and Expression in the Age of Emerson and Whitman. New York: Oxford University Press, 1941.
"Whitman--Only a Language Experiment," pp. 517-
625.

1642 _____. The Responsibilities of the Critic. New
York: Oxford University Press, 1952. "Whitman,
His Poetry and Prose," pp. 218-223.

1643 MAXWELL, J. C. "Swinburne and the 'Cult of the
Calamus.'" Notes and Queries, 6 (December, 1959),
452.

1644 MAXWELL, William. "Some Personalist Elements in
the Poetry of Walt Whitman." Personalist, 12 (July,
1931), 190-199.

1645 MAYER, Frederick. "Whitman's Social Philosophy."
Sociology and Social Research, 33 (March-April,
1949), 275-310.

1646 MAYFIELD, John S. "Shake the Hand That Shook the
Hand of Whitman." Manuscripts, 10 (Fall, 1958),
50-52.

1647 _____. "John Quincy Adams, Walt Whitman, Charles
E. Feinberg, William White, and Joseph Ishill."
Courier, 11 (September, 1961), 10-11.

1648 _____. "Walt Whitman, Theodore Roosevelt, and
'The New Inferno.'" Courier, 35 (September, 1970),
19-23. Humor: Art Young cartoon and verses by
Arthur Guiterman.

1649 MAYNARD, Laurens. "Walt Whitman and Elbert Hub-
bard." Conservator, 28 (December, 1917), 151-152.

1650 MAYNARD, Mila Tupper. Walt Whitman: The Poet of
the Wider Selfhood. Chicago: Kerr, 1903.

1651 MAZZARO, Jerome L. "Whitman's Democratic Vistas:
The Vast General Principle and Underlying Unity."
Walt Whitman Review, 8 (1962), 89-90.

1652 MEAD, Leon. "Walt Whitman." Conservator, 11 (August, 1900), 90-92.

1653 MEGNA, B. Christian. "Sociality and Seclusion in the
Poetry of Walt Whitman." Walt Whitman Review,
17 (1971), 55-57.

1654 MEHROTNA, Arvind K. "The Bard and the Foundry:
A Reaction to Whitman's Black Poems." Research
Studies, 39 (1971), 33-39.

1655 MENCKEN, Henry L. "Memorial Service," in Prejudices: First Series. New York: Knopf, 1919. Reprinted in Mencken Chrestomathy (1949), p. 484.
Pp. 249-250.

1656 _____. "In Memoriam," in Selected Prejudices.
New York: Knopf, 1927. Pp. 57-58.

1657 _____. "Whitman," in Mencken Chrestomathy. New
York: Knopf, 1949. Pp. 482-883.

1658 MENDELSON, Maurice O. "Walt Whitman." New
World (Moscow), 22 (March, 1945), 183-188.

1659 _____. "Walt Whitman in Russia." Voks Bulletin,
5 (1954), 111-112.

1660 _____. "Leaves of Grass." Soviet Literature (Moscow), 7 (1955), 161-166.

1661 _____. "'He Dreamed of the Brotherhood of People':
On the 150th Anniversary of the Birth Date of Walt
Whitman." Translated from Russian by Frank J.
Corliss, Jr. Walt Whitman Review, 16 (1970), 57-
59. Reprinted from Pravda, May 30, 1969.

1662 _____. "Whitman and the Oral Indian Tradition."
American Dialog, 7 (1972), 25-28.

1663 _____. The Life and Work of Walt Whitman: A
Soviet View. Translated from Russian by Andrew
Bromfield. Moscow: Progress Publishers, 1976.

1664 MENGELING, Marvin E. "Whitman and Ellison: Older
Symbols in a Modern Mainstream." Walt Whitman
Review, 12 (1966), 67-70. Discusses The Invisible
Man, Chapter 5, and "When Lilacs...."

1665 MERCER, Dorothy Frederica. "Leaves of Grass and
the Bhagavad Gita: A Comparative Study." Ph. D.
diss., California (Berkeley), 1933.

1666 _____. "Walt Whitman on Reincarnation." Vedanta
and the West, 9 (November-December, 1946), 180-
185.

1667 _____. "Walt Whitman on Learning and Wisdom."
Vedanta, 10 (March-April, 1947), 57-59.

1668 _____. "Walt Whitman on God and the Self." Vedanta, 10 (May-June, 1947), 80-87.

1669 _____. "Walt Whitman on Love." Vedanta, 10
(July-August, 1947), 107-113.

1670 _____. "Walt Whitman on Karma Yoga." Vedanta,
10 (September-October, 1947), 150-153.

1671 MEREDITH, William. "Whitman to the Poet," in White,

William, ed. , <u>Walt Whitman in Our Time</u> (1970),
pp. 9-11.

1672 MERRILL, Stuart. "Une Lettre ... à propos de Walt
Whitman. " <u>Mercure de France</u>, 102 (April, 1913),
890-892. In French.

1673 _____. "La question de Walt Whitman." <u>Mercure
de France</u>, 106 (November, 1913), 329-336.

1674 MERSCH, Arnold. "Teilhard de Chardin and Whitman's
'A Noiseless Patient Spider.'" <u>Walt Whitman Review</u>,
17 (1971), 99-100.

1675 _____. "Cosmic Contrast: Whitman and the Hindu
Philosophy." <u>Walt Whitman Review</u>, 19 (1973), 49-
63.

1676 _____. "Whitman and the Age of Aquarius: A Message for the 'Woodstock Generation.'" <u>Walt Whitman
Review</u>, 19 (1973), 138-146.

1677 _____. "Whitman and Buber: In the Presence of
Greatness." <u>Walt Whitman Review</u>, 21 (1975), 120-
125.

1678 METZGER, Charles Reid. <u>Thoreau and Whitman: A
Study of Their Esthetics.</u> Seattle: University of
Washington Press, 1961.

1679 _____. "Walt Whitman's Philosophical Epic." <u>Walt
Whitman Review</u>, 15 (1969), 91-96.

1680 MEYER, A. N. "Two Portraits of Whitman." <u>Put-
nam's Magazine</u>, 4 (September, 1908), 707-710.

1681 MEZEY, Robert. "Happy Birthday, Old Man." <u>Ameri-
can Dialogue</u>, 5 (1969), 28.

1682 MICHEL, Pierre. "Whitman Revisited." <u>Revue des
Langues Vivantes</u> (Brussels), 29 (January-February,
1963), 79-83.

1683 MIDDLEBROOK, Diane Wood. "The Mythology of Imagination: A Study of the Poetry of Walt Whitman and
Wallace Stevens." Ph.D. diss., Yale, 1968. <u>DA</u>,
29 (1969), 4011A-4012A.

1684 _____. Walt Whitman and Wallace Stevens. Ithaca, N.Y.: Cornell University Press, 1974.

1685 MILES, Josephine. "The Poetry of Praise." Kenyon Review, 23 (Winter, 1961), 104-125. Reprinted in revised form in Pearce, ed., Walt Whitman: A Collection (1962), pp. 163-175.

1686 MILLER, Edwin Haviland. "Walt Whitman's Correspondence with Whitelaw Reid, Editor of the New York Tribune." Studies in Bibliography, 8 (1956), 242-249.

1687 _____. "Whitman's First Letter to Anne Gilchrist: A Few Cautionary Remarks." Walt Whitman Newsletter, 4 (September, 1958), 92-93.

1688 _____. "New Letters of Walt Whitman." Missouri Historical Society Bulletin, 16 (January, 1960), 99-113.

1689 _____. "Whitman's Correspondence with Edwin Booth." Walt Whitman Review, 6 (1960), 49-50.

1690 _____. "A Whitman Note to John Swinton." Walt Whitman Review, 6 (1960), 72-73.

1691 _____. "Walt Whitman as a Lobbyist." Yale University Library Gazette, 35 (January, 1961), 134-136.

1692 _____. "Walt Whitman and Ellen Eyre." American Literature, 33 (March, 1961), 64-68.

1693 _____. "Walt Whitman and Louis Fitzgerald Tasistro." Walt Whitman Review, 7 (1961), 14-15.

1694 _____. "Walt Whitman as a Letter Writer." American Book Collector, 11 (May, 1961), 15-20.

1695 _____. "A Whitman Letter to Hiram J. Ramsdell." Walt Whitman Review, 10 (1964), 97-98.

1696 _____. "A New Whitman Letter to Josiah Child." Walt Whitman Review, 13 (1967), 32-33.

1697 _____. "Amy Haslam Dowe and Walt Whitman." Walt Whitman Review, 13 (1967), 73-79. Reprinted

biographical material of the 1930s from an unpublished
account, "A Child's Memories of the Whitmans," by
Amy Haslam Dowe, niece of Mrs. George Whitman.

1698 _____ . Walt Whitman's Poetry: A Psychological
Journey. Boston: Houghton Mifflin, 1968.

1699 _____ . "And Gladly Edit," in White, William, ed.,
Walt Whitman in Our Time (1970), pp. 13-16.

1700 _____ . "The Radical Vision of Whitman and Pollack,"
in Artistic Legacy (1970), pp. 56-71.

1701 _____ . "A Backward Glance: A Bibliography of
Gay Wilson Allen," in Artistic Legacy (1970), pp.
153-160.

1702 _____ , and Rosalind S. Miller. "Preparing a Checklist of Walt Whitman's Correspondence." Bulletin of
New York Public Library, 61 (March, 1957), 113-116.

1703 _____ , and Rosalind S. Miller. Walt Whitman's
Correspondence: A Checklist. New York: New York
Public Library, 1957. Description and location of
some 3,500 letters by Whitman.

1704 _____ , ed. The Correspondence, 1842-1867, Vol. I.
New York: New York University Press, 1961.

1705 _____ , ed. The Correspondence, 1868-1875, Vol.
II. New York: New York University Press, 1961.
First two volumes of a projected 14 volume CEAA
Collected Writings of Walt Whitman.

1706 _____ , ed. The Correspondence, 1876-1885, Vol.
III. New York: New York University Press, 1964.

1707 _____ , ed. The Correspondence, 1886-1889, Vol.
IV. New York: New York University Press, 1969.

1708 _____ , ed. The Correspondence, 1890-1892, Vol.
V. New York: New York University Press, 1969.
Completes 5 volumes, 2,721 letters. See supplement
volume below (1977).

1709 _____ , ed. A Century of Whitman Criticism. Bloomington: Indiana University Press, 1969. Reprints 46
critics.

1710   _____, ed. Leaves of Grass: Selections. New
         York: Appleton-Century-Crofts, 1970.

1711   _____, ed. The Artistic Legacy of Walt Whitman:
         A Tribute to Gay Wilson Allen. New York: New
         York University Press, 1970.

1712   _____, ed. with Introduction. The Correspondence,
         Vol. VI. A Supplement with a composite index to
         Volumes I-VI. New York: New York University
         Press, 1977.

1713 MILLER, F. De Wolfe. "Melville, Whitman, and the
         Forty Immortals," in Miller, F. De Wolfe, ed.,
         English Studies in Honor of James Southall Wilson.
         Charlottesville: University Virginia Press, 1951.
         Pp. 23-24. See Benjamin de Casseres, Forty Im-
         mortals (1926).

1714   _____. "The 'Long Foreground' of Whitman's Elegies
         on Lincoln." Lincoln Herald, 58 (Spring-Summer,
         1956), 3-7.

1715   _____. "Lincoln and Whitman: The Author's Re-
         joinder." Lincoln Herald, 59 (Spring-Summer, 1957),
         16, 24.

1716   _____. "Known Copies of Drum-Taps." Walt Whit-
         man Newsletter, 3 (June, 1957), 25-26.

1717   _____. "The Battle of a Book." Walt Whitman
         Newsletter, 4 (March, 1958), 79-80. Refers to
         Drum-Taps.

1718   _____. "Before The Good Gray Poet." Tennessee
         Studies in Literature and Language, 3 (1958), 89-98.

1719   _____. "The First Advertisement of Drum-Taps."
         Walt Whitman Review, 5 (1959), 15.

1720   _____. "Whitman's Talley, Put at Random." Tennes-
         see Studies in Literature, 6 (1961), 151-161. Also pub-
         lished in David, Richard Beale, and John Leon Lievsay,
         eds., Studies in Honor of Hodges and Thaler. Knoxville:
         University of Tennessee Press, 1961. Pp. 151-161.

1721   _____. "Whitman's 16-4 Diary." American Book
         Collector, 11 (May, 1961), 21-24.

1722 _____. "Malcolm Cowley Edits the First Leaves."
Walt Whitman Review, 7 (1961), 35-36.

1723 _____. "New Glimpses of Walt Whitman in 1886."
Tennessee Studies in Literature, 8 (1963), 71-80.

1724 _____. "The Reception of Whitman's Correspondence."
Walt Whitman Review, 9 (1963), 27-30. 24 reviews
of Miller, ed., Correspondence, Vols. I and II
(1961), are discussed.

1725 _____. "A Note on Memoranda." Walt Whitman
Review, 9 (1963), 67-68. Refers to publication of
war material, sent to publisher as early as 1863,
as "Memoranda of a Year," and finally published
as "Memoranda of the War," in 1874.

1726 _____. "Whitman Bibliography in Russia." Walt
Whitman Review, 11 (1965)

1727 _____. "The Partitive Studies of 'Song of Myself.'"
American Transcendental Quarterly, 12 (1971), 11-17.

1728 _____, ed. with Introduction. Walt Whitman's Drum-
Taps (1865), and Sequel to Drum-Taps (1865-1866).
Gainesville, Fla.: Scholars Facsimiles and Reprints,
1959.

1729 MILLER, F. H. "Some Unpublished Letters of Walt
Whitman." Overland Monthly, 43 (January, 1904),
61-63.

1730 MILLER, Henry. The Books in My Life. New York:
New Directions Press, 1952. Whitman, pp. 221-243.

1731 _____. Stand Still Like the Hummingbird. New
York: New Directions Press, 1962. Whitman, pp.
107-110.

1732 MILLER, James Edwin, Jr. "'Song of Myself' as Inverted Mystical Experience." PMLA, 70 (September,
1955), 636-661.

1733 _____. A Critical Guide to Leaves of Grass. Chicago: University of Chicago Press, 1957.

1734 _____. "Four Cosmic Poets." University of Kansas

City Review, 23 (Summer, 1957), 312-320.   Refers
to Whitman, D. H. Lawrence, Hart Crane, Dylan
Thomas.

1735   .   "Whitman's 'Calamus':   The Leaf and the
          Root." PMLA, 72 (March, 1957), 249-271.

1736   .   "Whitman and Eliot: The Poetry of Mysti-
          cism." Southwest Review, 43 (Spring, 1958), 113-
          123. Reprinted in Miller, J. E., Quests Surd and
          Absurd (1967), pp. 112-136.

1737   .   "Whitman and the Province of Poetry."
          Arizona Quarterly, 14 (Spring, 1958), 5-19.

1738   .   "Whitman in Italy."   Walt Whitman Review,
          5 (1959), 28-30.

1739   .   "Walt Whitman and the Secret of History."
          Centennial Review, 3 (Summer, 1959), 321-336.
          Nineteenth- and twentieth-century writers' image of
          Whitman.

1740   .   "The Mysticism of Whitman: Suggestions
          for a Seminar Discussion." Emerson Society Quar-
          terly, 22 (1961), 15-18.

1741   .   "America's Epic," reprinted excerpt from
          Miller, A Critical Guide (1957), pp. 174-186, in
          Pearce, ed., Whitman: A Collection (1962), pp. 60-
          65.

1742   .   "Whitman and Dylan Thomas: The Yawp
          and the Gab," in Lewis, R. W. B., ed., The Pres-
          ence of Walt Whitman (1962), pp. 137-163.

1743   .   Quests Surd and Absurd.   Chicago: Univer-
          sity of Chicago Press, 1967.   "Walt Whitman: The
          Quest for Identity," pp. 95-102; "Walt Whitman: The
          Quest for Spirit," pp. 103-111; and "Whitman and
          Eliot: The Poetry of Mysticism (reprint from 1958),"
          pp. 112-136.

1744   .   "Walt Whitman: 'Song of Myself,'" in Co-
          hen, Henig, ed., Landmarks of American Literature.
          New York: Basic Books, 1969.   Pp. 144-156.

Miller   148

1745 _____. "Whitman: Dead or Alive?" in White, Wil-
        liam, ed., Whitman in Our Time (1970), pp. 17-20.

1746 _____. "Walt Whitman's Omnisexual Vision," in
        Bruccoli, ed., The Chief Glory of Every People
        (1973), pp. 231-262.

1747 _____, Karl Shapiro, and Bernice Slote. Start with
        the Sun: Studies in Cosmic Poetry. Lincoln: Uni-
        versity of Nebraska Press, 1960. The Whitman tra-
        dition in D. H. Lawrence, Hart Crane, and Dylan
        Thomas.

1748 _____, ed. with Introduction. Complete Poetry and
        Selected Prose. Boston: Houghton Mifflin, 1959.

1749 _____, ed. Walt Whitman. New York: Twayne,
        1962. Collection of reprinted criticism.

1750 _____, ed. "Walt Whitman," in Foerster and Falk,
        eds., Eight American Writers: An Anthology (1963),
        pp. 971-1168.

1751 _____, ed. Song of Myself: Origin, Growth, Mean-
        ing. New York: Dodd, Mead, 1964.

1752 MILLER, Perry. "The Shaping of the American Char-
        acter." New England Quarterly, 28 (December,
        1955), 435-454. Reprinted in Pearce, ed., Walt
        Whitman: A Collection (1962), pp. 132-145.

1753 _____. "The Romantic Dilemma in American Na-
        tionalism and the Concept of Nature." Harvard The-
        ological Review, 48 (1955), 239-253.

1754 _____. "The Commonlaw and Codification in Jack-
        sonian America." Proceedings of the American Phil-
        osophical Society, 103 (1959), 463-468.

1755 _____, ed. Major Writers of America, 2 vols.
        New York: Harcourt, Brace, and World, 1962.
        "Walt Whitman," by R. W. B. Lewis, Vol. I, pp.
        969-1119.

1756 MILLER, Tracey R. "The Boy, the Bird, and the Sea:
        An Archetypal Reading of 'Out of the Cradle....'"
        Walt Whitman Review, 19 (1973), 93-103.

1757 MILLETT, Fred B. "Man--Liberator--Visionary."
Nocturne, 7 (Spring, 1955), 12.

1758 MILLS, Barriss. "Whitman's Poetic Theory." Emerson Society Quarterly, 55 (1969), 42-47.

1759 MILNE, W. Gordon. "William Douglas O'Connor and
the Authorship of The Good Gray Poet." American
Literature, 25 (March, 1953), 31-42.

1760 MIMS, Edward. "Prophets and Seers," in Mims, Great
Writers as Interpreters of Religion. Nashville,
Tenn.: Abingdon-Cokesbury, 1947. Pp. 73-109.

1761 MINER, Earl R. "The Background, Date, and Composition of Whitman's 'A Broadway Pageant.'" American Literature, 27 (November, 1955), 403-405.

1762 MIRSKY, D. A. "Walt Whitman: Poet of American
Democracy," translated by B. G. Guerney. Dialectics, 1 (1937), 11-29. Retranslated by Samuel Putnam, and reprinted in Allen, ed., Walt Whitman
Abroad (1955), pp. 169-186.

1763 MITCHELL, Roger. "A Prosody for Whitman?" PMLA,
84 (1969), 1606-1612.

1764 MITILINEOS, Peter. "A Phyllum of Chloë." Walt
Whitman Review, 22 (1976), 51-61. On a contemporary Greek translation of Whitman.

1765 MIZE, Lou Stem. "A Study of Selected Choral Settings
of Walt Whitman Poems." Ph.D. diss., Florida
State, 1967. DA, 28 (1969), 3706A.

1766 MOE, Christian. "Playwright Lawrence Takes the Stage
in London." D. H. Lawrence Review, 2 (1969), 93-97.

1767 MOE, Sigrid. "Walt Whitman and Wergeland: A Comparative Study." Ph.D. diss., New York University,
1951.

1768 MOHRMANN, Gerald P. "The Impact of Rhetorical
Theory and Practice upon the Poetry of Walt Whitman." Ph.D. diss., Florida, 1965.

1769 MOLINOFF, Katharine. "Walt Whitman at Smithtown."
Long Island Forum, 4 (August, 1941), 179-180, 182-
184.

1770 _____. Introduction by Oscar Cargill. Some Notes
on Whitman's Family. Brooklyn, N. Y.: Comet
Press (privately printed by the author), 1941. 43-
page pamphlet.

1771 _____. Monographs on Unpublished Whitman Material, 3 vols. Brooklyn, N. Y.: Comet Press (privately printed by the author), 1941-1942.

1772 _____. Whitman's Teaching at Smithtown, 1837-1838.
Brookville, N. Y.: Privately published, 1942.

1773 _____. Walt Whitman at Southold. Brookville, N. Y.:
Privately published, 1966.

1774 _____, ed. Introduction by Oscar Cargill. An Unpublished Whitman MS: The Record Book of the
Smithtown Debating Society, 1837-1838. Brooklyn,
N. Y.: Comet Press (privately printed by the author),
1941.

1775 MÖLLER, Tyge. "Walt Whitman." Conservator, 20
(January, 1910), 165-168.

1776 MONAHAN, M. "Walt Whitman--Two Notes," in Nem-
esis. New York: Frank-Maurice, 1926.

1777 MONROE, Harriet. "Walt Whitman." Poetry, 14 (May,
1919), 89-94.

1778 _____. "Walt Whitman," in Poets and Their Art.
New York: Macmillan, 1926. Pp. 179-184.

1779 MONROE, W. S. "Recent Walt Whitman Literature in
America." Revue Anglo-Américaine, 7 (December,
1930), 138-141.

1780 _____. "Swinburne's Recantation of Walt Whitman."
Revue Anglo-Américaine, 8 (April, 1931), 347-352.

1781 MONTEIRO, George. "A New Whitman Letter." Walt
Whitman Review, 11 (1965), 102-103.

1782 MONTOLIU, Cebriá. "Walt Whitman's Philosophy,"

translated by Fernando Alegria, in Allen, ed., Walt
Whitman Abroad (1955), pp. 213-220.

1783 MOODY, James. "Whitman," in Slatoff, Walter J.,
ed., With Respect to Readers: Dimensions of Literary Responses. Ithaca, N.Y.: Cornell University
Press, 1970. Pp. 191-207.

1784 MOORE, Jack B. "Review of Roger Asselineau's Evolution of Walt Whitman." Shenandoah, 12 (Spring,
1961), 49-55.

1785 MOORE, John Brooks. "The Master of Whitman."
Studies in Philology, 23 (January, 1926), 77-89.

1786 MOORE, John Robert. "Walt Whitman: A Study in
Brief." Sewanee Review, 25 (January, 1917), 80-92.

1787 MOORE, Rayburn S. "The Literary World Gone Mad:
Hayne on Whitman." Southern Literary Journal, 10
(1977), 75-83. Refers to poet Paul Hamilton Hayne.

1788 MOORE, William Luther. Haughty This Song. Eight-
act television drama, broadcast on Czechoslovakian
TV, 1969. First act published in Calamus, 4 (1970).
One Act in each subsequent issue.

1789 _____, ed. Walt Whitman's Poems: Song of Myself, By Blue Ontario's Shore. Introduction in English; Japanese text. Tokyo: Kenkyusha, 1957.

1790 _____, ed. Complete Leaves of Grass, with Prose
Essences and Annotations. Tokyo: Taibundo, 1966.
Moore's paraphrases in English.

1791 _____, ed. Calamus: An International Whitman
Quarterly. Published in Japan in English by the International Christian University, Tokyo. 1969--date.

1792 MORAN, Ronald. "'Walt Whitman at Bear Mt.' and
the American Illusion." Concerning Poetry, 2 (1969),
5-9.

1793 MORDELL, Albert, ed. Notorious Literary Attacks.
New York: Boni and Liveright, 1926. "Walt Whit-
man," pp. 214-220. Reprinted from Saturday Review
(London), March 18, 1876.

1794 MORE, Paul Elmer. "Walt Whitman, " in Shelburne
     Essays: Fourth Series. Boston: Houghton Mifflin,
     1906. Pp. 180-211.

1795 _____. "Walt Whitman, " excerpt from Shelburne
     Essays: Fourth Series (1906), in More, Shelburne
     Essays on American Literature. Selected from the
     11 series of Shelburne essays (1904-1921), and edited
     by Daniel Aaron. New York: Harcourt, Brace,
     1963. Pp. 230-253. Published posthumously; More
     died in 1937.

1796 MORGAN, Charles H. "A New Look at Whitman's
     'Crisis.'" South Atlantic Bulletin, 36 (1971), 41-52.

1797 MORGAN, Claude. "Walt Whitman and Howard Fast."
     Parallèle, 5, No. 108 (October 15, 1948), 5. In
     French.

1798 MORGAN, Jennie A. "Early Reminiscences of Walt
     Whitman." American Literature, 13 (March, 1941),
     9-17.

1799 _____. "A Reply." American Literature, 13 (Jan-
     uary, 1942), 414-416. In response to Louise Pound
     article, American Literature, 13 (January, 1942),
     411-413.

1800 MORGAN, Paul. "New Significance to Whitman's 'The
     Song of the Exposition.'" University of Texas Li-
     brary Chronicle, 4 (Summer, 1952), 137-150.

1801 MORLEY, Christopher Darlington. "Walt Whitman
     Miniatures, " in Mince Pie: Adventures on the Sunny
     Side of Grub Street. New York: Doubleday, Doran,
     1919. Pp. 272-291. Reprinted in Forty-Four Essays
     (1925), pp. 240-255.

1802 _____. "Fulton Street and Walt Whitman, " in Plum
     Pudding. New York: Doubleday and Page, 1921.
     Pp. 57-62.

1803 _____. "Moby Walt, " in Forty-Four Essays. New
     York: Harcourt, Brace, 1925. Pp. 204-207.

1804 _____. "Whitman Centennial, " in Essays. New
     York: Doubleday, Doran, 1928. Pp. 435-441.

1805 _____ . "1855 Preface to Leaves of Grass," in Essays (1928), pp. 694-707.

1806 _____ . "Notes on Walt," in Streamlines. New York:
Doubleday, Doran, 1936.

1807 _____ . "Atom Splitter," in Ironing Board. New
York: Doubleday, 1949.

1808 _____ , ed. Walt Whitman in Camden: A Selection
of Prose from Specimen Days. Camden, N.J.:
Haddon Craftsmen, 1938.

1809 MORRIS, Harrison Smith. Walt Whitman: A Brief
Biography with Reminiscences. Cambridge: Harvard
University Press, 1929.

1810 MORRIS, Wright. Territory Ahead. New York: Harcourt, Brace, 1958. "Open Road: Walt Whitman,"
pp. 51-66.

1811 _____ . Earthly Delights, Unearthly Adornments.
New York: Harper, 1978. "Whitman," pp. 25-32.

1812 MORSBERGER, Robert E. "Whitman's Hermit Thrush:
An Ornithological Note." Walt Whitman Review, 20
(1974), 111-113.

1813 MORTON, Richard M. "Artifice of Passage: An Inquiry into the Search for Complement in Walt Whitman." Ph.D. diss., Georgia, 1970. DA, 31
(1971), 4173A-4174A.

1814 MOTHER Mary Eleanor. "The Debate of the Body and
Soul." Renascence, 12 (Summer, 1960), 192-197.

1815 MOURAY, Gabriel. "Walt Whitman." Conservator, 21
(May, June, 1910), 37, 53.

1816 MOYNE, Ernest J. "Walt Whitman and Folger McKinsey or Walt Whitman in Elkton, Maryland: A Study
of Public Taste in the 1880's." Delaware Notes,
29 (1956), 103-117.

1817 _____ . "Leaves of Grass and Granite Bowlders:
Walt Whitman and Finland," in Studies Presented to
Tauno F. Mustanoja on the Occasion of His Sixtieth

Birthday. Published by the Neuphilologische Mittei-
lungen magazine (Helsinki, Finland), 1972. Pp. 235-
244.

1818 _____. "Folger McKinsey and Walt Whitman."
Walt Whitman Review, 21 (1975), 135-144.

1819 MUFSON, Thomas. "Walt Whitman, Poet of the New
Age." Twentieth Century, 2 (July, 1910), 325-330.

1820 MULQUEEN, James E. "Organic Growth of Leaves of
Grass." Walt Whitman Review, 15 (1969), 85-91.

1821 _____. "'Song of Myself': Whitman's Hymn to
Eros." Walt Whitman Review, 20 (1974), 60-67.

1822 _____. "Walt Whitman: Poet of the American Cul-
ture-Soul." Walt Whitman Review, 22 (1976), 156-
162.

1823 MUMFORD, Lewis. The Golden Day. New York:
Boni and Liveright, 1926. "Whitman: High Noon,"
pp. 121-137. Reprinted in Untermeyer, Louis, ed.,
The Poetry and Prose of Walt Whitman. New York:
Simon and Schuster, 1949. Pp. 1083-1087.

1824 _____. "Whitman," in Piercy, Josephine Ketcham,
ed., Modern Writers at Work. New York: Macmillan, 1930. Pp. 175-183.

1825 _____. "The Golden Day," excerpt in Mumford,
Interpretations and Forecasts, 1922-1972. New York:
Harcourt, Brace, and Jovanovitch, 1973. Pp. 35-50.

1826 MURDOCK, Kenneth B., ed. A Leaf of Grass from
Shady Hill. Cambridge: Harvard University Press
for John Barnard Associates, 1928. Contains "A
Leaf of Grass," a poem by Charles Eliot Norton,
found in his copy of the 1855 Leaves of Grass; also
the anonymous review of Whitman's work that appeared in Putnam's Monthly, 1855.

1827 MURPHY, Francis, ed. Walt Whitman: A Critical
Anthology. Middlesex, England: Penguin Books,
1962. Reprinted with new Introduction, Baltimore:
Penguin, 1970.

1828 _____, ed. with Notes. Walt Whitman: The Complete Poems. Middlesex, England: Penguin, 1975.

1829 MURPHY, Kevin Christopher. "Poetics of the New World: A Study of Walt Whitman's 'Song of Myself.'" Ph.D. diss., University of Rochester, 1974. DA, 36 (1975), 281A.

1830 MURPHY, Robert Cushman. "The Poet Through a Naturalist's Eyes." Walt Whitman Review, 13 (1967), 39-44.

1831 MURRY, John Middleton. "Walt Whitman: The Prophet of Democracy," in Hindus, ed., Leaves of Grass: One Hundred Years (1955), pp. 123-144.

1832 _____. Excerpt from "Prophet of Democracy," in Murry, Unprofessional Essays. London: Jonathan Cape, 1956. Reprinted in Murry, Selected Criticism, 1916-1957. Selected with an Introduction by Richard Rees. New York: Oxford University Press, 1960. Pp. 270-289.

1833 MUSGROVE, Sydney. T. S. Eliot and Walt Whitman. Wellington: New Zealand University Press, 1952; Cambridge, England: Cambridge University Press, 1953. Reprinted, New York: Haskell House, 1970.

1834 MUZZEY, D. S. "The Ethical Message of Walt Whitman." Ethical Record, 4 (May, 1903), 147-151.

1835 MYERS, Henry Alonzo. "Whitman's Conception of the Spiritual Democracy, 1855-1856." American Literature, 6 (November, 1934), 239-253.

1836 _____. "Whitman's Consistency." American Literature, 8 (November, 1936), 243-257. Reprinted in Myers, Tragedy: A View of Life. Ithaca, N.Y.: Cornell University Press, 1956. Pp. 78-97.

1837 MYERSON, Joel, ed. Studies in the American Renaissance: 1977. Boston: Twayne, 1978. Whitman, passim.

1838 _____, ed. Studies in the American Renaissance: 1978. Boston: Twayne, 1978. Whitman, passim.

1839 _____, ed. Studies in the American Renaissance: 1979. Boston: Twayne, 1979. Whitman, passim.

1840 NABESHIMA, Norihiro. "Walt Whitman in Japan." Studies in English Literature (Tokyo), English number (1965), 47-57.

1841 NABESHIMA, Yoshihiro. "On Whitman's 'When Lilacs Last in the Dooryard Bloom'd.'" Studies in Arts and Culture, 14 (March, 1961), 25-46.

1842 NAGLE, John M. "Toward a Theory of Structure in 'Song of Myself.'" Walt Whitman Review, 15 (1969), 162-171.

1843 NAMBIAR, O. K. Walt Whitman and Yoga. Bangalore, India: Jevan Publications, 1966.

1844 _____. "Whitman's Twenty-Eight Brothers: A Guessing Game," in Mukherjee, Sujit, and D. V. K. Raghavacharyulu, eds., Indian Essays in American Literature: Papers in Honor of Robert E. Spiller. Bombay: Popular Prakashan, 1969.

1845 NANDAKUMAR, Prema. "Whitman's 'Out of the Cradle.'" Literary Criterion (India), 5 (1962), 79-84.

1846 NATHAN, Hans. "Walt Whitman and the Marine Band." More Books, 18 (February, 1943), 47-56.

1847 NATHANSON, J. "Walt Whitman: The Poet as a Seer," in Forerunners of Freedom: The Re-creation of the American Spirit. New York: American Council on Public Affairs, 1941.

1848 NAUMBURG, Edward, Jr. "A Collector Looks at Walt Whitman." Princeton University Library Chronicle, 3 (November, 1941), 1-18.

1849 NEILSON, Kenneth P. "The World of Whitman Music." Walt Whitman Bulletin, 2 (April, 1959), 8-10.

1850 _____. "Calamus: Search and Discovery." Walt Whitman Bulletin, 4 (October, 1960), 13-19.

1851 _____. "More About Calamus." Walt Whitman Bulletin, 4 (January, 1961), 15-18.

1852 _____ . "The 'Voice' of Walt Whitman." American
     Book Collector, 19 (1968), 20-22.

1853 _____ . "A Discovery Rediscovered in the Search
     for Walt Whitman Music." Walt Whitman Review,
     19 (1973), 114-118. Discusses "Ode to the Prison
     Ship Martyrs."

1854 _____ . "Lab Theatre Production of Joseph Scott
     Kierland's 'Drum-Taps.'" Walt Whitman Review,
     21 (1975), 76-78.

1855 NEILSON, Shaw. "Free Verse Old and New." South-
     erly (Australia), 17 (1956), 38.

1856 NELSON, Carl. "Whitman's Dynamic Form: The Im-
     age of the Divine." Walt Whitman Review, 20
     (1974), 121-132.

1857 NELSON, Cary. "Whitman in Vietnam: Poetry and
     History in Contemporary America." Massachusetts
     Review, 16 (1975), 55-71. Relates Whitman to poets
     affected by the war.

1858 NELSON, Charles Alan. "Patterns of Water Imagery
     in Walt Whitman's Leaves of Grass." Ph.D. diss.,
     Wisconsin, 1974. DA, 35 (1975), 4444A-4445A.

1859 NELSON, Herbert B. "Walt Whitman and the Westward
     Movement." Ph.D. diss., Washington, 1945.

1860 NELSON, Jane A. "Ecstasy and Transformation in
     Whitman's 'Lilacs.'" Walt Whitman Review, 18
     (1972), 113-123.

1861 NEUMAN, Mary A. "'Song of Myself' Section 21: An
     Explication." Walt Whitman Review, 13 (1967), 98-99.

1862 NEUMANN, Henry. "Walt Whitman." American Scholar,
     2 (May, 1933), 261-268.

1863 NEVINSON, H. W. "Voice of America (Whitman)," in
     Essays in Freedom and Rebellion. New Haven:
     Yale University Press, 1921. Pp. 100-107.

1864 NEWTON, A. E. "Walt Whitman," in Magnificent Farce
     and Other Diversions of a Book Collector. Boston:
     Little, Brown, 1921. Pp. 140-159.

1865 _____ . "Carolyn Wells and Her Books," in End
Papers: Literary Recreations. Boston: Little,
Brown, 1933. Pp. 209-212. See Carolyn Wells
below.

1866 NICHOLSON, Homer K. Jr. "O Altitudo: A Comparison of the Writings of Walt Whitman, D. H. Lawrence,
and Henry Miller." Ph. D. diss., Vanderbilt, 1956.
DA, 17 (1957), 2614.

1867 NILSEN, Helge Normann. "The Mystic Message: Whitman's 'Song of Myself.'" Edda, 69 (1969), 400-409.

1868 NIST, John. "Two American Poets and a Spider."
Walt Whitman Bulletin, 4 (January, 1961), 8-11.

1869 NOEL, Roden. "A Study of Walt Whitman." Dark Blue
(October-November, 1871). Reprinted in Essays on
Poetry and Poets. London: Kegan Paul and Trench,
1886. Pp. 304-341.

1870 NOGUCHI, Yone. "Whitmanism and Its Failure."
Bookman, 49 (March, 1919), 95-97.

1871 NORTH, Joseph. "'I am the Hounded Slave....'"
American Dialogue, 5 (1969), 1-4.

1872 _____ , et al., eds. "Walt Whitman: 1819-1969."
American Dialogue, 5 (1969), 1-38.

1873 NOTT, G. William. "Walt Whitman in New Orleans."
Reviewer, 4 (April, 1924), 183-187.

1874 NOVERR, Douglas A. "'Aboard at a Ship's Helm':
A Minor Sea Drama, the Poet, and the Soul." Walt
Whitman Review, 17 (1971), 23-25.

1875 _____ . "Poetic Vision and Locus in Whitman's 'Our
Old Feuillage.'" Walt Whitman Review, 22 (1976),
118-122.

1876 NOYES, Alfred. "Walt Whitman and American Individualism," in Opalescent Parrot: Essays. New York:
Sheed and Ward, 1929.

1877 _____ . "Walt Whitman," in Pageant of Letters.
New York: Sheed and Ward, 1940. Pp. 236-245.

1878 NOYES, Carleton. An Approach to Walt Whitman.
      Boston: Houghton Mifflin, 1910.

1879 NUHN, Fern. "Leaves of Grass Viewed as an Epic."
      Arizona Quarterly, 7 (Winter, 1951), 324-338.

1880 OAKES, Frances E. "The Whitman Controversy in
      France." Ph.D. diss., Florida State, 1954. DA,
      15 (1955), 1621.

1881 _____. "Toward Destroying a Myth." Walt Whitman
      Newsletter, 2 (September, 1956), 19-21. Argues that
      Whitman was not homosexual.

1882 _____. "Whitman and Dixon: A Strange Case of
      Borrowing." Georgia Review, 11 (Fall, 1957), 330-
      340. Refers to Thomas Dixon, The Clansman, 1905.

1883 O'BRIEN, Michael W. "Between Language and Voice:
      A Study of Aesthetic Experimentation in Blake, Whit-
      man, Cummings, and Concrete Poetry." Ph.D.
      diss., Illinois (Urbana), 1973. DA, 34 (1974), 5985A.

1884 O'CONNELL, Richard. "Whitman's Tomb." ETC: A
      Review of General Semantics, 32 (1975), 276. An
      original poem.

1885 O'CONNOR, William Douglas. The Good Gray Poet:
      A Vindication. New York: Bunce and Huntington,
      1866. Reprinted in Bucke, R. M., Walt Whitman.
      Philadelphia: David McKay, 1883. Pp. 99-130.
      Reprinted in Loving, Walt Whitman's Champion
      (1978), pp. 157-203.

1886 _____. "Walt Whitman. Is He Persecuted?" New
      York Tribune, April 22, 1876. Reprinted in Lov-
      ing, Walt Whitman's Champion (1978), pp. 204-
      216.

1887 _____. "Suppressing Walt Whitman." New York
      Tribune, May 27, 1882. Reprinted in Loving, Walt
      Whitman's Champion (1978), pp. 217-225.

1888 _____. "Emerson and Whitman." New York Tribune,
      June 18, 1882. Reprinted in Loving, Walt Whitman's
      Champion (1978), pp. 226-232.

1889 _____. Three Tales. Preface by Walt Whitman. Boston: Houghton Mifflin, 1892. Includes "The Ghost," "The Brazen Android," and "The Carpenter."

1890 ODESSKY, Marjory H. "Sooner or Later Delicate Death." Journal of Historical Studies, 1 (1968), 355-359.

1891 OGILVIE, John Thayer. "The Art of Leaves of Grass: A Critical Analysis of the Final Text with Particular Attention to Imagery, Symbolism, and Structure." Ph.D. diss., Indiana, 1958. DA, 19 (1959), 2339-2340.

1892 O'HIGGINS, Harvey Jerrold, and Edward Hiram Reede. "Walt Whitman," in O'Higgins and Reede, American Mind in Action. New York: Harper, 1924. Pp. 202-234.

1893 _____. "Alias Walt Whitman." Harper's Magazine, 158 (May, 1929), 698-707.

1894 OKAMOTO, Kazuko. "On One's Self: An Address to University Students in Rebellion." Calamus, 1 (1969), 6-23.

1895 O'LEARY, R. D. "Swift and Whitman as Exponents of Human Nature." International Journal of Ethics, 24 (January, 1914), 183-201.

1896 OLIVER, Egbert S. "Walt Whitman's 'Passage to India.'" Journal of University of Poona (India), 5 (1955), 84-88.

1897 _____. "'The Seas Are All Cross'd': Whitman on American and World Freedom." Western Humanities Review, 9 (August, 1955), 303-312. Reprinted in American Review (New Delhi), 1 (October, 1956), 18-29.

1898 _____. "Walt Whitman and Asia." Emerson Society Quarterly, 22 (1961), 18-20.

1899 OPPENHEIM, James. "Whitman," in Macy, John, ed., American Writers on American Literature (1931), pp. 258-273.

1900 ORAGE, A. R. "Whitman in Short," in Orage, Selected

Essays and Critical Writings. London: George Allen,
1935. P. 73.

1901 ORIGO, Iris. "Additions to the Keats Collection."
Times Literary Supplement, April 23, 1970. Pp.
457-458.

1902 ORTH, Michael. "Walt Whitman, Metaphysical Teapot:
The Structure of 'Song of Myself.'" Walt Whitman
Review, 14 (1968), 16-24.

1903 OSMASTON, F. P. "The 'Coarseness' of Whitman."
Quest, 3 (July, 1912), 766-770.

1904 OTA, Saburo. "Walt Whitman and Japanese Literature,"
in Frenz, Horst, ed., Asia and the Humanities: Papers presented at the Second Conference on Oriental-
Western literary and cultural relations. Bloomington:
Indiana University Press, 1959. Pp. 62-69.

1905 _____. "The Introduction of Walt Whitman." Gakuen,
234 (September, 1959), 20-36.

1906 _____. "Notes on a 'Whitman Journey.'" Sylvan,
5 (December, 1959), 89-94.

1907 PADOVER, S. K. "The American as Poet: Walt Whit-
man," in Padover, The Genius of America: Men
Whose Ideas Shaped Our Civilization. New York:
McGraw-Hill, 1960. Pp. 206-218.

1908 PAINE, Gregory. "The Literary Relations of Whitman
and Carlyle with Especial Reference to Their Contrasting Views on Democracy." Studies in Philology,
36 (July, 1939), 550-563.

1909 PALANDRI, Angela Chih-Ying Jung. "Whitman in Red
China." Walt Whitman Newsletter, 4 (September,
1958), 94-97.

1910 PALLIKUNNEN, Augustine G. "Eastern Influence on
Whitman's Mysticism," in Eastern Influence on Whit-
man's Mysticism and Other Essays in Literature.
Alwaye, India: Pontifical Institute Publishers, 1975.
Pp. 1-21.

1911 PALMER, David D. "An Image of the 'Self' in the
First Three Editions of Whitman's Leaves of Grass."
Ph.D. diss., Pennsylvania State, 1971. DA, 32
(1972), 6446A.

1912 PAPINI, Giovanni. "Walt Whitman and Leaves of
Grass," in Papini, Four and Twenty Minds, trans.
from Italian by Ernest Hatch Wilkins. London:
George C. Harrap and Company, 1923. Pp. 130-168.

1913 _____. "Whitman (opening excerpt)," trans. by Roger
Asselineau, in Allen, ed., Walt Whitman Abroad
(1955), p. 189.

1914 PARKS, Edd Winfield. "The Public and the Private
Poet." South Atlantic Quarterly, 54 (August, 1957),
480-485.

1915 _____, et al. "Problems of the Complete or Collected Editions." Mississippi Quarterly, 15 (Summer,
1962), 95-125.

1916 PARRINGTON, Vernon Louis. Main Currents in American Thought, 3 vols. New York: Harcourt, Brace,
and World, 1927-1930. Reissued in one-volume edition, c. 1949. "The Afterglow of the Enlightenment:
Walt Whitman," Vol. III, pp. 69-86.

1917 PARRY, Albert. "Walt Whitman in Russia." American
Mercury, 33 (September, 1934), 100-107.

1918 PARSONS, Olive W. "Whitman, the Non-Hegelian."
PMLA, 58 (December, 1943), 1073-1093.

1919 PASCAL, Richard F. "The Radiant Gist: Romantic
Strains in 'Song of Myself' and Paterson." Ph.D.
diss., Cornell, 1971. DA, 32 (1972), 6996A-6997A.
Refers to poem by William Carlos Williams, 1946.

1920 PASTERNAK, Melvin J. "Walt Whitman's Conception
of the Social Function of the Ideal American Poet in
the 1855 Edition of Leaves of Grass." Ph.D. diss.,
Wisconsin, 1972. DA, 34 (1973), 284A.

1921 PATTEE, Fred Lewis. A History of American Literature Since 1870. Boston: Silver Burdett and Company, 1896. Revised and reissued, New York: Cen-

tury Company, 1909, 1915. Whitman, pp. 376-384.

1922 _____. Side-Lights on American Literature. New York: Century Company, 1922. Whitman, passim.

1923 _____. The New American Literature, 1890-1930. New York: Century Company, 1930. Whitman, passim.

1924 _____. The First Century of American Literature, 1770-1870. New York and London: Appleton-Century, 1935. Reprinted, New York: Cooper Square Publishers, 1966. Whitman, passim; see also "Romanticism," pp. 285-298.

1925 _____. The Feminine Fifties. New York: Appleton-Century, 1940. "Melville and Whitman," pp. 28-49.

1926 PATTERSON, Margaret C. "'Lilacs' A Sonata." Walt Whitman Review, 14 (1968), 46-50.

1927 PAUL, Sherman, ed. Six Classic American Authors: An Introduction. Minneapolis: University of Minnesota Press, 1971. "Walt Whitman," by Richard Chase, pp. 195-232.

1928 PAVESE, Cesare. "Whitman--Poetry of Poetry Writing," (1951), trans. from Italian by Roger Asselineau, in Allen, ed., Walt Whitman Abroad (1955), pp. 189-198.

1929 _____. American Literature: Essays and Opinions, trans. from Italian by Edwin Fussell. Berkeley: University of California Press, 1970. "Interpretation of Walt Whitman, Poet," pp. 117-141. Original published in La Cultura, 12 (September, 1933), pp. 584-604.

1930 PAXTON, Claire. "Unamuno's Indebtedness to Whitman." Walt Whitman Review, 9 (1963), 16-19. See Unamuno's The Tragic Sense of Life in Men and Peoples, 1913.

1931 PEARCE, Howard D. "'I Lean and Loafe': Whitman's Romantic Posture." Walt Whitman Review, 15

(1969), 3-12.   Relates Whitman to Emerson and
Wordsworth.

1932 PEARCE, Roy Harvey. "Toward an American Epic."
Hudson Review, 12 (August, 1959), 362-377. Reprinted in Yu, A. C., ed., Parnassus Revisited.
Chicago: American Library Association, 1973. Pp.
342-353.

1933 _____. "Ezra Pound's Appraisal of Walt Whitman:
Addendum." Modern Language Notes, 74 (January,
1959), 23-28. See articles by Charles B. Willard
(1957).

1934 _____. The Continuity of American Poetry. Princeton, N. J.: Princeton University Press, 1961. Whitman, pp. 164-174.

1935 _____. "Whitman Justified: The Poet in 1860."
Minnesota Review, 1 (April, 1961), 261-294. Reprinted in Lewis, R. W. B., ed., The Presence of
Walt Whitman (1962), pp. 72-109. Also reprinted
in Pearce, ed., Whitman: A Collection (1962), pp.
37-59.

1936 _____. "Whitman: The Poet in 1860," in Allen,
Don Cameron, and Henry T. Rowell, eds., The
Poetic Tradition. Baltimore: Johns Hopkins Uni-
versity Press, 1968. Pp. 123-140. Reprinted in
Pearce, Historicism (1969), pp. 200-239.

1937 _____. Historicism Once More. Princeton, N. J.:
Princeton University Press, 1969. Reprints "Whitman: The Poet in 1860," pp. 200-239 (cited above).
Also includes "Whitman and Our Hope for Poetry,"
pp. 327-350.

1938 _____, ed. with Introduction. Leaves of Grass.
Facsimile edition of the 1860 text. Ithaca, N. Y.:
Cornell University Press, 1961. Great Seal Books.

1939 _____, ed. with Introduction. Whitman: A Collection of Critical Essays. Englewood Cliffs, N. J.:
Prentice-Hall, 1962. Twentieth-Century Views series.

1940 PEATTIE, R. W. "Postscript to Charles Kent on Whitman." Walt Whitman Review, 15 (1969), 107-111.

Refers to a review written by Charles Kent of William M. Rossetti's edition of Leaves of Grass.

1941 PEAVY, Linda S. "'Wooded Flesh and Metal Bone': A Look at the Riddle of the Broad-Axe." Walt Whitman Review, 20 (1974), 152-154.

1942 PECKHAM, Morse. "Toward a Theory of Romanticism." PMLA, 66 (1951), 5-23. Whitman, passim.

1943 _____. Beyond the Tragic Vision. New York: George Braziller, 1962. Whitman, Emerson, Melville, passim. Detailed discussion of transcendentalism.

1944 PEEK, George A., Jr. "Walt Whitman and Politics." Michigan Alumnus Quarterly Review, 62 (Spring, 1956), 254-261.

1945 PEEPLES, Ken, Jr. "The Paradox of the 'Good Gray Poet': Walt Whitman on Slavery and the Black Man." Phylon, 35 (1974), 22-32.

1946 PENTECOST, H. O. "Walt Whitman's View of Life." Truth Seeker, March 7, 1914.

1947 PEPPER, Stephen C. World Hypotheses: A Study in Evidence. Berkeley: University of California Press, 1957. "Organicism," pp. 280-314. Important background material to Whitman and other Romantics.

1948 PERRY, Bliss. Walt Whitman: His Life and Works. Boston: Houghton Mifflin, 1906. Reprinted, St. Clair Shores, Mich.: Scholarly Press, 1971.

1949 PETERS, Robert L. "Edmund Grosse's Two Whitmans." Walt Whitman Review, 11 (1965), 19-21. Gosse's varying reactions to Whitman.

1950 PETERSEN, William J. "The Walt Whitman Club." Palimpsest, 51 (1970), 323-348.

1951 PETTERSON, Dale E. "Vladimir Mayakovsky and Whitman: The Icon and the Mosaic." Slavic Review, 28 (1970), 416-425.

1952 PFEIFER, Edward J. "The Theory of Evolution and

Whitman's 'Passage to India.'" Emerson Society Quarterly, 42 (1966), 31-35.

1953 PHELPS, William Lyon. "Whitman," in Howells, James, Bryant, and Other Essays. New York: Macmillan, 1924. Pp. 31-65.

1954 PHILLIPS, Elizabeth. "'Song of Myself': The Numbers of the Poem in Relation to Its Form." Walt Whitman Review, 16 (1970), 67-81.

1955 PHILLIPS, William. "Review of Newton Arvin's Whitman." Partisan Review, 6 (Spring, 1939), 114-117.

1956 PICI, Joseph. "An Editing of Walt Whitman's 'When Lilacs....'" University of Dayton Review, 9 (1972), 35-45.

1957 PITZ, H. C. "Gil Wilson--Painter of Themes." The American Artist, 21 (April, 1957), 30-35. Concentrates on Moby-Dick and Leaves of Grass.

1958 PLATT, Isaac Hull. "The Silence of Whitman." Conservator, 13 (June, 1902), 56-57.

1959 _____. Walt Whitman. Boston: Small, Maynard, 1904. Reprinted, Folcroft, Pa.: Folcroft Press, 1969.

1960 _____. "Whitman's Superman." Conservator, 16 (February, 1906), 182-183.

1961 _____. "A Poet Who Could Wait." Book News, 24 (April, 1906), 545-549.

1962 POCHMANN, Henry A. "Walt Whitman," in Pochmann, German Culture in America: 1600-1900. Madison: University of Wisconsin Press, 1950. Pp. 461-474.

1963 _____, and Gay Wilson Allen. Introduction to Masters of American Literature. Carbondale: Southern Illinois University Press, 1969. Whitman, pp. 108-112. Based on Pochmann and Allen, eds., Masters of American Literature: Anthology, 2 vols. (1949).

1964 POIRIER, Richard. A World Elsewhere: The Place of Style in American Literature. New York: Oxford University Press, 1966. Whitman, passim.

1965 POIRIER, Suzanne. "'A Song of the Rolling Earth' as
      Transcendental and Poetic Theory." Walt Whitman
      Review, 22 (1976), 67-74.

1966 POLLARD, Marguerite. "The Universality of Whitman."
      Theosophist, 35 (December, 1913), 373-381.

1967 POLLET, Maurice. "Whitman in Dakar." The Long-
      Islander, special issue, July 1976. Reprinted in
      Walt Whitman Review, 22 supplement (1976), 27.

1968 POLLEY, Robert L., ed. America the Beautiful: In
      the Words of Walt Whitman. Waukesha, Wis.:
      Country Beautiful Corporation, 1970.

1969 POLLIN, Burton R. "'Delightful Sights': A Possible
      Whitman Article in Poe's Broadway Journal." Walt
      Whitman Review, 15 (1969), 180-187.

1970 POLLOCK, Georgiana. "The Relationship of Music to
      Leaves of Grass." College English, 15 (April, 1954),
      384-394.

1971 PONGS, H. "Walt Whitman and Stefan George." Com-
      parative Literature, 4 (Fall, 1952), 289-322. Trans.
      by Seeymour L. Flaxman and reprinted in Allen, ed.,
      Walt Whitman Abroad (1955), pp. 17-55.

1972 PONTE, Durant da. "Whitman's 'Young Fellow Named
      Da Ponte.'" Walt Whitman Review, 5 (1959), 16-17.

1973 PORTER, Carolyn J. "Form and Process in American
      Literature." Ph.D. diss., Rice, 1972. DA, 34
      (1973), 1291A. Includes Emerson, Whitman, et al.

1974 POSEY, Meredith N. "Walt Whitman's Debt to the
      Bible with Special Reference to the Origins of His
      Rhythm." Ph.D. diss., Texas, 1938.

1975 POUND, Louise. "Walt Whitman and the Classics."
      Southwest Review, 10 (January, 1925), 75-83.

1976 _____. "Walt Whitman's Neologisms." American
      Mercury, 4 (February, 1925), 199-201.

1977 _____. "Walt Whitman and Italian Music." Amer-
      ican Mercury, 6 (September, 1925), 58-62.

1978 _____ . "Walt Whitman and the French Language. "
American Speech, 1 (May, 1926), 421-429.

1979 _____ . "Note on Walt Whitman and Bird Poetry. "
English Journal, 19 (January, 1930), 31-36.

1980 _____ . "Doubtful Whitman Lore. " American Literature, 13 (January, 1942), 411-413. See "A Reply, "
by Jennie A. Morgan, American Literature, 13 (January, 1942), 414-416.

1981 _____ , ed. Specimen Days, Democratic Vistas, and
Other Prose. Garden City, N.Y.: Doubleday, 1935.

1982 POWELL, Lawrence Clark. "Leaves of Grass and
Granite Boulders. " Carmelite, 4 (October 22, 1931),
8-9. See article by Moyne (1971).

1983 _____ . "Of Whales and Grass, " in Powell, Books
in My Baggage. Cleveland: World, 1960. Pp. 49-
55.

1984 POWERS, Richard Gid. "Leaves of Grass: The Evolution of an Epic. " Books at Brown, 24 (1971), 107-
118.

1985 POWYS, John Cowper. "Whitman, " in Powys, Visions
and Revisions: A Book of Literary Devotions. New
York: G. A. Shaw, 1915. Pp. 281-289. Reprinted
in Powys, The Enjoyment of Literature. New York:
Simon and Schuster, 1938. Reprinted, London: Mac-
Donald, 1955. Pp. 342-364.

1986 PRASSAD, Thakur Guru. "'America' in American Poetry, " in Menon, K.P.K. , M. Manuel, and K. Ayyappa
Daniker, eds. , Literary Studies: Homage to Dr. A.
S. Aiyer. Trivandrum, India: St. Joseph's Press
for the Dr. Aiyer Memorial Community, 1972. Pp.
149-162.

1987 PRATT, J. W. "Whitman and Masters: A Contrast. "
South Atlantic Quarterly, 16 (April, 1917), 155-158.

1988 PRESSLEY, Ruth Peyton. "Walt Whitman's Debt to
Emerson. " Ph.D. diss. , Texas, 1930.

1989 PREUSCHEN, Karl Adalbert. "Walt Whitman's Unde-

livered Oration, 'The Dead in This War.'" Etudes
Anglaises, 24 (1971), 147-151. Also in Calamus,
5 (April, 1972), 21-28.

1990 PRITCHARD, John Paul. "Walt Whitman," in Pritchard,
Criticism in America. Norman: University of Oklahoma Press, 1956. Pp. 112-120.

1991 _____. Literary Wise Men of Gotham: Criticism in
New York, 1815-1860. Baton Rouge: Louisiana State
University Press, 1963. Whitman, passim.

1992 PRITCHETT, V. S. "Books in General" (title of column).
New Statesman and Nation, 28 (September 30, 1944),
223-224.

1993 _____. "Two Writers and Modern War," in Pritchett,
The Living Novel. New York: Reynal and Hitchcock,
1947. Excerpt reprinted in Daiches, David, ed.,
Century of the Essay: British and American. New
York: Harcourt, Brace, 1951. Pp. 432-444. Also
reprinted in Pritchett, The Living Novel and Later
Appreciations. New York: Random House, 1964.
Pp. 225-237.

1994 PUCCIANI, Oreste Francesco. "The Literary Reputation of Walt Whitman in France." Ph.D. diss.,
Harvard, Romance Languages, 1943.

1995 _____. "Walt Whitman and the Nineteenth Century."
Twice a Year, 16-17 (1948), 245-258.

1996 PUGH, C. Scott. "The End as Means in 'A Riddle
Song.'" Walt Whitman Review, 23 (1977), 82-85.

1997 PULLING, Albert Van S. "An Appraisal of Walt Whitman (1819-1892)." Rendevous, 3 (1968), 16-22.

1998 PULOS, C. E. "Whitman and Epictetus: The Stoical
Element in Leaves of Grass." Journal of English
and Germanic Philology, 55 (January, 1956), 75-84.

1999 QUINN, Arthur Hobson, ed. The Literature of the
American People: An Historical and Critical Survey.
New York: Appleton-Century-Crofts, 1915. Reissued,
1951. "The Establishment of a National Literature,"

by Arthur Hobson Quinn, pp. 175-568. Includes
Emerson, Hawthorne, Melville, Thoreau, and Whit-
man; Whitman also discussed in "Democracy in Free
Verse," by Clarence Gohdes, pp. 598-621.

2000 QUINN, James E. "Yeats and Whitman, 1887-1925."
Walt Whitman Review, 20 (1974), 106-109.

2001 RAFFANIELLO, William. "Pasquale Jannaconne and
'The Last Invocation.'" Walt Whitman Review, 14
(1968), 41-45. See Jannaconne.

2002 RAHV, Philip. "Paleface and Redskin." Kenyon Re-
view, 1 (Summer, 1939), 251-256. Reprinted in
Rahv, Image and Idea. New York: New Directions
Press, 1949. Pp. 1-10.

2003 _____, ed. Literature in America: An Anthology
of Literary Criticism. New York: Meridian, 1957.
"'Ones Self I Sing.'" by Richard Chase, pp. 150-167;
"Concerning Walt Whitman," by Henry David Thoreau,
pp. 148-149.

2004 RAILTON, Stephen, ed., with Foreword by Daniel Mag-
gin. Walt Whitman's Autograph Revision of the Analysis of Leaves of Grass. New York: New York
University Press, 1974. Contains facsimile of two
chapters and appendix from Part 2 of Walt Whitman,
by R. M. Bucke, with Whitman's notes for revision.
Also contains articles by Anderson and Kinnell.

2005 RAJASEKHARAIAH, T. R. The Roots of Whitman's
Grass. Introductory note by Gay Wilson Allen.
Rutherford, N.J.: Fairleigh Dickinson University
Press, 1970.

2006 RAMSEY, Roger. "Whitman Rhapsode." Research
Studies, 45 (1977), 243-248.

2007 RAND, G. I. "Tennyson's Gift to Walt Whitman--a
New Letter." Emerson Society Quarterly, 24 (1961),
106-109.

2008 RANDALL, Alec W. G. "Notes on Modern German
Poetry: Walt Whitman in Germany--Arno Holz."
Egoist, 2 (November 1, 1915), 172-173.

2009 _____. "Notes on Modern German Poetry: Walt
      Whitman in Germany--Johannes Schlaf." Egoist, 2
      (December 1, 1915), 187.

2010 RANDALL, Huberta F. "Whitman and Verhaeren--
      Priests of Human Brotherhood." French Review,
      16 (October, 1942), 36-43.

2011 RANDEL, William. "Walt Whitman and American
      Myths." South Atlantic Quarterly, 59 (Winter, 1960),
      103-113.

2012 RAO, Rayapati. "Vedantic Parallels in Whitman's
      Thought and Art." The Ayran Path, 38 (July, Au-
      gust, 1967), 290-295; 353-357.

2013 RASCOE, Burton. "Whitman, the Prophet," in Rascoe,
      Titans of Literature: From Homer to the Present.
      New York: Putnam's, 1932. Pp. 391-394.

2014 RATCLIFFE, S. K. "Walt Whitman." Literature, 4
      (February 16, 1901), no page.

2015 RATTAN, Narinder Kumar. "Utopian Vision of Walt
      Whitman." Banasthali Patrika, 20 (1976), 31-36.

2016 RAY, Gordon N., ed. with Foreword. Introduction by
      C. Waller Barrett. The American Writer in Eng-
      land. Charlottesville: University Press of Virginia,
      1969. Whitman, et al., passim.

2017 RAYMOND, George L. Art in Theory. New York:
      Putnam's, 1909. Whitman, passim.

2018 READ, Sir Herbert E. "Figure of Grammar: Whitman
      and D. H. Lawrence," in Read, The True Voice of
      Feeling. London: Pantheon, 1953. Pp. 87-100.

2019 READER, Dennis J. "Drum-Taps: Walt Whitman and
      the Civil War." Ph.D. diss., California (San Diego),
      1970. DA, 32 (1971), 2068A-2069A.

2020 REDMOND, L. "A Dream Marched to the Swing of
      His Words," in Stefferud, A., ed., Wonderful World
      of Books. Illustrated by Robert Osborn. Boston:
      Houghton Mifflin, 1952. Pp. 96-97.

2021 REED, Harry B. "The Heraclitan Obsession of Walt
Whitman." Personalist, 15 (Spring, 1934), 125-138.

2022 REED, Michael D. "First Person Persona and the
Catalogue in 'Song of Myself.'" Walt Whitman Review, 23 (1977), 147-155.

2023 REEVES, Harrison. "À propos de Walt Whitman."
Mercure de France, 103 (June 16, 1913), 893-895.
In French.

2024 REEVES, J., and M. Seymour-Smith, eds. Selected
Poems of Walt Whitman. London: Harper, 1976.

2025 REEVES, Paschal. "The Silhouette of the State in
Democratic Vistas--Hegelian or Whitmanian." Personalist, 43 (Summer, 1962), 374-382.

2026 REID, Alfred S. "The Structure of 'Song of Myself'
Reconsidered." Southern Humanities Review, 8
(1974), 507-514. Contains an appendix summarizing
earlier studies by Strauch, Allen, James E. Miller,
Cowley, and Pearce.

2027 REINARTZ, Kay F. "Walt Whitman and Feminism."
Walt Whitman Review, 19 (1973), 127-137.

2028 REISIGER, Hans. "'A Child Went Forth.'" (Berlin,
1922), trans. by Horst Frenz, in Allen, ed., Walt
Whitman Abroad (1955), pp. 7-15.

2029 REISS, Edmund. "Whitman's Debt to Animal Magnetism."
PMLA, 78 (March, 1963), 80-88.

2030 _____. "Recent Scholarship on Whitman and Emily
Dickinson," in Leary, ed., The Teacher and American Literature (1965), pp. 115-127.

2031 _____. "Whitman's Poetic Grammar: Style and
Meaning in 'Children of Adam.'" American Transcendental Quarterly, 12 (1970), 32-41.

2032 REISSMAN, Rose Cherie. "Recurrent Motifs in Good-
Bye, My Fancy." Walt Whitman Review, 21 (1975),
28-35. Refers to 31 poems of the "Second Annex"
added to Leaves of Grass in 1891.

2032a REMENYI, Joseph. "Walt Whitman in Hungarian Lit-
      erature. " American Literature, 16 (November, 1944),
      181-185.

2033 RENNER, Dennis Kent. "Walt Whitman's Religion of the
      Republic: A Study of His Journalistic Writings and
      the First Three Editions of Leaves of Grass in Re-
      lation to Sectionalism and the Prospect of Civil War
      in America. " Ph. D. diss. , Iowa, 1975. DA, 36
      (1975), 2208A.

2034 RENNER, Dennis Kent. "The Conscious Whitman: Al-
      legorical Manifest Destiny in 'Song of Myself. ' "
      Walt Whitman Review, 24 (1978), 149-155.

2035 RESNICK, Nathan. Walt Whitman and the Authorship
      of 'The Good Gray Poet. ' Brooklyn, N. Y.: Long
      Island University Press, 1948.

2036 _____ . "Image Makers and Restorers. " Walt Whit-
      man Review, 6 (1960), 29-31.

2037 REUBEN, Paul P. "Whitman in B. O. Flowers' Arena. "
      Walt Whitman Review, 19 (1973), 11-19.

2038 REXROTH, Kenneth. "Walt Whitman. " Saturday Re-
      view, 49 (September 3, 1966), 43. Reprinted in
      Classics Revisited. New York: Quadrangle, 1968.
      Pp. 249-253.

2039 REYNOLDS, Michael S. "Whitman's Early Prose and
      'The Sleepers. ' " American Literature, 41 (1969),
      406-414.

2040 RHODES, S. A. "The Influence of Walt Whitman on
      André Gide. " Romanic Review, 31 (April, 1940),
      156-171.

2041 RHYS, Ernest. "Walt Whitman's Leaves of Grass. "
      Everyman, 1 (February 28, and March 7, 1913),
      623; 656-657.

2042 _____ . "Walt Whitman--1819-1892. " Bookman
      (London), 56 (May, 1919), 66-68.

2043 RICHARDSON, Charles F. American Literature: 1607-

1885, 2 vols. New York: Putnam's, 1889. Whitman, Vol. I, pp. 275-280.

2044 RICHARDSON, R. D., Jr. Myth and Literature in the
American Renaissance. Bloomington: Indiana University Press, 1978. Whitman, pp. 138-164.

2045 RICKETT, A. "Walt Whitman," in Vagabond in Literature. New York: Dutton, 1906. Pp. 169-205.

2046 RIDDEL, Joseph N. "Walt Whitman and Wallace Stevens:
Functions of a 'Literatur.'" South Atlantic Quarterly,
61 (August, 1962), 506-520.

2047 RIDGELY, J. V. "Whitman, Emerson, and Friend."
Columbia Library Columns, 10 (November, 1960),
15-19. "Friend" refers to Moncure Conway.

2048 RIDLEY, Hilda M. "Walt Whitman and Anne Gilchrist."
Dalhousie Review, 11 (January, 1932), 521-526.

2049 _____. "The Good Gray Poet." Dalhousie Review,
35 (January, 1956), 370-373.

2050 RIETHMUELLER, Richard Henri. "Walt Whitman and
the Germans." German-American Annals, n.s., 4
(1906), 1-127. Also published Philadelphia: Ameri-
cana/Germanica Press, 1906.

2051 RILEY, Woodbridge. The Meaning of Mysticism.
Peterborough, N.H.: Richard R. Smith, 1930.
Whitman, p. 64 et passim.

2052 RINGE, Donald A. "Bryant and Whitman: A Study in
Artistic Affinities." Boston University Studies in
English, 2 (Summer, 1956), 85-94.

2052a RISING, Clara. "Vistas of a Disillusioned Realist."
Walt Whitman Review, 7 (1961), 63-71.

2053 RIVERS, W. C. Walt Whitman's Anomaly. London:
George Allen, 1913.

2054 RIVIÈRE, Jean. "Howells and Whitman After 1881."
Walt Whitman Review, 12 (1966), 97-100.

2055 ROBBINS, J. Albert. "America and the Poet: Whitman, Hart Crane, and Frost," in Brown, John Russell, Irvin Ehrenpreis, and Bernard Harris, eds., American Poetry. London: Edward Arnold, 1965. Pp. 45-67. Stratford-on-Avon Studies, No. 7.

2056 _____. "The Narrative Form of 'Song of Myself.'" American Transcendental Quarterly, 12 (1971), 17-20.

2057 _____, ed. American Literary Manuscripts: A Checklist of Holdings in Academic, Historical, and Public Libraries, Museums, and Authors' Homes in the U.S. (1960). Second edition, revised. Athens: University of Georgia Press, 1977.

2058 ROBINSON, David. "The Poetry of Dialogue in 'Song of Myself.'" American Poetry and Poetics, 1 (1974), 34-50.

2059 ROBINSON, Victor. "Walt Whitman." Altruria Magazine, May, 1907. Pp. 14-25.

2060 ROBINSON, W. J. "Walt Whitman and Sex." Conservator, 24 (June, 1913), 53-55.

2061 RODGERS, Cleveland. "Walt Whitman, the Politician." Literary Review, 4 (1923), 57-58.

2062 _____. "Walt Whitman and Independence Day." Walt Whitman Bulletin, 2 (October, 1958), 7-8.

2063 _____. "The Good Gray House Builder." Walt Whitman Review, 5 (December, 1959), 63-69.

2064 _____, and John Black, eds. The Gathering of the Forces. New York: Putnam's, 1920. Whitman's writings in the Brooklyn Daily Eagle, 1846-1847.

2065 ROESLER, Sister Miriam Clare, O.S.F. "The Sea and Death in Whitman's Leaves of Grass." Ph.D. diss., Catholic, 1962. DA, 24 (1963), 1606.

2066 _____. "The Sea and Death in Leaves of Grass." Walt Whitman Review, 10 (March, 1964), 14-16.

2067 ROGERS, Cameron. The Magnificent Idler: The Story of Walt Whitman. Garden City, N.Y.: Doubleday, Page, 1926. Fictionalized biography.

Rogers   176

2068 ROGERS, Fred B. "Walt Whitman: A Fardel of Ad-
      mirers." New Jersey Historical Society Proceed-
      ings, 83 (September, 1965), 275-286. Physicians
      who admired Whitman.

2069 ROMIG, Edna Davis. "Walt Whitman: 1819-1919."
      Outlook, 122 (May 7, 1919), 34-37.

2070 _____. "The Paradox of Walt Whitman." Univer-
      sity of Colorado Studies, 5 (June, 1926), 95-132.

2071 _____. "More Roots for Leaves of Grass," in
      Elizabethan Studies and Other Essays in Honor of
      George F. Reynolds. Boulder: University of Col-
      orado Studies in the Humanities, No. 4, 1945. Pp.
      322-327.

2072 ROOS, Carl, ed. "Walt Whitman's Letters to a Danish
      Friend." Orbio Litterarum, 7 (1949), 31-60.

2073 ROREM, Ned. "Words Without Song," in Miller, Ed-
      win H., ed., The Artistic Legacy (1970), pp. 9-19.

2074 ROSE, Alan H. "Destructive Vision in the First and
      Last Versions of 'Song of Myself.'" Walt Whitman
      Review, 15 (1969), 215-222.

2075 ROSENBERRY, Edward H. "Walt Whitman's All-Amer-
      ican Poet." Delaware Notes, 32 (1959), 1-12.

2076 ROSENBLATT, Louise M. "Whitman's Democratic
      Vistas and the New 'Ethnicity.'" Yale Review, 67
      (1978), 187-204.

2077 ROSENFELD, Alvin H. "The Poem as Dialogical
      Process: A New Reading of 'Salut au Monde!'"
      Walt Whitman Review, 10 (1964), 34-40.

2078 _____. "Emerson and Whitman: Their Personal
      and Literary Relationships." Ph.D. diss., Brown,
      1967. DA, 28 (1968), 3197A.

2079 _____. "Whitman's Open Road Philosophy." Walt
      Whitman Review, 14 (1968), 3-16.

2080 _____. "The Eagle and the Axe: A Study of Whit-
      man's 'Song of the Broad-Axe.'" American Imago,
      25 (1968), 354-370.

2081 _____. "Whitman and the Providence Literati. "
       Books at Brown, 24 (1971), 82-106.

2082 ROSENTHAL, M. L.   "The Idea of Revolution in Poe-
       try. " Nation, 223 (1976), 117-119.

2083 ROSENTHAL, Peggy Z.   "Whitman Music: The Prob-
       lem of Adaptation. " Books at Brown, 20 (1965), 71-
       97.

2084 _____. "1. Ceremony in The Two Noble Kinsmen.
       2. Toward the Beyond; A Study of Whitman's Diction
       in His Early Writing.   3. The Rhetoric of Women's
       Lib. " Ph. D. diss. , Rutgers, 1970. DA, 32 (1971),
       3267A.

2085 _____. "The Language of Measurement in Whitman's
       Early Writing. " Texas Studies in Literature and
       Language, 15 (1973), 461-470.

2086 _____. " 'Dilation' in Whitman's Early Writings. "
       Walt Whitman Review, 20 (1974), 3-15.

2087 ROSS, Donald.   "Emerson's Stylistic Influence on Whit-
       man. " American Transcendental Quarterly, 25 (1975),
       41-51.   Also printed in Strauch, Carl F. , ed. , Char-
       acteristics of Emerson: Transcendental Poet. Hart-
       ford, Conn.: Transcendental Books, 1975. Pp. 41-
       51.

2088 ROSS, E. C.   "Whitman's Verse. " Modern Language
       Notes, 45 (June, 1930), 363-364.

2089 ROSS, Morton L.   "Walt Whitman and the Limits of
       Embarrassment. " Forum, (Houston), 6 (1968), 29-34.

2090 ROSSETTI, William Michael, ed. Poems by Walt Whit-
       man. London: John Camden Horten, 1868.

2091 ROSTOV, Elspeth D.   "Review of Joseph Beaver's Walt
       Whitman--Poet of Science. " New England Quarterly,
       24 (September, 1951), 383-385.

2092 ROTCHFORD, C. M.   "Walt Whitman's Modern Music. "
       Music Journal, 19 (March, 1961), 44, 82.

2093 ROUGEMONT, Denis de. Love in the Western World.

Rountree 178

Trans. from French by Montgomery Belgion. London: Cresset, 1940. Whitman, passim.

2094 ROUNTREE, Thomas J. "Whitman's Indirect Expression and Its Application to 'Song of Myself.'" PMLA, 73 (December, 1958), 549-555.

2095 ROY, Claude. "Sur Whitman." Europe, 30 (January, 1952), 66-70.

2096 ROY, G. R. "Walt Whitman, George Sand, and Certain French Socialists." Revue de Littérature Comparée, 29 (October-December, 1955), 550-561.

2097 RUBIN, Joseph Jay. "Whitman in 1840: A Discovery." American Literature, 9 (May, 1937), 239-242. A political "card" in the Long Island Democrat, October 6, 1840.

2098 _____. "Whitman and the Boy-Forger." American Literature, 10 (May, 1938), 214-215.

2099 _____. "Whitman and Carlyle: 1846." Modern Language Notes, 53 (May, 1938), 370-371. Whitman's review of Carlyle's Letters and Speeches of Oliver Cromwell (1845).

2100 _____. "Whitman, on Byron, Scott, and Sentiment." Notes and Queries, 176 (March 11, 1939), 171.

2101 _____. "Whitman's New York Aurora." American Literature, 11 (May, 1939), 214-217.

2102 _____. "The Early Years of Walt Whitman." Ph.D. diss., Yale, 1940.

2103 _____. "John Neal's Poetics as an Influence on Whitman and Poe." New England Quarterly, 14 (June, 1941), 359-362.

2104 _____. "Tupper's Possible Influence on Whitman's Style." American Notes and Queries, 1 (October, 1941), 101-102.

2105 _____. "Whitman as a Dramatic Critic." Quarterly Journal of Speech, 28 (February, 1942), 45-49. Whitman in the Brooklyn Eagle.

2106 _____ . "Whitman: Equal Rights in the Foreground. "
Emerson Society Quarterly, 22 (1961), 20-23.

2107 _____ . The Historic Whitman. University Park:
Penn State University Press, 1973.

2108 _____ . "Plea to the Media, " in White, William, ed.,
"The Bi-centennial Walt Whitman: Essays from The
Long-Islander, " June 24, 1976. Reprinted in Walt
Whitman Review, 22 supplement (1976), 29-30.

2109 _____ , and Charles H. Brown, eds. Walt Whitman
of the 'New York Aurora,' Editor at 22: A Collection of Recently Discovered Writings. University
Park: Penn State University Press, 1950.

2110 RUDE, Carolyn Detjen. "Whitman's Concept of the
Poet in Society. " Ph.D. diss., Illinois (Urbana-
Champaign), 1976. DA, 36 (1976), 6104A.

2111 RULAND, Richard. The Rediscovery of American Literature. Cambridge: Harvard University Press,
1967. Whitman, pp. 231-282 et passim.

2112 RULE, Henry B. "Walt Whitman and George Caleb
Bingham. " Walt Whitman Review, 15 (1969), 248-
253. Also in Journal of the American Studies Association of Texas, 1 (June, 1970), 43-47.

2113 _____ . "Walt Whitman and Thomas Eakins: Variations on Some Common Themes. " Texas Quarterly,
17 (1974), 371-391.

2114 RUNDEN, John P. "Whitman's 'The Sleepers' and the
'Indiana' Section of Crane's The Bridge. " Walt Whitman Review, 15 (1969), 245-248.

2115 RUNES, Dagobert D., ed. Twentieth Century Philosophy. New York: Philosophical Library, 1947. Reprinted, Greenwood, Conn.: Greenwood Press, 1968.

2116 RUPP, Richard H., ed. Critics on Whitman. Coral
Gables: University of Miami Press, 1972.

2117 RUSCH, Frederik L. "Of Eidolons and Orgone. " Walt
Whitman Review, 13 (1967), 11-15. Relates Whitman
to Wilhelm Reich.

2118 RUSSELL, Charles Edward. An Hour of American
      Poetry. Philadelphia: Lippincott, 1929. Whitman,
      pp. 87-90.

2119 RUSSELL, David, and Delvan McIntire. "In Paths Un-
      trodden: A Study of Walt Whitman." One: The
      Homosexual Magazine, 2 (July, 1954), 4-15.

2120 RUSSELL, Jack. "Israel Potter and 'Song of Myself.'"
      American Literature, 40 (1968), 72-77.

2121 SABO, William J. "The Ship and Its Related Imagery
      in 'Inscriptions' and 'Song of Myself.'" Walt Whit-
      man Review, 24 (1978), 118-123.

2122 SACHITHANANDAN, V. "Bharati and Whitman." Lit-
      erary Criterion, 5 (1963), 85-94.

2123 _____. "Whitman and the Serpent Power." Walt
      Whitman Review, 16 (1970), 50-55.

2124 _____. "Whitman and Bharati as Vedantists," in
      Thani, Nayagan, et al., eds., Proceedings of the
      First International Conference Seminar of Tamil
      Studies. Kualalumpur: Department of Indian Studies,
      University of Malaya, 1968-1969. Pp. 247-259.

2125 _____. "A Poet in Search of God," in Menon, K.
      P. K., M. Manuel, and K. Ayyappa Daniker, eds.,
      Literary Studies: Homage to Dr. A. S. Aiyer.
      Trivandrum, India: St. Joseph's Press for the Dr.
      Aiyer Memorial Community, 1972. Pp. 112-118.

2126 _____. Whitman and Bharati: A Comparative Study.
      Bombay: Macmillan, 1978.

2127 SACHS, Viola. "Whitman and the Orientals." Kwartal-
      nik Neofilogiczny (Warsaw), 9 (1962), 147-160.

2128 SADER, Marion, ed. Comprehensive Index to Little
      Magazines: 1890-1970, 8 vols. Millwood, N.Y.:
      Kraus Thompson Organization, 1976. Whitman, Vol.
      8, pp. 4859-4861. Lists reviews and articles; espe-
      cially good for listings of reviews.

2129 St. ARMAND, Barton L. "Franklin Evans: A Sportive

Temperance Novel." Books at Brown, 24 (1971),
134-147.

2130 SAINTSBURY, George E. B. Historical Manual of English Prosody. London and New York: Macmillan,
1910. Whitman, pp. 33, 314.

2131 SAKAMOTO, Masayuki. "The Dissociation of Ideas in
Whitman's Democratic Vistas," in Miner, E. R.,
ed., English Criticism in Japan. Tokyo: University
Press, 1972. Distributed by Princeton University
Press. Pp. 259-270.

2132 SALLEE, Jonel Curtis. "Circles of the Shelf." Ph.D.
diss., Kentucky, 1977. DA, 38 (1978), 6730A.

2133 SANDBURG, Carl, ed. Leaves of Grass. Illustrated
by Valenti Angelo. New York: Random House, 1944.
Modern Library edition.

2134 SANDEEN, Ernest E. "Ego in New Eden: Walt Whit-
man," in Gardiner, Harold C., S.J., ed., American
Classics Reconsidered: A Christian Appraisal. New
York: Scribner's, 1958. Pp. 229-263.

2135 SANDERLIN, W. Stephen Jr. "The Growth of Leaves
of Grass, 1856-1860: An Analysis of the Relationship of the Valentine-Barrett Mss. to the Third Edition." Ph.D. diss., Virginia, 1955. DA, 15 (1955),
1857-1858.

2136 SANDERS, Mary K. "Leaves of Grass in the Prophetic
Tradition: A Study of Walt Whitman's Poetic Method."
Ph.D. diss., North Carolina, 1967. DA, 28 (1968),
4646A.

2137 _____. "Shelley's Promethean Shadow on Leaves of
Grass." Walt Whitman Review, 14 (1968), 151-159.

2138 SANFORD, John. View from This Wilderness: American Literature as History. Foreword by Paul Mar-
iani. Santa Barbara, Calif.: Capra Press, 1977.
Whitman, p. 108.

2139 SANTAYANA, George. "Poetry of Barbarism," in
Santayana, Interpretations of Poetry and Religion.
New York: Scribner's, 1900. Reprinted, New York:

Harper Brothers, 1957. Pp. 166-216. Article reprinted in Santayana, Essays in Literary Criticism, selected and edited by Irving Singer. New York: Scribner's, 1956. Pp. 149-178.

2140 _____. "Genteel American Poetry." New Republic 3 (May 29, 1915), 94-95.

2141 _____. "Transcendental Absolutism," in The Philosophy of George Santayana. Evanston, Ill.: Northwestern University Press, 1942. Pp. 525-530. Reprinted in Runes, ed., Twentieth Century Philosophy (1968), pp. 313-320.

2142 SARRAZIN, Gabriel. "Walt Whitman," trans. by Harrison S. Morris, in Traubel, et al., eds., In Re Walt Whitman (1893), pp. 159-194.

2143 SASTRI, P. S. "Whitman: Two Approaches," in Menon, K. P. K., M. Manuel, and K. Ayyappa Daniker, eds., Literary Studies: Homage to Dr. A. S. Aiyer. Trivandrum, India: St. Joseph's Press for the Dr. Aiyer Memorial Community, 1972. Pp. 78-88.

2144 SASTRY, C. N. "Walt Whitman's 'Reconciliation' and Wilfred Owens' 'Strange Meeting.'" American Studies Research Centre Newsletter (Hyderabad), 11 (1969), 54-56.

2145 _____. "Walt Whitman and Rabindranath Tagore: A Study in Comparison and Contrast." Triveni, 38 (1969), 22-31.

2146 SATYANARAYANA, T. V. "Walt Whitman, Poet and Prophet." Ph.D. diss., Andhra, India. No date.

2147 SAUNDERS, Henry S., ed. Parodies of Walt Whitman. New York: American Library, 1923. Reprinted, New York: AMS Press, 1970.

2148 SAWYER, Roland D. Walt Whitman: The Prophet-Poet. Boston: Houghton Mifflin, 1918.

2149 SAXENA, M. C. "Walt Whitman and Democracy." Triveni, 39 (1971), 43-49.

2150 SCHEICK, William J. "Whitman's Grotesque Half-

Breed." Walt Whitman Review, 23 (1977), 133-
136.

2151 SCHIFFMAN, Joseph. "Walt Whitman and the People
Across the Street." Nassau County Historical Journal, 19 (Winter, 1958), 17-25.

2152 SCHILLER, Andrew. "Thoreau and Whitman: The
Record of a Pilgrimage." New England Quarterly,
28 (June, 1955), 186-197.

2153 _____. "Review of Allen's Walt Whitman Abroad."
Western Review, 20 (Autumn, 1955), 71-75.

2154 _____. "An Approach to Whitman's Metrics."
Emerson Society Quarterly, 22 (1961), 23-25.

2155 SCHINZ, Albert. "Walt Whitman, a World Poet?" Lippincott's Magazine, October, 1913. Pp. 466-474.

2156 _____. "À propos de Walt Whitman." Mercure de
France, 107 (February 1, 1914), 669-671.

2157 SCHMITZ, Neil. "Exhuming Whitman: The Body in the
Text." Paunch, 48-49 (1977), 133-139.

2158 SCHNEPS, Maurice. "Walt Whitman and His Critics."
Today's Japan, 4 (March, 1959), 54-58.

2159 SCHNEIDER, Herbert Wallace. "Liberty and Union,"
in A History of American Philosophy. New York:
Columbia University Press, 1946. Pp. 159-177.
Whitman, passim.

2160 SCHNEIDER, Suzanne Beth. "'Porches of the Sun':
The Problem of Form in Whitman's 'Song of Myself.'"
Ph.D. diss., Yale, 1976. DA, 38 (1977), 268A-269A.

2161 SCHNITTKIND, Henry Thomas. "Walt Whitman, Dreamer
of the Great American Dream," in Story of the United
States. New York: Doubleday, 1938. Pp. 239-250.

2162 _____, and D. A. Schnittkind (Henry Thomas and
Dana Lee Thomas, pseudonymns). "Walt Whitman,"
in Living Biography of Great Poets. New York:
Doubleday, 1940. Pp. 279-293.

2163 SCHOLNICK, Robert J. "Whitman and the Magazines: Some Documentary Evidence." American Literature, 44 (1972), 222-246.

2164 _____. "The Selling of the 'Author's Edition': Whitman, O'Connor, and the West Jersey Press Affair." Walt Whitman Review, 23 (1977), 3-23.

2165 SCHONFELD, Judge M. "No Exit in 'Passage to India': Existence Precedes Essence in Section 5." Walt Whitman Review, 19 (1973), 147-151.

2166 SCHROTH, Raymond A., S.J. The "Eagle" and Brooklyn. Westport, Conn.: Greenwood Press, 1974. Whitman, pp. 39-58. Whitman's connection with the paper.

2167 SCHUMANN, Detlev W. "Enumerative Style and Its Significance in Whitman, Rilke, and Werfel." Modern Language Quarterly, 3 (June, 1942), 171-204.

2168 SCHWAB, Arnold T. "James Huneker on Whitman: A Newly Discovered Essay." American Literature, 38 (May, 1966), 208-218.

2169 SCHWARTZ, Arthur. "The Each and All of Whitman's Verse." Emerson Society Quarterly, 22 (1961), 25-26.

2170 SCHWEDA, Donald N. "The Journey and the Voyage Motif in Selected Major Poems, Clusters, and Short Lyrics of the Final Edition (1891-1892), of Walt Whitman's Leaves of Grass." Ph.D. diss., Loyola (Chicago), 1972. DA, 34 (1973), 286A.

2171 SCHYBERG, Frederik. Walt Whitman. Copenhagen, 1933. Based on Ph.D. diss., University of Copenhagen. Translated from Danish by Evie Allison Allen; Introduction by Gay Wilson Allen. New York: Columbia University Press, 1951.

2172 _____. "Leaves of Grass: 1855-1889," in Murphy, ed., Walt Whitman: A Critical Anthology (1962), pp. 231-238.

2173 SCOTT, Dixon. "Walt Whitman." Bookman (London), 46 (May, 1914), 81-85.

2174 SCOTT, Fred Newton. "A Note on Walt Whitman's
      Prosody." Journal of English and Germanic Philo-
      logy, 7 (1908), 134-153.

2175 SCOVEL, J. M. "Walt Whitman as I Knew Him."
      National Magazine, 20 (May, 1904), 165-169.

2176/7 SEAMON, Roger. "Sinners in the Hands of a Happy
        God: Hierarchical Values in 'Song of Myself.'" Ca-
        nadian Association of American Studies Bulletin, 2
        (1967), 3-18. See also article by Buitenhuis (1967).

      SELINCOURT, Basil de see DE SELINCOURT.

2178 SEWELL, Elizabeth. "Science and Literature." Com-
      monweal, 84 (May 13, 1966), 218-221.

2179 SEWELL, Richard H. "Walt Whitman, John P. Hale,
      and the Free Democracy: An Unpublished Letter."
      New England Quarterly, 34 (June, 1961), 239-242.

2180 SHAHANE, V. A. "Aspects of Walt Whitman's Symbol-
      ism." Literary Criterion, 5 (1962), 72-78.

2181 SHAPIRO, Karl Jay. "The First White Aboriginal." Walt
      Whitman Review, 5 (September, 1959), 43-52. Re-
      printed in Shapiro, In Defense of Ignorance. New York:
      Random House, 1960. Pp. 187-204. Also reprinted
      in Miller, J. E., Karl Shapiro, and Bernice Slote,
      Start with the Sun (1960), pp. 57-70. Reprinted in
      Shapiro, The Poetry Wreck: Selected Essays, 1950-
      1970. New York: Random House, 1975. Pp. 156-174.

2182 _____ . "Whitman Today." Walt Whitman Review,
      6 (1960), 31-32.

2183 _____ . "Is Poetry an American Art?" College
      English, 25 (1964), 395-405. Says No, and cites
      Whitman as an example.

2184 SHARMA, D. R. "George Santayana's Assessment of
      Whitman." Banasthali Patrika, 14 (1970), 13-22.

2185 SHARMA, Inder Jit. "Whitman: The Poet of Democ-
      racy," in Maini, Darshan Singh, ed., Variations on
      American Literature. New Delhi: U.S. Educational
      Foundation in India, 1968. Pp. 11-16.

2186 SHARMA, Mohan Lal. "Whitman, Tagore, Iqbal:
      Whitmanated, Under-Whitmanated, and Over-Whit-
      manated Singers of Self." Walt Whitman Review,
      15 (1969), 230-237.

2187 SHARMA, Om Prakash. "Walt Whitman and the Doc-
      trine of Karman." Philosophy East and West (Hon-
      olulu), 20 (1970), 169-174.

2188 SHARMA, Som Parkash. "A Study of Themes: Self,
      Love, War, and Death, in Relationship to Form in
      the Poetry of Walt Whitman." Ph.D. diss., Wis-
      consin, 1963. DA, 24 (1964), 4703-4704.

2189 _____. "Self, Soul, and God in 'Passage to India.'"
      College English, 27 (February, 1966), 394-399.

2190 SHARPLESS, Parvin, ed. The Myth of the Fall: Lit-
      erature of Innocence and Experience. Rochelle Park,
      N.J.: Hayden, 1974. Whitman, passim.

2191 _____, ed. Symbol and Myth in Modern Literature.
      Rochelle Park, N.J.: Hayden, 1976. Whitman,
      passim.

2192 _____, ed. Romanticism: A Literary Perspective.
      Rochelle Park, N.J.: Hayden, 1979. Whitman, passim.

2193 SHAY, Frank. The Bibliography of Walt Whitman.
      New York: Friedman's Publishing Company, 1920.
      Lists primary materials only, 46 pages.

2194 SHEFFAUER, Herman. "Whitman in Whitman's Land."
      Fortnightly Review, 91 (January, 1915), 128-137.

2195 SHEPARD, Odell. Pedlar's Progress: The Life of
      Bronson Alcott. Boston: Little, Brown, 1937.
      Whitman, passim.

2196 SHEPHARD, Esther. "Walt Whitman's Pose." Ph.D.
      diss., Washington, 1937.

2197 _____. Walt Whitman's Pose. New York: Har-
      court, Brace, 1938.

2198 _____. "An Error of Omissions in Mabbott and Sil-
      ver's 'Walt Whitman's 'Tis But Ten Years Since.'"
      American Literature, 15 (January, 1944), 421.

2199 _____ . "An Inquiry into Whitman's Method of Turn-
ing Prose into Poetry." Modern Language Quarterly,
14 (March, 1953), 43-59.

2200 _____ . "Possible Sources of Some of Whitman's
Ideas and Symbols in Hermes Mercurius Trismegistus
and Other Works." Modern Language Quarterly, 14
(March, 1953), 60-81. Refers to an English translation of an ancient Egyptian work.

2201 _____ . "The Photoduplicates of Whitman's Cardboard
Butterfly." PMLA, 70 (September, 1955), 876.

2202 _____ . "Walt Whitman's Whereabouts in the Winter
of 1842-1843." American Literature, 29 (November,
1957), 289-296.

2203 _____ . "Whitman's Copy of George Sand's Consuelo."
Walt Whitman Review, 9 (1963), 34-36.

2204 _____ . "A Fact Which Should Have Been Included in
'Whitman's Earliest Known Notebook: A Clarifica-
tion' by John C. Broderick." PMLA, 86 (1971), 266.

2205 _____ . "The Inside Front and Back Covers of Whitman's Earliest Known Notebook: Some Observations
on Photocopy and Verbal Descriptions." PMLA, 87
(1972), 1119-1122.

2206 SHERMAN, Stuart Pratt. "Walt Whitman," in Americans. New York: Scribner's, 1922. Pp. 153-185.

2207 _____ . "Emotional Discovery of America," in American Academy of Arts and Letters: Four Addresses
in Commemoration of Its Twentieth Anniversary,
1924. Pp. 144-188. Reprinted in Sherman, The
Emotional Discovery of America and Other Essays,
ed. Jacob Zeitlin. New York: Farrar and Straus,
1932. Pp. 3-34. Published posthumously; Sherman
died in 1926. Also reprinted in Loomis, R. S.,
and D. L. Clark, eds., Modern English Readings.
New York: Farrar and Straus, 1934. Pp. 131-143.

2208 _____ , ed. Leaves of Grass. New York: Scribner's, 1922.

2209 SHIMIZU, Haruo. "A Study of Whitman's Imagery."

Walt Whitman Review, 5 (1959), 26-28.   English
summary of author's book in Japanese.

2210 SHIPLEY, Maynard. "Walt Whitman's Message."   Conservator, 17 (September, 1906), 102-105.

2211 _____ . "Democracy as Religion: The Religion of
Walt Whitman." Open Court, 33 (July, 1919), 385-
393.

2212 SHOEMAKER, C. Brant, Jr. "Walt Whitman's Biographers." Ph. D. diss., Pennsylvania, no date.

2213 SHOLES, C. W. "Walt Whitman: His Poetry and Philosophy." Pacific Monthly, 6 (September, 1901),
141-143.

2214 SHUMAN, R. Baird. "Clarence Darrow's Estimate of
Whitman." Walt Whitman Review, 8 (1962), 86-87.

2215 SHYRE, Paul. "A Whitman Portrait." Nassau Review,
1 (Spring, 1965), 19-79. Dramatic narrative acted
at Whitman celebration; announced for New York
production, 1966-1967.

2216 SIDWELL, Rolin. "Formal 'Rowdyism' in Whitman and
Pavese." Ph. D. diss., Indiana, 1976. DA, 37
(1976), 2171A.

2217 SILLEN, Samuel. "Walt Whitman: The War Years."
New Masses, 42 (March 31, 1942), 22-23.

2218 _____ , ed. with Introduction. Walt Whitman: Poet
of American Democracy. New York: International
University Publishers, 1955. Selections from the
poetry and prose.

2219 SILVER, Rollo G. "Whitman and Dickens." American
Literature, 5 (January, 1934), 370-371.

2220 _____ . "Concerning Walt Whitman." Notes and
Queries, 167 (August 11, 1934), 96.

2221 _____ . "A Parody on Walt Whitman." Notes and
Queries, 167 (September 1, 1934), 150.

2222 _____ . "A Note About Whitman's Essay on Poe."

American Literature, 6 (January, 1935), 435-436.

2223 _____. "Seven Letters of Walt Whitman." American Literature, 7 (March, 1935), 76-81.

2224 _____. "Oscar Makes a Call." Colophon, 5 (March, 1935), part 20. Oscar Wilde's visit to America in 1882.

2225 _____. "Whitman." New York Times, November 3, 1935. Section 4, page 9.

2226 _____. "Walt Whitman's Lecture in Elkton." Notes and Queries, 170 (March 14, 1936), 190-191. On President Lincoln.

2227 _____. "For the Bright Particular Star." Colophon, n. s., 2 (Winter, 1937), 197-216. Refers to Mary Costelloe.

2228 _____. "Whitman Interviews Himself." American Literature, 10 (March, 1938), 84-87.

2229 _____. "Walt Whitman: First Appearance of 'Virginia--the West.'" Notes and Queries, 175 (November 12, 1938), 348-349.

2230 _____. "Whitman in 1850: Three Uncollected Articles." American Literature, 19 (January, 1948), 301-317. Letters to National Era signed 'Paumanok.'

2230a _____, ed. Seven Letters of Walt Whitman. Durham, N. C.: Duke University Press, 1935. Pamphlet.

2231 _____, ed. with Introduction. Letters Written by Walt Whitman to His Mother, 1866-1872. New York: Alfred E. Goldsmith, 1936. 71-page excerpt reprinted from edition by Harned (1902).

2232 _____, ed. "Thirty-One Letters of Walt Whitman." American Literature, 8 (January, 1937), 417-438.

2233 SIMON, Gary. "Craft, Theory, and the Artist's Milieu: The Myth-Maker and Wordsworth." Walt Whitman Review, 22 (1976), 58-66. Whitman, passim.

2234 SIMON, Myron. "'Self' in Whitman and Dickinson."
College English Association Critic, 30 (December,
1937), 8.

2235 _____. "Dunbar and Dialect Poetry," in Martin,
Jay, ed., A Singer in the Dawn: Reinterpretations
of Paul Lawrence Dunbar. New York: Dodd, Mead,
1975. Pp. 114-134.

2236 SIMONDS, W. E. "Walt Whitman: Fifty Years After."
Dial, 41 (November 16, 1906), 317-320.

2237 SIMPSON, Grace Pow. "'Susannah and the Elders':
A Source for 'Song of Myself' Section 11." Walt
Whitman Review, 20 (1974), 109-111.

2238 SINGH, Amritzit. "Walt Whitman in India: 1976."
Special issue of The Long Islander, June, 1976.
Reprinted in Walt Whitman Review, 22 supplement
1976), 31-33.

2239 SINGH, Raman K. "Whitman, Avatar of Shri Krishna?"
Walt Whitman Review, 15 (1969), 97-102.

SISTER Barbara A. Brumleve, S.S., N.D. see
BRUMLEVE.

SISTER Donez Xiques, M.C., N.D. see XIQUES.

2240 SISTER Eva Mary, O.S.F. "Shades of Darkness in
'The Sleepers.'" Walt Whitman Review, 15 (1969),
187-190.

2241 SISTER Flavia Marie, C.S.J. "'Song of Myself': A
Presage of Modern Teilhardian Paleontology." Walt
Whitman Review, 15 (1969), 43-49.

SISTER Margaret Patrice Slattery see SLATTERY.

SISTER Marie Yestadt see YESTADT.

2242 SISTER Mary Eleanor. "Hedge's Prose Writers of
Germany as a Source of Whitman's Knowledge of
German Philosophy." Modern Language Notes, 61
(June, 1946), 381-388. Refers to Frederick Henry
Hedge, work published in 1848.

SISTER Mary Kathleen Heavill, R.S.M. see HEA-
VILL.

SISTER Mary W. Brady see BRADY

SISTER Miriam Clare Roesler, O.S.F. see ROESLER.

2243 SIXBEY, George L. "Walt Whitman's Middle Years."
Ph.D. diss., Yale, 1941.

2244 _____ . "'Chanting the Square Deific'--A Study in
Whitman's Religion." American Literature, 9 (May,
1937), 171-195.

2245 SKINNER, C. M. "Walt Whitman as Editor." Atlantic
92 (November, 1903), 679-686.

2246 SKIPP, Francis E. "Whitman's 'Lucifer': A Footnote
to 'The Sleepers.'" Walt Whitman Review, 11 (1965),
52-53.

2247 _____ . "Whitman and Shelley: A Possible Source
for 'The Sleepers.'" Walt Whitman Review, 11
(1965), 69-74. Refers to "The Witch of Atlas."

2248 SLATTERY, Sister Margaret Patrice. "Patterns of
Imagery in Whitman's 'There Was a Child Went
Forth.'" Walt Whitman Review, 15 (1969), 112-114.

2249 SLOCHOWER, Harry. Mythopoesis: Mythic Patterns
in the Literary Classics. Detroit: Wayne State
University Press, 1970. "A Note on Mark Twain
and Walt Whitman," pp. 343-345.

2250 SLONIM, Ruth. "Walt Whitman's 'Open Road.'" Research Studies of the State College of Washington,
25 (March, 1957), 69-74.

2251 SLOTE, Bernice, and James E. Miller. "Of Monkeys,
Nudes, and the Good Gray Poet: Dylan Thomas and
Walt Whitman." Western Humanities Review, 13
(August, 1959), 339-353.

Start with the Sun (1960). Listed under Miller,
James E., Karl Shapiro, and Bernice Slote.

2252 _____ . "Willa Cather and Walt Whitman." Walt

Whitman Review, 12 (March, 1966), 3-5. Reprints
Willa Cather's essay of January, 1896.

2253 _____ . "Whitman and Dickinson." Review of Current Scholarship in American Literary Scholarship,
1969-1974. Pp. 56-76, 55-76, 59-74, 59-72, 85-98,
61-74.

2254 SMITH, Alberta Helen. "Origin and Interpretation of
the Hero in 'Song of Myself.'" Walt Whitman Review, 17 (1971), 45-54.

2255 _____ . "Water Imagery in Leaves of Grass." Walt
Whitman Review, 17 (1971), 82-92.

2256 _____ . "The Development of Walt Whitman's Concept
of Heroism." Ph.D. diss., New York (Albany),
1972. DA, 34 (1973), 1295A.

2257 _____ . "Walt Whitman's 'Personality' Figure."
Ball State University Forum, 16 (1975), 23-28.

2258 SMITH, Bernard. "Democracy and Realism," in Smith,
Forces in American Criticism. New York: Harcourt, Brace, 1939. Pp. 134-184.

2259 SMITH, F. Lannom. "The American Reception of
Leaves of Grass: 1855-1882." Walt Whitman Review, 22 (1976), 137-156.

2260 SMITH, Fred M. "Whitman's Poet-Prophet and Carlyle's
Hero." PMLA, 55 (December, 1940), 1146-1164.

2261 _____ . "Whitman's Debt to Carlyle's Sartor Re-
sartus." Modern Language Quarterly, 3 (March,
1942), 51-65.

2262 SMITH, G. J. "Emerson and Whitman." Conservator,
14 (June, 1903), 53-55.

2263 _____ . "Whitman's Reading of Life." Poet Lore,
17 (August, 1906), 79-94.

2264 SMITH, Henry Nash. Virgin Land: The American
West as Symbol and Myth. Cambridge: Harvard
University Press, 1950. Whitman, Chapter 4 et
passim.

2265 SMITH, Logan Pearsall. "Knowing Walt Whitman," in
      Balch, M., ed., Modern Short Biographies and Auto-
      biographies. New York: Harcourt, Brace, 1935.
      Pp. 169-176.

2266 _____. "Walt Whitman," in Unforgotten Years.
      Boston: Little, Brown, 1939. Pp. 79-108.

2267 SMITH, Michael John. "The Changing Nature of Whit-
      man's 'Song of Myself.'" Ph.D. diss., Nebraska
      (Lincoln), 1975. DA, 36 (1976), 5305A.

2268 SMITH, Patrick D. "A Critical Reappraisal of Walt
      Whitman: 1950-1965." Ph.D. diss., North Colo-
      rado, 1971. DA, 33 (1972), 733A.

2269 SMITH, Ray. "Whitman: The Leaves of Grass Bicen-
      tennial 2055." Approach, 18 (1956), 7-12.

2270 SMITH, Thomas K. "Walt Whitman's Leaves of Grass:
      Style and Subject-Matter, with Special Reference to
      Democratic Vistas." Ph.D. diss., Konigsberg (Ger-
      many), 1914.

2271 SMITHLINE, Arnold. "Walt Whitman," in Smithline,
      Natural Religion in American Literature. New Haven:
      College and University Press, 1966. Pp. 127-165.
      Discusses Ethan Allen, Paine, Jefferson, Freneau,
      Theodore Parker, and Whitman.

2272 SMUTS, Jan Christian. Walt Whitman: A Study in the
      Evolution of Personality. New edition, edited by
      Alan L. McLeod. Detroit: Wayne State University
      Press, 1973. Work written in 1894-1895 but unable
      to find a publisher; author later incorporated some
      of the material into Holism and Evolution.

2273 _____. Holism and Evolution. New York: Mac-
      millan, 1926.

2274 SNYDER, J. E. "Walt Whitman's Woman." The So-
      cialist Woman, February 10, 1909. P. 8.

2275 SNYDER, John R. "The Two Modes of Communion in
      Walt Whitman's Poetry and Prose." Ph.D. diss.,
      Claremont, 1971. DA, 32 (1972), 5751A.

2276 _____. "The Irony of National Union: Violence and
Compassion in 'Drum-Taps.'" Canadian Review of
American Studies, 4 (1973), 169-183.

2277 _____. The Dear Love of Man: Tragic and Lyrical
Communion in Walt Whitman. The Hague: Mouton
and Company, 1975. American studies in literature,
number 28.

2278 SOULE, George. "Rupert Brooke and Whitman." Little
Review, 1 (April, 1914), 15-16.

2279 SOULE, George H., Jr. "Walt Whitman's 'Pictures':
An Alternative to Tennyson's 'Palace of Art.'" Emerson Society Quarterly, 22 (1976), 39-47.

2280 SOUTHARD, Sherrylu G. "Whitman and Language: His
'Democratic' Words." Ph.D. diss., Purdue, 1972.
DA, 33 (1973), 5143A.

2281 SPECTOR, Robert D. "The Reality of War in Walt
Whitman's Specimen Days." Notes and Queries, 196
(June 9, 1951), 254-255.

2282 SPENCER, Benjamin T. "Walt Whitman," in Spencer,
The Quest for Nationality. Syracuse, N.Y.: Syracuse University Press, 1957. Pp. 219-241.

2283 _____. "'Beautiful Blood and Beautiful Brain': Whit-
man and Poe," in Strauch, Carl F., ed., Critical
Symposium on American Romanticism. Hartford,
Conn.: Transcendental Books, 1964. Pp. 45-49.
Also published in Emerson Society Quarterly, 35
(1964), 45-49.

2284 SPIEGELMAN, Julia. "Walt Whitman and Music."
South Atlantic Quarterly, 41 (April, 1942), 167-176.

2285 SPILLER, Robert E. The Cycle of American Literature. New York: Macmillan, 1955. Reprinted,
New York: New American Library, 1957. "Romantic Crises: Melville, Whitman," pp. 89-110.

2286 _____. The Third Dimension. New York: Macmillan, 1965.

2287 _____. The Oblique Light. New York: Macmillan,
1968.

2288 _____ . Milestones in American Literary History. Foreword by Robert H. Walker. Westport, Conn.: Greenwood Press, 1977. 32 reviews by Spiller, 1923-1960. Whitman, passim.

2289 _____ , et al., eds. Literary History of the United States, 3 vols. New York: Macmillan, 1948. "Whitman," by Henry Seidel Canby, Vol. I, pp. 472-498; Whitman Bibliography," by Thomas H. Johnson, Vol. III, pp. 759-768.

2290 SPITZ, Leon. "Walt Whitman and Judaism." Chicago Jewish Forum, 13 (Spring, 1955), 174-177.

2291 SPITZER, Leo. "'Explication de Texte' Applied to Whitman's 'Out of the Cradle....'" English Literary History, 16 (September, 1949), 229-249. Reprinted in abridged form in Hatcher, Anna, ed., Essays on English and American Literature. Princeton, N.J.: Princeton University Press, 1962. Pp. 14-36.

2292 SPRINGER, Otto. "Walt Whitman and Ferdinand Freiligrath." American-German Review, 11 (December, 1944), 22-25. Refers to Whitman's first German critic and translator; Whitman translated into German, 1856.

2293 SQUIRE, Sir John Collings. "Mutual Compliments," in Books in General, Second Series. New York: William Heinemann, 1920. Pp. 75-76.

2294 _____ . "Walt Whitman," in Life and Letters. New York: William Heinemann, 1921. Pp. 196-202.

2295 _____ . "Supplement to Whitman," in Books Reviewed: Critical Essays on Books and Authors. New York: William Heinemann, 1922. First appeared weekly in The Observer (London), 1920. Reprinted, Port Washington, N.Y.: Kennikat Press, 1968. Pp. 252-259.

2296 STAFFORD, John. The Literary Criticism of "Young America": A Study in the Relationship of Politics and Literature, 1837-1850. Berkeley: University of California Press, 1952. Whitman, passim.

2297 STANTON, Theodore. "Walt Whitman in Germany." The Literary Review (Literary supplement of the New York Evening Post), September 30, 1922.

Discusses Hans Reisiger's study of Whitman in
German, 1922.

2298 STARK, Lewis M., and John D. Gordon, eds. Walt
Whitman's Leaves of Grass: A Centenary Exhibition
from the Lion Whitman Collection and the Berg Collection of the New York Public Library. New York:
New York Public Library, 1955.

2299 STARK, Myra. "Walt Whitman and Anne Sexton: A
Note on the Uses of Tradition." Notes on Contemporary Literature, 8 (1978), 7-8.

2300 STARKE, Aubrey H. "Lanier's Appreciation of Whitman." American Scholar, 2 (October, 1933), 398-
408.

2301 STARR, William T. "Jean Giono and Walt Whitman."
French Review, 14 (December, 1940), 118-129.

2302 STAUFFER, Donald Barlow. A Short History of American Poetry. New York: Dutton, 1974. "Whitman
and Dickinson," pp. 137-158.

2303 _____. "Textual Emendations to Whitman's 'Cham-
pagne in Ice.'" Walt Whitman Review, 22 (1976),
132.

2304 _____. "Walt Whitman and Old Age." Walt Whitman Review, 24 (1978), 142-148.

2305 STAUFFER, Ruth. "Whitman's 'Passage to India.'"
Explicator, 9 (May, 1951), item 50.

2306 STAVROU, Constantine Nicholas. Whitman and Nietz-
sche: A Comparative Study of Their Thought. Chapel
Hill: University of North Carolina Press, 1964.
University of North Carolina Studies in the Germanic
Language and Literatures, No. 48.

2307 STEADMAN, John M. "Whitman and the King James
Bible." Notes and Queries, n.s., 3 (December,
1956), 538-539.

2308 STEDMAN, Edmund Clarence. Poets of America, 2
vols. Boston: Houghton Mifflin, 1885. Whitman,
Vol. I, pp. 349-395.

2309 _____. The Nature and Elements of Poetry. Boston: Houghton Mifflin, 1892. Reprinted, Upper Saddle River, N.J.: Gregg Press, 1970. Whitman, passim.

2310 _____, ed. An American Anthology. Boston: Houghton Mifflin, 1902.

2311 _____, and Ellen M. Hutchinson, eds. A Library of American Literature, 11 vols. New York: Charles L. Webster, 1888-1892. Whitman, Vol. 7, pp. 501-513; Vol. 9, p. 52.

2312 STEELL, Willis. "Walt Whitman's Early Life on Long Island." Munsey's Magazine, 40 (January, 1909), 497-502.

2313 STEENSMA, Robert C. "Whitman and General Custer." Walt Whitman Review, 10 (1964), 41-42. Discusses "From Far-Dakota's Canóns."

2314 STEIN, Marian L. "'Comrade' or 'Camerado' in Leaves of Grass." Walt Whitman Review, 13 (1967), 123-125.

2315 _____. "Affirmations and Negations: Lawrence's 'Whitman' and Whitman's 'Open Road.'" Walt Whitman Review, 18 (1972), 63-67.

2316 STEIN, William Bysshe. "Whitman: The Divine Ferryman." Walt Whitman Review, 8 (1962), 27-33.

2317 STEINBRINK, Jeffrey. "'To Span Vast Realms of Space and Time': Whitman's Vision of History." Walt Whitman Review, 24 (1978), 45-62.

2318 STEPANCHEV, Stephen. "Whitman in Russia," in Allen, ed., Walt Whitman Abroad (1955), pp. 144-155.

2319 _____. "Other Slavic Countries," in Allen, ed., Walt Whitman Abroad (1955), pp. 156-158.

2320 _____. "Leaves of Grass in the Soviet Camp." Walt Whitman Newsletter, 2 (March-June, 1956), 3-4.

2321 STEPHENS, Rosemary. "Elemental Imagery in 'Children of Adam.'" Walt Whitman Review, 14 (1968), 26-28.

2322 STERN, Madeleine B. Heads and Headlines: The
      Phrenological Fowler. Norman: University of Ok-
      lahoma Press, 1971. "Walt Whitman, in Care of
      Fowler and Wells, " pp. 99-123.

2323 _____. "The Long and the Short of It. " American
      Book Collector, 26 (1976), 23-24.

2324 STERN, Philip van Doren, ed. Soldier Life in the
      Union and Confederate Armies. Bloomington: In-
      diana University Press, 1961. Whitman, pp. 212-
      223.

2325 STEVENSON, Lionel. "An English Admirer of Walt
      Whitman. " American Literature, 29 (January, 1958),
      470-473. Refers to Edward Lamplough, author of a
      book of poems, Hull and Yorkshire Frescoes: A
      Poetical Year-Book of 'Specimen Days. '

2326 STEVENSON, Philip. "Walt Whitman's Democracy. "
      New Masses, 27 (June 14, 1933), 129-133.

2327 STEVENSON, Robert Louis. "The Gospel According
      to Walt Whitman. " New Quarterly, 10 (1879), 461-
      481.

2328 _____. Familiar Studies of Men and Books. London:
      Chatto and Windus, 1882; New York: Scribner's,
      1895. Whitman, pp. 87-115.

2329 _____. "Walt Whitman, " in Scott, F. W. and J.
      Zeitlin, eds. , Essays, Formal and Informal. Peter-
      borough, N. H.: Richard R. Smith, 1930. Pp. 220-
      246.

2330 _____. "Walt Whitman, " excerpt from Familiar
      Studies (1882), in Stevenson, Essays, ed. Malcolm
      Elwin. New York: Coward-McCann, 1950. Pp. 36-
      59.

2331 STEWART, George R. , Jr. "Whitman and His Own
      Country. " Sewanee Review, 33 (April, 1925), 210-
      218.

2332 STIBITZ, E. Earle. "Walt Whitman Answers a Col-
      lector. " Illinois Studies, 1 (1974), 141-144.

2332a STILLGOE, John R. "Possible Lockean Influence in
'The World Below the Brine.'" Walt Whitman Review, 21 (1975), 150-155.

2333 STODDARD, Donald R. "Horace Traubel: A Critical
Biography." Ph.D. diss., Pennsylvania, 1970. DA,
32 (1971), 402A.

2334 STORY, Irving C. "The Growth of Leaves of Grass:
A Proposal for a Variorum Edition." Pacific University Bulletin, 37 (February, 1941), 1-11.

2335 _____. "The Structural Pattern of Leaves of Grass."
Pacific University Bulletin, 38 (January, 1942), 2-
12.

2336 STOTT, Jon C. "The Mocking-Bird in 'Out of the
Cradle....'" Walt Whitman Review, 16 (1970),
119-120.

2337 STOVALL, Floyd. "Main Drifts in Whitman's Poetry."
American Literature, 4 (March, 1932), 3-22. Re-
printed in Untermeyer, ed., Poetry and Prose of
Whitman (1949), pp. 1119-1136.

2338 _____. "On Whitman's Calamus Poems." Princeton
University Library Chronicle, 3 (February, 1942),
68-69.

2339 _____. American Idealism. Norman: University
of Oklahoma Press, 1943. Whitman, pp. 79-96.

2340 _____. "Whitman's Knowledge of Shakespeare."
Studies in Philology, 49 (October, 1952), 643-664.

2341 _____. "Whitman, Shakespeare, and Democracy."
Journal of English and Germanic Philology, 51 (October, 1952), 457-472.

2342 _____. "Whitman, Shakespeare, and the Baconians."
Philological Quarterly, 31 (1952), 27-38.

2343 _____. "Notes on Whitman's Reading." American
Literature, 26 (November, 1954), 337-362.

2344 _____. "Walt Whitman and the American Tradition."

Virginia Quarterly Review, 31 (August, 1955), 540-
557.

2345   . "Walt Whitman: The Man and the Myth. "
South Atlantic Quarterly, 54 (November, 1955), 538-
551.

2346   . "Leaves of Grass. " University of North
Carolina Extension Bulletin, 35 (January, 1956), 19-
29.

2347   . "On Editing Whitman Papers. " Mississippi
Quarterly, 15 (1962), 120-125.

2348   . "Dating Whitman's Early Notebooks. " Studies in Bibliography (Virginia University Bibliographical Society), 24 (1971), 197-204.

2349   . "Whitman and the Poet in Leaves of Grass, "
in Woodress, James, ed. , Essays Mostly on Periodical Publication in America: Essays in Honor of
Clarence F. Gohdes. Durham, N. C. : Duke University Press, 1973. Pp. 3-21.

2350   . The Foreground of Leaves of Grass. Charlottesville: University Press of Virginia, 1974.

2351   . "Walt Whitman as American, " in Crawley,
Thomas Edward, ed. , Four Makers. Durham, N. C. :
Duke University Press, 1976. Pp. 43-63.

2352   , ed. with Introduction, Bibliography, and Notes.
Walt Whitman: Representative Selections. New
York: American Book Company, 1934. Revised
edition, 1939. Reprinted, New York: Hill and Wang,
1961. American Writers Series.

2353   , ed. Eight American Authors. New York:
Modern Language Association, 1956. Reprinted,
New York: Norton, 1963. "Whitman, " by Willard
Thorp, pp. 271-318. Revised edition, ed. by James
Woodress, New York: Norton, 1971. "Whitman, " by
Roger Asselineau, pp. 225-272.

2354   , ed. with Notes. Prose Works, 1892: Vol.
I, Specimen Days, in The Collected Writings of Walt
Whitman. New York: New York University Press,
1963.

2355 _____, ed. with Notes. Prose Works, 1892: Vol. II, Collect and Other Prose Writings, in The Collected Writings of Walt Whitman. New York: New York University Press, 1964.

2356 STOWELL, Robert. "Stephen Crane's Use of Colour in The Red Badge of Courage." Literary Criterion, 9 (1970), 36-39. Relates to Whitman, passim.

2357 STRAUCH, Carl F. "The Structure of Walt Whitman's 'Song of Myself.'" English Journal (College edition), 27 (September, 1938), 597-607.

2358 _____, ed. "Symposium on Walt Whitman." Emerson Society Quarterly, 22 (1961), 2-29.

2359 _____, ed. Critical Symposium on American Romanticism. Hartford, Conn.: Transcendental Books, 1964. Also published in Emerson Society Quarterly, 35 (1964), 2-60.

2360 STROHL, Beverly Luziette. "An Interpretation of 'Out of the Cradle....'" Walt Whitman Review, 10 (1964), 83-87.

2361 STROM, Susan. "'Face to Face': Whitman's Biblical Reference in 'Crossing Brooklyn Ferry.'" Walt Whitman Review, 24 (1978), 7-16.

2362 STRONG, Augustus H. American Poets and Their Theology. Philadelphia and Boston: Griffith and Rowland Press, 1916. Whitman, pp. 419-470.

2363 STUBBLEFIELD, Charles. "The Great Circle: Whitman's 'Passage to India.'" Prairie Schooner, 49 (1975), 19-30.

2364 STUEHLER, David M. "Significant Form in Whitman's 'Out of the Cradle....'" Calamus, 10 (1975), 28-39.

2365 SUGG, Richard P. "Whitman's Symbolic Circle and 'A Broadway Pageant.'" Walt Whitman Review, 16 (1970), 35-40.

2366 SULFRUDGE, Cynthia. "Meaning in Whitman's Use of 'Electric.'" Walt Whitman Review, 19 (1973), 151-153.

2367 SULLIVAN, Art. "Incident at Sunken Meadow."

Nassau Review, 1 (Spring, 1965), 99-100. An original
poem about Whitman.

2368 SULLIVAN, Donald J. "To Go Unsworn: The Political
Pilgrimage of Walt Whitman." Ph.D. diss., Michigan, 1972. DA, 33 (1973), 5202A.

2369 SULLIVAN, Edward E., Jr. "Thematic Unfolding in
Whitman's Drum-Taps." Emerson Society Quarterly,
31 (1963), 42-45.

2370 SUMMERHAYES, Don. "Joyce's Ulysses and Whitman's
'Self': A Query." Wisconsin Studies in Contemporary Literature, 4 (Spring-Summer, 1963), 216-224.

2371 SUTCLIFFE, Emerson G. "Whitman, Emerson, and
the New Poetry." New Republic, 19 (May 24, 1919),
114-116.

2372 SUTTON, Larry. "Structural Music in Whitman's 'Out
of the Cradle....'" Walt Whitman Review, 15
(1969), 57-59.

2373 SUTTON, Walter. "The Analysis of Free Verse Form,
Illustrated by a Reading of Whitman." Journal of
Aesthetics and Art Criticism, 18 (December, 1959),
241-254. Reprinted in Pearce, ed., Walt Whitman:
A Collection (1962), as "Whitman's Poetic Ensembles,"
pp. 119-131.

2374 SWAN, Tom. "Walt Whitman: The Man, His Book,
His Message." Open Road, 1 (July, August, November, 1907), no page.

2375 SWAYNE, Mattie. "Structural Unity in Leaves of Grass."
Ph.D. diss., Texas, 1938.

2376 _____. "Whitman's Catalogue Rhetoric." University
of Texas Studies in English, 21 (July, 1941), 162-
178.

2377 SWEET, Robert B. "A Writer Looks at Whitman's
'A Sight in Camp in the Daybreak Gray and Dim.'"
Walt Whitman Review, 17 (1971), 58-62.

2378 SWINBURNE, Algernon Charles. "Under the Micro-
scope," in Gosse, Sir Edmund, and Thomas J. Wise,

eds., Complete Works of Swinburne, 20 vols. (Bon-
church edition, 1925-1927. Reprinted, New York:
Russell and Russell, 1968. Vol. 16, pp. 377-444.

2379 SYMONDS, John Addington. Walt Whitman: A Study.
London: George Routledge; New York: Dutton, 1893.
Reprinted, New York: John C. Nimmo, 1946.

2380 _____. "Walt Whitman," in Kiell, ed., Psychological Studies (1964), pp. 255-270.

2381 SYMONS, Arthur. "Note on Walt Whitman." Bellman,
24 (February 9, 1918), 154-155.

2382 TAGORE, Rabindranath. "Walt Whitman," written in
Bengali in 1891. Translated with notes by Rameshwar
K. Gupta. Walt Whitman Review, 19 (1973), 3-11.

2383 TAINE, Hippolyte A. Histoire de la littérature anglaise
(4 vols. 1863-1864). Translated from French by H.
Van Laun, as History of English Literature, 4 vols.
Philadelphia: Henry Altemus Company, 1908.

2384 TAKANO, Fumi. "Walt Whitman's Spiritual Pilgrimage."
Studies in English Literature (Tokyo), 34 (1957), 59-
75.

2385 TAKAYAMA, R. "A Japanese Estimate of Walt Whitman." Calamus, 2 (1970), 1-5. Reprint of 1904
essay.

2386 TALBOT, N. C. "Walt Whitman, the Monster and the
Critics," in Adams, Marion, ed., Australasian University Languages and Literature Association. Melbourne, Australia: University of Melbourne, 1964.
Pp. 61-62.

2387 TANASOCA, Donald. "Poe and Whitman." Walt Whitman Bulletin, 2 (April, July, 1959), 3-7, 6-11.

2388 TANIGUCHI, Toshiro. "Whitman Seen from the Zen
Viewpoint." Jimbungaku, 108 (1968), 28-45. Text
in Japanese; English abstract, pp. 81-82.

2389 TANNENBAUM, Earl. "Pattern in Whitman's 'Song of
Myself': A Summary and a Supplement." College

Language Association Journal, 6 (September, 1962), 44-49.

2390 TANNER, James Thomas Fontenst. "The Lamarckian Theory of Progress in Leaves of Grass." Walt Whitman Review, 9 (1963), 3-11.

2391 _____. "Walt Whitman: Poet of Lamarckian Evolution." Ph.D. diss., Texas Tech (Lubbock), 1965. DA, 26 (1966), 5446.

2392 _____. "The Superman in Leaves of Grass." Walt Whitman Review, 11 (1965), 85-100.

2393 _____. "Walt Whitman Bibliographies: A Chronological Listing, 1902-1964." Bulletin of Bibliography, 25 (1968), 131-132. Contains 68 items.

2394 _____, with Introduction. Walt Whitman: A Supplementary Bibliography, 1961-1967. Kent, Ohio: Kent State University Press, 1968. 59-page pamphlet. Serif series in bibliography, No. 5.

2395 _____. "A Note on Whitman's 'A Sight in Camp.'" Emerson Society Quarterly, 58 (1970), 123-124.

2396 _____. "Walt Whitman and William James." Calamus, 2 (1970), 6-23.

2397 TANNER, Stephen L. "Star-Gazing in Whitman's Specimen Days." Walt Whitman Review, 19 (1973), 158-161.

2398 _____. "Whitman as Urban Transcendentalist." South Dakota Review, 14 (1976), 6-18.

2399 TANNER, Tony. "An Introduction to the Modern World." Time and Tide, 42 (March 16, 1961), 430-431.

2400 _____. The Reign of Wonder: Naiveté and Reality in American Literature. Cambridge, England: Cambridge University Press, 1965. "Walt Whitman's Ecstatic First Step," pp. 64-86. Reissued, 1977.

2401 TANSELLE, G. Thomas. "Whitman's Short Stories: Another Reprint." Papers of the Bibliographical Society of America, 56 (1962), 115.

2402 TAPSCOTT, Stephen J. "Leaves of Myself: Whitman's
      Egypt in 'Song of Myself.'" American Literature,
      50 (March, 1978), 49-73.

2403 _____. "American Beauty: Whitman, Williams, and
      Poetic Form." Ph.D. diss., Cornell, 1976. DA,
      38 (1978), 4172A-4173A.

2404 TAYLOR, Estelle W. "Analysis and Comparison of the
      1855 and 1891 Versions of Whitman's 'To Think of
      Time.'" Walt Whitman Review, 13 (1967), 107-122.

2405 _____. "Moments of Silence in Leaves of Grass."
      Walt Whitman Review, 21 (1975), 145-150.

2406 TELLER, Walter. "Whitman at Timber Creek," in
      Brown, E. Francis, ed., Page 2: The Best of
      "Speaking of Books" from The New York Times Book
      Review. New York: Holt, Rinehart, and Winston,
      1969. Pp. 201-205.

2407 _____, ed. with Introduction. Walt Whitman's Cam-
      den Conversations. New Brunswick, N.J.: Rutgers
      University Press, 1973. 217 pages selected from
      Traubel's With Walt Whitman in Camden.

2408 TEMPLEMAN, W. D. "Hopkins and Whitman: Evidence
      of Influence and Echoes." Philological Quarterly, 33
      (January, 1954), 48-65.

2409 _____. "On Whitman's 'Apple-Peelings.'" Philolog-
      ical Quarterly, 35 (April, 1956), 200-202.

2410 TEMPLIN, Lawrence. "The Quaker Influence on Walt
      Whitman." American Literature, 42 (1970), 165-180.

2411 THAYER, William Roscoe. "Personal Recollections of
      Walt Whitman." Scribner's Magazine, 65 (June,
      1919), 674-687.

2412 THOMAS, John L. "Romantic Reform in America,
      1815-1865." American Quarterly, 17 (1965), 656-
      681.

2413 THOMPSON, Bert A. "Edward Wilkins: Male Nurse
      to Walt Whitman." Walt Whitman Review, 15 (1969),
      194-196.

2414 THOMPSON, G. R. "An Early Unrecorded Printing of
     Walt Whitman's 'Death in the School-Room.'" Walt
     Whitman Review, 19 (1973), 64-65. Refers to Whit-
     man's short story published in the New York Mirror:
     A Weekly Gazette of Literature and Fine Arts, Au-
     gust 21, 1841.

2415 THOMPSON, Leslie M. "Promise of America in Whit-
     man and Thomas Wolfe: 'Song of Myself' and You
     Can't Go Home Again." Walt Whitman Review, 12
     (1966), 27-43.

2416 THOMSON, James (1834-1882). Walt Whitman: The
     Man and the Poet. First published in Thomson, Bio-
     graphical and Critical Studies. London: Reeves,
     1896. Later published separately with Introduction
     by Bertram Dobell. London: Bertram Dobell, 1910.
     Reprinted, Folcroft, Pa.: Folcroft Publishers, 1970;
     also reprinted, New York: Haskell House, 1971.

2417 THOREAU, Henry David. "Concerning Walt Whitman
     (A Letter to Harrison Blake)," in Rahv, Philip, ed.,
     Literature in America (1957), pp. 148-149.

2418 _____. "Walt Whitman," in Warfel, et al., eds.,
     The American Mind (1947), p. 576. Also in Leary,
     ed., American Literary Essays (1960), pp. 115-116.

2419 THORNSTENBERG, Edward. "The Walt Whitman Cult
     in Germany." Sewanee Review, 19 (January, 1911),
     71-86.

2420 THORP, Willard. "Walt Whitman," in Stovall, ed.,
     Eight American Authors (1956), pp. 271-318.

2421 _____. "Do Princeton Students Read Whitman?"
     Walt Whitman Review, 6 (1960), 32-33.

2422 _____, ed. with Introduction. Great Short Works
     of the American Renaissance. New York: Harper
     & Row, 1968.

2423 TIMMIS, Jessica H. "Walt Whitman: An Impressionist
     Experiment?" Ph.D. diss., Ohio, 1972. DA, 34
     (1973), 2582A.

2424 TISIKER, Monica R. "Jacob Boehme's Influence on

Some Poems in Leaves of Grass." Walt Whitman
Review, 20 (1974), 15-27.

2425 TODD, Edgeley W. "Indian Pictures and Two Whitman
Poems." Huntington Library Quarterly, 19 (November, 1955), 1-11.

2426 TOLLES, Frederick B. "A Quaker Reaction to Leaves
of Grass." American Literature, 19 (May, 1947),
170-171.

2427 TOMLINSON, Henry Major. "News from the Front,"
in Waiting for Daylight. New York: Knopf, 1922.
Pp. 74-79.

2428 TOPEROFF, Sam. "Reconciliation of Polarity in Whitman's Drum-Taps." Emerson Society Quarterly, 31
(1963), 45-47.

2429 _____. "Whitman's Raft Metaphor." Emerson Society Quarterly, 38 (1965), 130-132. Refers to
"Crossing Brooklyn Ferry."

2430 TOWNSEND, Frank H. "Literary Nationalism in Walt
Whitman: Theory and Practice of Poetry." Ph.D.
diss., Chicago, 1953.

2431 TRACHTENBERG, Alan. Brooklyn Bridge: Fact and
Symbol. New York: Oxford University Press, 1965.
Refers principally to Hart Crane; Whitman, passim.

2432 _____. "The Rainbow and the Grid," in Cohen, H.,
ed., The American Culture (1968), pp. 1-17.

2433 TRAIL, George Y. "Whitman's 'Spear of Summer
Grass': Epic Invocations in 'Song of Myself.'"
Walt Whitman Review, 23 (1977), 120-125.

2434 TRAUBEL, Horace. "Leaves from Whitman's Later
Life." Critic, 41 (October, 1902), 319-327.

2435 _____. "Walt Whitman at Fifty Dollars a Volume
and How He Came To It." Era, 11 (June, 1903),
523-529.

2436 _____. "Walt Whitman's Respect for the Body."
Physical Culture, 10 (September, 1903), 246-250.

2437 _____. "The Good Gray Poet at Home." Saturday
Evening Post, May 13, June 3, August 1, 1905.

2438 _____. With Walt Whitman in Camden, 5 vols.
Vol. I (March 28-July 14, 1888). Boston: Small,
Maynard, 1906. Vol. II (July 16-October 31, 1888).
New York: Appleton, 1908. Vol. III (November 1,
1888-January 20, 1889). New York: Mitchell Ken-
nerly, 1914. Vols. I-III, reprinted, New York: Row-
man and Littlefield, 1961. Vol. IV (January 21-
April 7, 1889), ed. by Sculley Bradley. Philadel-
phia: University of Pennsylvania Press, 1953. Vol.
V (April 8-September 14, 1889), ed. by Gertrude
Traubel. Carbondale: University of Southern Illi-
nois Press, 1964.

2439 _____. "With Walt Whitman in Camden" articles
published in part in the following:

Century, 71 (November, 1905), 82-98.
Forum, 46 (October, November, December, 1911),
400-414, 589-600, 709-719.
Forum, 47 (January, 1912), 78-89.
Forum, 54 (July, August, September, 1915), 77-85,
187-199, 318-327.
Seven Arts, 2 (September, 1917), 627-638.
Conservator, 12-30 (January, 1900-June, 1919),
passim.

2440 _____. "The Code of a Gentleman." Conservator,
17 (January, 1907), 168-172.

2441 _____. "Talks with Walt Whitman." American Magazine, 64 (July, 1907), 281-288.

2442 _____. "Whitman in Old Age." Century, 74 (September, October, 1907), 740-755, 911-922.

2443 _____. "Estimates of Well-Known Men." Century,
83 (December, 1911), 250-256.

2444 _____. "Getting Whitman Right and Wrong." Conservator, 25 (July, 1914), 77.

2445 _____. "Walt Whitman's New Publishers." Conservator, 28 (August, 1917), 92.

2446 _____. "Walt Whitman's America." Conservator,
28 (November, 1917), 134-136.

2447 _____. "Whitmania." Conservator, 29 (May, 1918),
40-42.

2448 _____. "Walt Whitman on Himself." American Mercury, 3 (October, 1924), 186-192.

2449 _____. "Whitman on His Contemporaries." American Mercury, 2 (July, 1924), 328-332.

2450 _____, ed. Camden's Compliment to Walt Whitman,
May 31, 1889. Philadelphia: David McKay, 1889.

2451 _____, ed. "An American Primer" with Facsimiles
of the Original Manuscript. Boston: Small, Maynard,
1904. 35-page pamphlet.

2452 _____, Richard M. Bucke, and Thomas B. Harned,
eds. In Re Walt Whitman. Philadelphia: David
McKay, 1893.

2453 _____, Richard M. Bucke, and Thomas B. Harned,
eds. The Complete Writings of Walt Whitman, 10
vols. New York: Putnam's, 1902. Considered the
"Standard" Whitman until superseded by Blodgett and
Bradley, eds., The Collected Writings of Walt Whitman, projected 18 vols. New York University Press,
1965--date.

2454 TRENT, Josiah C., M.D. "Walt Whitman--A Case
History." Surgery, Gynecology, and Obstetrics, 87
(July, 1948), 113-121. Reprinted in Kiell, ed.,
Psychological Studies (1964), pp. 226-242.

2455 TRENT, William P., and John Erskine. Great American Writers. New York: Henry Holt, 1912. Whitman, pp. 212-231.

2456 _____, et al., eds. Cambridge History of American
Literature, 4 vols. New York: Macmillan, 1917-
1921. Reprinted in one-volume edition, 1944. Whitman, by Emory Holloway and Henry S. Saunders,
Vol. II, pp. 258-274.

2457 TRIGGS, Oscar Lovell. "Walt Whitman." Poet-Lore,
5 (June-July, 1893), 289-305.

2458 _____ . Browning and Whitman: A Study in Democracy. Chicago: University of Chicago Press, 1893.

2459 _____ . "The Growth of Leaves of Grass, " in Traubel, et al. , eds. , Complete Writings (1902), Vol.
10, pp. 99-134.

2460 _____ . "Bibliography of Walt Whitman, " in Traubel,
et al. , eds. , Complete Writings (1902), Vol. 10,
pp. 139-233. Lists primary sources.

2461 _____ , et al. "Walt Whitman and the Critics. "
Chap-Book, 7 (August 1, 1897), 192-195.

2462 TRILLING, Lionel. "Sermon on a Text from Whitman. "
Nation, 160 (February 24, 1945), 214-220.

2463 TRIMBLE, Annie E. "Concordance Making in New
Zealand. " Atlantic, 104 (September, 1909), 364-367.
Refers to a concordance made by Mr. and Mrs. W.
H. Trimble of Leaves of Grass. Not published;
manuscript is in Brown University Library.

2464 TRIMBLE, W. H. Walt Whitman and Leaves of Grass:
An Introduction. London: Watts, 1905. Based on
lectures given in New Zealand.

2465 TRIMMER, Joseph F. "The Kinetic Structure of 'Song
of Myself. ' " Calamus, 4 (December, 1970), 1-8.

2466 TROWBRIDGE, John Townsend. "Reminiscences of
Walt Whitman. " Atlantic, 89 (February, 1902), 163-
175.

2467 _____ . My Own Story: With Recollections of Noted
Persons. Boston: Houghton Mifflin, 1903. Whitman,
pp. 360-401.

2468 TRUEBLOOD, D. E. "The Fullness of the Godhead
Dwelt in Every Blade of Grass, " in West, J. , ed. ,
The Quaker Reader. New York: Viking Press,
1962. Pp. 332-334.

2469 TSANOFF, Radoslav Andrea. "Moral Outlook of New
England and the Spreading American Scene, " in
Moral Ideals of Our Civilization. New York: Dut-
ton, 1942. Pp. 450-471.

2470 TURNER, Lorenzo D. "Walt Whitman and the Ne-
      gro." Chicago Jewish Forum, 15 (Fall, 1956), 5-
      11.

2471 TURNER, Mary Ann. "Reconciliation of Love and Death
      in 'Out of the Cradle' and Other Poems." Walt Whit-
      man Review, 18 (1972), 123-132.

2472 TUTTLE, Robert Clifford. "The Identity of Walt Whit-
      man: Motive, Theme, and Form in Leaves of Grass."
      Ph.D. diss., Washington, 1965. DA, 26 (1965),
      2763.

2473 UNAMUNO, Miguel de. "Adamic Song," (1930) trans-
      lated from Spanish by Fernando Alegria, in Al-
      len, ed., Walt Whitman Abroad (1955), pp. 220-
      223.

2474 UNTERMEYER, Louis. "Whitman Centenary." New
      Republic, 18 (March 22, 1919), 245-247.

2475 _____. "Walt Whitman," in Untermeyer, Makers
      of the Modern World. New York: Simon and Schus-
      ter, 1955. Pp. 34-46. Includes the lives of 92
      writers important in shaping the twentieth cen-
      tury.

2476 _____. "Walt Whitman's Role Today." Walt Whit-
      man Review, 6 (1960), 34-35.

2477 _____, ed. Poetry and Prose of Whitman. New
      York: Simon and Schuster, 1949. "High Noon," by
      Lewis Mumford, pp. 1083-1087.

2478/9 VALENTE, John, ed. with Introduction. Leaves of
      Grass. New York: Macmillan, 1928.

2480 VANDERBILT, Kermit. "'Hear America Singing':
      Whitman and Democratic Culture." Walt Whitman
      Review, 21 (1975), 22-28. Response to a TV
      show.

2481 VANDERHAAR, Margaret W. "Whitman, Paine, and
      the Religion of Democracy." Walt Whitman Review,
      16 (1970), 14-22.

2482 VAN DOREN, Carl. The Roving Critic. New York:
Knopf, 1923. "Whitman in His Crises," pp. 40-44.

2483 _____, and Carl L. Carmer. American Scriptures.
New York: Boni and Gaer, 1946. "Lincoln and
Whitman," pp. 51-57.

2484 VAN DOREN, Mark. "Walt Whitman, Stranger."
American Mercury, 35 (July, 1935), 277-285. Re-
printed in Van Doren, The Private Reader. New
York: Holt, Rinehart, 1942. Pp. 69-86.

2485 _____. "The Poet," in Allen, Gay Wilson, Mark
Van Doren, and David Daiches, Walt Whitman: Man,
Poet, Philosopher. Three lectures presented under
the auspices of the Gertrude Clarke Whittall Poetry
and Literature Fund. Washington, D.C.: Library
of Congress, 1955. Pp. 15-33.

2486 _____. The Happy Critic and Other Essays. New
York: Hill and Wang, 1961. "Leaves of Grass:
1855-1955," pp. 25-49.

2487 _____, ed. There Were Giants in the Land. New
York: Farrar and Rinehart, 1942. "Walt Whitman:
1819-1892," pp. 84-89.

2488 _____, ed. The Portable Walt Whitman. New York:
Viking Press, 1945. Revised edition by Malcolm
Cowley; Chronology and Bibliographical Checklist by
Gay Wilson Allen. New York: Viking Press, 1974.

2489 VAN DYKE, Henry. "Greater Comet," in The Man
Behind the Book. New York: Scribner's, 1929.
Pp. 57-90.

2490 VAN EGMOND, Peter G. "Walt Whitman's Study of
Oratory and Uses of It in Leaves of Grass." Ph.D.
diss., North Carolina, 1966. DA, 27 (1967), 2510A.

2491 _____. "Walt Whitman on the Platform." Southern
Speech Journal, 32 (Spring, 1967), 215-224.

2492 _____. "Herzog's Quotation of Walt Whitman."
Walt Whitman Review, 13 (1967), 54-56.

2493 _____. "Bryn Mawr College Library Holdings on

Whitman's Books." Walt Whitman Review, 20 (1974), 41-50.

2494 _____, ed. with Introduction. Memoirs of Thomas B. Harned: Walt Whitman's Friend and Literary Executor. Hartford, Conn.: Transcendental Books, 1972. Also listed in Harned.

2495 VAN NOSTRAND, A. D. Everyman His Own Poet: Romantic Gospels in American Literature. New York: McGraw-Hill, 1968. "The Drift of Whitman," pp. 44-62.

2496 VAN TASSEL, David Dirck. "Regarding America's Past: American Historical Writing, 1607-1889." Ph.D. diss., Wisconsin, 1955. DA, 15 (1956), 1131. Whitman, passim.

2497 VINCE, R. W. "A Reading of 'The Sleepers.'" Walt Whitman Review, 18 (1972), 17-28.

2498 VINCENT, Leon Henry. American Literary Masters. Boston: Houghton Mifflin, 1906. Whitman, pp. 485-506.

2499 VIRK, Sarudeep Singh. "Symbolism in Whitman," in Maini, Darshan Singh, ed., Variations on American Literature. New Delhi: U.S. Educational Foundation in India, 1968.

2500 VOIGHT, Gilbert P. The Religious and Ethical Element in the Major American Poets. Columbia: South Carolina University Press, 1925.

2501 VON ENDE, Amelia. "Whitman's Following in Germany." Conservator, 14 (April, 1903), 23-25.

2502 _____. "Walt Whitman in Germany." Conservator, 14 (January, February, 1904), 167, 183.

2503 _____. "Walt Whitman and Arno Holz." Poet-Lore, 16 (Summer, 1905), 61-65. Refers to a German poet, 1863-1929.

2504 _____. "Walt Whitman and the Germans Today." Conservator, 18 (June, 1907), 55-57.

2505 W. "Walt Whitman: A Sketch." Universal Brotherhood Path, 16 (December, 1901), 502-511.

2506 WAGGONER, Hyatt H. "Signing for Soul and Body,"
in American Poets from the Puritans to the Present.
Boston: Houghton Mifflin, 1968. Pp. 149-180.
Whitman's relation to Emerson.

2507 _____. "The Last Stand of the Genteel Tradition:
Or, How Brown Acquired the Saunders Whitman Col-
lection: A Short Story with Several Possible Morals."
Books at Brown, 24 (1971), 148-155.

2508 WAITE, William. "Whitman on Carlyle: A New Letter." Walt Whitman Review, 20 (1974), 74.

2509 WALCUTT, Charles Child. "Whitman's 'Out of the
Cradle....'" College English, 10 (February, 1949),
277-279.

2510 WALDHORN, Arthur. "Walt Whitman's Leaves of
Grass." Critical Quarterly, 8 (Winter, 1966), 368-
373.

2511 WALDRON, Randall H., ed. Mattie: The Letters of
Martha Mitchell Whitman. New York: New York
University Press, 1977. Refers to Brother Jeff's
wife.

2512 WALLACE, James K. "Whitman and Life Illustrated:
A Forgotten 1855 Review of Leaves." Walt Whitman
Review, 17 (1971), 135-138.

2513 WALLACE, J. W. "Whitman's Personality." Bookman
(London), 56 (May, 1919), 68-69.

2514 _____. Walt Whitman and the World Crises. Manchester, England: National Labour Press, 1920.

2515 WALLING, William English. Whitman and Traubel.
New York: Albert and Charles Boni, 1916. Reprinted, New York: Haskell House, 1969.

2516 WALT WHITMAN BULLETIN, established April, 1958;
ran four years to April, 1961.

2517 WALT WHITMAN NEWSLETTER, established in 1955;
ran four years to 1958.

2518 WALT WHITMAN REVIEW, established 1955 as Walt
       Whitman Newsletter; changed name in 1959 to Review
       with Vol. 5.   Runs to present.

2519 WANG, Alfred S.   "Walt Whitman and Lao-Chuang."
       Walt Whitman Review, 17 (1971), 109-122.

2520 WANKHADE, Manohar Namdeo.   "Walt Whitman and
       Tantrism: A Comparative Study." Ph.D. diss.,
       Florida, 1965. DA, 26 (1966), 6029.   Refers to
       the doctrines of the Sanskrit Tantras.

2521 WANN, Louis.   "Robinson Jeffers--Counterpart of Whit-
       man." Personalist, 19 (1938), 297-308.

2522 WANNAMAKER, John S.   "A New Musical Setting of
       'Song of Myself' by Robert L. Sanders." Walt Whit-
       man Review, 18 (1972), 28-31.

2523 WARE, Lois.   "Poetic Conventions in Leaves of Grass."
       Studies in Philology, 26 (January, 1929), 47-57.

2524 WARFEL, Harry R.   "Whitman's Structural Principles
       in 'Spontaneous Me.'" College English, 18 (January,
       1957), 190-195.

2525 _____ . "Whitman's Salut au Monde: The Ideal of
       Human Brotherhood." Phylon, 19 (Summer, 1958),
       154-156.

2526 _____ . "'Out of the Cradle....'" Tennessee Stud-
       ies in Literature, 3 (1958), 83-87.

2527 _____ . "The Structure of 'Eidólons.'" Walt Whit-
       man Newsletter, 4 (1958), 103-105.

2528 _____ . "Collecting Walt Whitman." American Book
       Collector, 11 (April, 1961), 27-28.

2529 _____ . "A Seminar in Leaves of Grass." Emerson
       Society Quarterly, 22 (1961), 27-28.

2530 _____ . "Walt's Tribute to Lincoln." South Atlantic
       Bulletin, 30 (1965), 1-3.

2531 _____ , ed. Studies in Walt Whitman's Leaves of
       Grass. Written by students at Philipps-Universität,
       Marburg/Lahn, Western Germany, 1953-1954. Gaines-

ville, Fla.: Scholars Facsimile and Reproductions
Press, 1954.

2532 _____, R. H. Gabriel, and Stanley T. Williams,
eds. The American Mind. New York: American
Book Company, 1947. "Walt Whitman," by Henry
David Thoreau, p. 576.

2533 WARNER, Ella. "A History of Walt Whitman's Reception in the British Isles." Ph.D. diss., Yale, 1916.

2534 WASKOW, Howard J. "Walt Whitman and the Problem
of Literary Form." Ph.D. diss., Yale, 1963.

2535 _____. Whitman: Explorations in Form. Chicago:
University of Chicago Press, 1966.

2536 WATERMAN, Arthur E. "A Criticism of 'When Lilacs....'" Walt Whitman Review, 8 (1962), 64-68.

2537 WATKINS, Patricia D. "Origins of and Influences upon
Black Slave Spirituals (The Validity of Two Schools
of Thought)." Black American Studies, 1 (Fall,
1970-Spring, 1971), 94-102.

2538 WATSON, Georgia M. So We Bought a Poet's Shrine.
New York: Pageant Press, 1955. Whitman's birthplace in Huntington, Long Island.

2539 WATT, Olivia B. "Humanitarianism in Walt Whitman."
Walt Whitman Review, 10 (1964), 60-67.

2540 WATTS-DUNTON, Theodore. "Walt Whitman." The
Athenaeum, April 2, 1892. Pp. 436-437.

2541 WEATHERS, Willie T. "Whitman's Poetic Translations
of His 1855 Preface." American Literature, 19
(March, 1947), 21-40.

2542 WEATHERS, Winston. "Seven Considerations of Whitman's Creative Spirit," in Zimmerman and Weathers,
eds., Papers (1970), pp. 1-5. Studies a group of
poems.

2543 WECTER, Dixon. "Walt Whitman as Civil Servant."
PMLA, 58 (December, 1943), 1094-1109.

2544 WEEKS, Lewis E., Jr. "Did Whittier Really Burn
Whitman's Leaves of Grass?" Walt Whitman Review,
22 (1976), 22-29.

2545 WEEKS, Robert P. "Dos Passo's Debt to Whitman,"
in Lanzinger, Klaus, ed., Americana-Austriaca,
Vol. 3. Stuttgart, Germany: Wilhelm Braumuller,
1974. Pp. 121-138.

2546 WEEKS, Ruth M. "Phrasal Prosody." English Journal,
10 (January, 1921), 11-19.

2547 WEIMER, David R. The City as Metaphor. New York:
Random House, 1966. Whitman, pp. 14-33.

2548 WEIRICK, Bruce. From Whitman to Sandburg in American Poetry. New York, 1924. Reprinted, New York:
Biblo and Tannen, 1967. Whitman, pp. 1-37.

2549 WELD, Ralph Foster. Brooklyn is America. New York:
Columbia University Press, 1950. Whitman, passim.
Good discussion of the Negro population in Brooklyn
in Whitman's time.

2550 WELLS, Carolyn, and Alfred F. Goldsmith. A Concise
Bibliography of the Works of Walt Whitman with a
Supplement of Fifty Books About Whitman. Boston:
Houghton Mifflin, 1922. Revised edition, 1930. Re-
printed in a volume containing Frey, Ellen Frances.
Catalogue of the Whitman Collection in the Duke Uni-
versity Library (1945). Reprinted, Port Washington,
N.Y.: Kennikat Press, 1965.

2551 _____, and _____. "On Collecting Whitman."
Colophon, new graphic series, 1 (1939-1940), 47-54.
Excerpt in Targ, W., ed., Bouillabaisse for Bibli-
ophiles. New York: World, 1955. Pp. 369-381.

2552 _____, and _____, eds. with Introduction. Rivu-
lets of Prose: Critical Essays by Walt Whitman.
New York, 1928. Reprinted, Freeport, New York:
Books for Libraries Press, 1969. Introduction,
"Walt Whitman and His Poems," pp. 1-18.

2553 WELLS, Charles, illustrator. "Walt Whitman, 1964."
Massachusetts Review, 5 (Summer, 1964), 722.

2554 WESTERFIELD, Hargis. "Walt Whitman's Reading."
     Ph.D. diss., Indiana, 1949. DA, 14 (1954), 2353-
     2354.

2555 _____. "A Whitman-John Pierpont Parallel." Walt
     Whitman Review, 5 (1959), 17.

2556 WESTLAKE, Neda M. "'A backward glance on my own
     road.'" Library Chronicle (University of Pennsyl-
     vania), 34 (1968), 100-102. Description of a manu-
     script.

2557 WHEAT, Edward McKinley. "A Study in Politics and
     Literature." Ph.D. diss., California (Santa Barbara),
     1975. DA, 36 (1976), 7615A.

2558 WHEATLEY, Elwood A. "Walt Whitman and the Bridge:
     An Unsuccessful Campaign to Change a Name."
     Churchman, 171 (March 1, 15, 1957), 6-7, 9-10.

2559 WHICHER, Stephen E. "Whitman's 'Out of the Cradle....'"
     Explicator, 5 (February, 1947), item 28.

2560 _____. "Whitman's Awakening to Death: Toward a
     Biographical Reading of 'Out of the Cradle....'"
     Studies in Romanticism, 1 (August, 1961), 9-28.
     Reprinted in Lewis, R. W. B., ed., The Presence
     of Walt Whitman (1962), pp. 1-27. Also reprinted
     in Golden, ed., Walt Whitman (1974), pp. 77-96.

2561 WHITE, Courtland Y. "A Whitman Ornithology." Cas-
     sinia: Proceedings of the Delaware Valley Ornithol-
     ogy Club, 35 (1945), 12-22.

2562 WHITE, Eliot. "Walt Whitman's Significance to a Rev-
     olutionist." Conservator, 22 (July, 1911), 71-72.

2563 _____. "Walt Whitman and the Living Present."
     Conservator, 24 (October, 1923), 117.

2564 WHITE, Fred D. "Whitman's Cosmic Spider." Walt
     Whitman Review, 23 (1977), 85-88.

2565 WHITE, Viola Chittenden. "Thoreau's Opinion of Whit-
     man." New England Quarterly, 8 (June, 1935), 262-
     264. Refers to Harrison Blake's letter from Thor-
     eau.

2566 WHITE, William. "Walt Whitman and Sir William Os-
      ler." American Literature, 11 (March, 1939), 73-
      77. Refers to Canadian physician, educator, and
      author, 1849-1919.

2567 _____. "Walt Whitman on Osler: 'He Is a Great
      Man.'" Bulletin of History of Medicine, 15 (Jan-
      uary, 1944), 79-90.

2568 _____. "Walt Whitman on New England Writers:
      An Uncollected Fragment." New England Quarterly,
      27 (September, 1954), 395-396.

2569 _____. "Walt Whitman and Osler: Three Unpublished
      Letters." Journal of the History of Medicine and
      Allied Science, 11 (1956), 348-349.

2570 _____. "More About the 'Pub' of the First Leaves
      of Grass." American Literature, 28 (January, 1957),

2571 _____. "The Walt Whitman Fellowship: An Account
      of Its Organization and Checklist of Its Papers."
      Papers of the Bibliographic Society of America, 51
      (1957), 67-84.

2572 _____. "Review of The Eighteenth Presidency."
      Papers of the Bibliographic Society of America, 51
      (1957), 101-102. Critical review of a text edited
      by Edward Grier and Charles Feinberg (1956). See
      also work by Jean Catel (1928).

2573 _____. "The Walt Whitman Fellowship: Additions
      and Corrections." Papers of the Bibliographic So-
      ciety of America, 51 (1957), 167-169.

2574 _____. "Lincoln and Whitman: A Note on the 'Van
      Rensellaer' Letter." Lincoln Herald, 59 (Summer,
      1957), 16-24.

2575 _____. "Sir Edmund Gosse on Walt Whitman."
      Victorian Studies, 1 (December, 1957), 180-183.

2576 _____. "Walt Whitman's Short Stories: Some Com-
      ments and a Bibliography." Papers of the Biblio-
      graphic Society of America, 52 (1958), 300-306.

2577 _____. "Logan Pearsall Smith on Walt Whitman:

A Correction and Some Unpublished Letters. " Walt
Whitman Newsletter, 4 (June, 1958), 87-90.

2578 _____. "'Kentucky': Unpublished Poetic Fragments
by Walt Whitman. " Prairie Schooner, 32 (Fall,
1958), 170-178.

2579 _____. "Mary Whitall Smith's Letters to Walt Whitman." Smith Alumni Quarterly, 49 (Winter, 1958),
86-88.

2580 _____. "Mr. Comstock as Cato the Censor." Walt
Whitman Review, 5 (1959), 54-56.

2581 _____. "A Walt Whitman Poster." American Book
Collector, 10 (November, 1959), 5-6. Facsimile
reproduction.

2582 _____. "Three Unpublished Whitman Fragments. "
Walt Whitman Review, 5 (1959), 77-78.

2583 _____. "'I am a Born Democrat': An Unpublished
Whitman Fragment." Notes and Queries, 6 (December, 1959), 454-455.

2584 _____. "Walt Whitman to U. S. Grant: An Unknown
Exchange." Prairie Schooner, 34 (Summer, 1960),
120-122.

2585 _____. "Walt Whitman's Short Stories: Two Addenda." Papers of the Bibliographic Society of America, 54 (1960), 126.

2586 _____. "Whitman's Prose." Harper's Monthly, 222
(March, 1961), 6-8.

2587 _____. "Fanny Fern to Walt Whitman: An Unpublished Letter." American Book Collector, 11 (May,
1961), 8-9.

2588 _____. "Whitmaniana." American Book Collector,
11 (May, 1961), 11-14.

2589 _____. "The Hempstead Tragedy." American Book
Collector, 11 (May, 1961), 27. A news story with
Whitman's notes.

2590 _____ . "Whitman in Paperback." American Book
        Collector, 11 (May, 1961), 28-30.

2591 _____ . "Walt Whitman in 'Ideals of Life.'" Amer-
        ican Book Collector, 11 (May, 1961), 30-31.

2592 _____ . "Trial Lines for the 1855 Leaves?" Walt
        Whitman Review, 7 (1961), 60.

2593 _____ . "Walt Whitman: 'Western Nicknames.'"
        American Speech, 36 (December, 1961), 296-298.

2594 _____ . "$400 for the Brooklyn Freeman?" Walt
        Whitman Review, 7 (1961), 80.

2595 _____ . "An Unpublished Notebook: Walt Whitman
        in Washington in 1863." American Book Collector,
        12 (January, 1962), 8-13.

2596 _____ . "Whitman as Short Story Writer: Two Un-
        published Manuscripts." Notes and Queries, 9
        (March, 1962), 87-89.

2597 _____ . "Whitman's Copy of Epictetus." Walt Whit-
        man Review, 8 (1962), 95-96.

2598 _____ . "Walt Whitman: Journalist." Journalism
        Quarterly, 39 (Summer, 1962), 339-346.

2599 _____ . "'Nationalism' Unpublished Whitman?"
        American Notes and Queries, 1 (January, 1963),
        67-68.

2600 _____ . "Whitman's First 'Literary' Letter." Amer-
        ican Literature, 35 (March, 1963), 83-85.

2601 _____ . "Robinson Jeffers' 'Space.'" Personalist,
        44 (April, 1963), 175-179. Contrast to Whitman.

2602 _____ . "A Thousand and One Mss. by Walt Whit-
        man." Orient West, 8 (1963), 69-80. Refers to
        the Feinberg collection in Detroit.

2603 _____ . "An Unpublished Whitman Notebook for 'Li-
        lacs.'" Modern Language Quarterly, 24 (June, 1963),
        177-180.

2604 _____ . "Whitman on American Poets: An Uncollected Piece." English Language Notes, 1 (September, 1963), 42-43.

2605 _____ . "Whitman's Poem on the Johnstown Flood." Emerson Society Quarterly, 33 (1963), 79-84. Refers to "A Voice from Death."

2606 _____ . "Some Uncollected Whitman Journalism." Emerson Society Quarterly, 33 (1963), 84-90.

2607 _____ . "A Week in the Feinberg Collection." Thoreau Society Bulletin, 85 (Fall, 1963), 2.

2608 _____ . "Addenda to Whitman's Short Stories." Papers of the Bibliographic Society of America, 57 (1963), 221-222.

2609 _____ . "The First (1855) Leaves of Grass: How Many Copies?" Papers of the Bibliographic Society of America, 57 (1963), 352-354.

2610 _____ . "A Strange Coincidence in Walt Whitman." Walt Whitman Review, 11 (1965), 100-102.

2611 _____ . "Whitman's Leaves of Grass: Notes on the Pocketbook (1889) Edition." Studies in Bibliography, 18 (1965), 280-281.

2612 _____ . "Morley on Whitman: Inédite." American Notes and Queries, 4 (May, 1966), 132-133. See articles by Christopher Morley.

2613 _____ . "Author at Work: Whitman's Specimen Days." Manuscripts, 18 (Summer, 1966), 26-28. Reprints rough draft of "The First Frost."

2614 _____ . " 'Ned-a-Phantasy': Uncollected Whitman." Emerson Society Quarterly, 47 (1967), 100-101.

2615 _____ . "Whitman to U. S. Grant: An Addendum." Walt Whitman Review, 13 (1967), 60-61.

2616 _____ . "The Collected Works of Walt Whitman: A Progress Report." Newsletter of American Studies at Research Centre (Hyderabad, India), 11 (December, 1967), 23-28. Address to scholars in India.

2617   . "Walt Whitman's Journalism: A Bibliography." Walt Whitman Review, 14 (1968), 67-141.
Lists 2,500 items, primary sources.

2618   . "Dreiser on Hardy, Henley, and Whitman."
English Language Notes, 6 (1968), 122-124.

2619   . "Variants of R. M. Bucke's Walt Whitman."
Serif, 5 (1968), 25-29.

2620   . "Lathrop's Unpublished Letter to Traubel on
Whitman." Renascence, 20 (1968), 165-166.

2621   . Walt Whitman's Journalism: A Bibliography.
Detroit: Wayne State University Press, 1969. Book
form of item above.

2622   . "Jeffers and Whitman, Briefly." Serif, 6
(1969), 32-33.

2623   . "Walt Whitman and the Sierra Grande Min-
ing Company." New Mexico Historical Review, 44
(1969), 223-230.

2624   . "Unpublished Henry James on Whitman."
Review of English Studies, 20 (1969), 321-322.

2625   . "On the Whitman-Symonds Correspondence."
Walt Whitman Review, 15 (1969), 125-126.

2626   . "Walt Whitman: An Unpublished Autobiographical Note." (1891). Notes and Queries, 16
(1969), 221-222. Reprint with short commentary.

2627   . "Whitman or Whitmaniana?" American
Transcendental Quarterly, 1 (1969), 120-121. Re-
prints "Walt Whitman for 1878," West Jersey Press,
January 16, 1878.

2628   . "Whitman on Himself: An Unrecorded Piece."
Papers on Language and Literature, 6 (1970), 202-
205. Reprint of "Foreign Criticism on an American
Poet."

2629   . "Some New Whitman Items." Prairie
Schooner, 44 (1970), 47-55. Poem and four letters.

2630 _____. "Four Recent Whitman Editions." Walt
Whitman Review, 16 (1970), 27-28.

2631 _____. "My Six Children: Whitman to Symonds."
Walt Whitman Review, 16 (1970), 31.

2632 _____. "Letter from Whitman's Mother, Text and
Holograph: 'Mrs. Walter Whitman, Sr. Writes to
Her Son.'" Walt Whitman Review, 16 (1970), 63-64.

2633 _____. "Tasisto and the Daybook." Walt Whitman
Review, 16 (1970), 89-90.

2634 _____. "Alcott and Chapman Revisited." Walt Whitman Review, 16 (1970), 90-91.

2635 _____. "Two Notes to R. Spence Watson." Walt
Whitman Review, 16 (1970), 122.

2636 _____. "Walt Whitman's Erotic Poetry: New as
Foam and Old as the Rock." Sewanee Review, 79
(1971), 650-654. Review of The Tenderest Lover:
Erotic Poetry of Walt Whitman, ed. with Introduction
by Walter Lowenfels. Illustrated by J. K. Lambert
(1970).

2637 _____. "Whitman and the MLA Bibliography: Addenda, 1969." Serif, 8 (1971), 18-20.

2638 _____. "Billy Duckett: Whitman Rogue." American
Book Collector, 21 (1971), 20-23.

2639 _____. "Two More Unpublished Whitman Letters."
American Notes and Queries, 10 (1971), 3-4.

2640 _____. "Walter Whitman: Kings County Democratic
Party Secretary." Walt Whitman Review, 17 (1971),
92-98.

2641 _____. "A Tribute to William Hartshorne: Unrecorded Whitman." American Literature, 42 (1971),
554-558.

2642 _____. "Walt Whitman on Trial: A Clipping from
His Daybook." Prairie Schooner, 46 (1972), 52-56.

2643 _____. "Whitman Letter to H. H. Furness, January

26, 1881." Walt Whitman Review, 18 (1972), 141-142.

2644 _____. "An Unknown Report on a Whitman Social." American Book Collector, 23 (1973), 22-24.

2645 _____. "Whitman Reprints from Haskell House and Others." Walt Whitman Review, 19 (1973), 30-32.

2646 _____. "Unknown Letter to W. S. Huntington." Walt Whitman Review, 19 (1973), 73.

2647 _____. "Editions of Leaves of Grass: How Many?" Walt Whitman Review, 19 (1973), 111-114.

2648 _____. "A New Whitman Letter to The Century." Walt Whitman Review, 19 (1973), 118.

2649 _____. "Textual Editing: A Whitman Note." American Notes and Queries, 12 (1974), 15-16.

2650 _____. "Errors in Leaves of Grass, Comprehensive Readers' Edition." Papers of the Bibliographic Society of America, 68 (1974), 439-442.

2651 _____. "Walt Whitman's Poetry in Periodicals: A Bibliography." Serif, 11 (1974), 31-38.

2652 _____. "Whitman to Carlyle: A New Letter." Walt Whitman Review, 20 (1974), 74.

2653 _____. "Whitman to Roden Noel: A New Letter." Walt Whitman Review, 20 (1974), 117.

2654 _____. "'Beat! Beat! Drums!' The First Version." Walt Whitman Review, 21 (1975), 43-44.

2655 _____. "Whitman in 1881: Five Frank Hill Smith Sketches." Walt Whitman Review, 21 (1975), 81-82.

2656 _____. "A New Whitman Letter to J. Q. A. Ward." Walt Whitman Review, 21 (1975), 131-132.

2657 _____. "Whitman to J. A. Symonds: Unpublished." Walt Whitman Review, 21 (1975), 168.

2658 _____. "Whitman's Short Stories: More Addenda."

Papers of the Bibliographic Society of America, 69
(1975), 402-403.

2659 _____. "A New Whitman Letter to Mary Whitall
Costelloe." Walt Whitman Review, 22 (1976), 42-43.

2660 _____. "An Unknown Whitman Ms. on the 1855
Leaves." Walt Whitman Review, 22 (1976), 172.

2661 _____. "A New Whitman Letter to Deborah Browning." Walt Whitman Review, 23 (1977), 143-144.

2662 _____, ed. Walt Whitman Newsletter, Quarterly,
Vols. I-IV, 1955-1958. "Whitman Current Bibliography" in each issue. Became Walt Whitman Review,
with Vol. V, in 1959.

2663 _____, ed. with Introduction. Walt Whitman in Our
Time. Detroit: Wayne State University Press, 1970.
Also published in Walt Whitman Review, 16 supple-
ment (1970). Reprinted criticism.

2664 _____, ed. The Long-Islander. Whitman Page,
June 1, 1972. Commemorates 100th anniversary of
Whitman's visit to Dartmouth.

2665 _____, ed. The Long-Islander. Whitman page,
May 29, 1975. "Women in the Life of Walt Whitman,"
pp. 16-17, 22.

2666 _____, ed. The Bicentennial Walt Whitman: Essays
from The Long-Islander. Detroit: Wayne State University Press, 1976. 36 page pamphlet.

2667 _____, and Herbert Bergman, eds. Journalism, 5
vols. in The Collected Writings of Walt Whitman.
New York: New York University Press, projected
date of publication. Has not been published as of
January, 1980.

2668 WHITE, William M. "The Dynamics of Whitman's
Poetry." Sewanee Review, 80 (1972), 347-360.

2669 WHITEHEAD, Graham G. R. "The Craftsmanship of
Sean O'Casey." Ph.D. diss., Toronto, 1973. DA,
34 (1974), 5377A. Whitman, passim.

2670 WHITTEMORE, R. C. "Walt Whitman," in Whittemore,
      Makers of the American Mind. New York: William
      Morrow, 1964. Pp. 251-261.

2671 WILBUR, Richard. "The Present State of Whitman,"
      in Wilbur, Responses: Prose Pieces, 1953-1976.
      New York: Harcourt, Brace, 1976. Pp. 146-151.

2672 WILD, P. H. "Flower Power: A Students' Guide to
      Pre-Hippie Transcendentalism." English Journal,
      58 (1969), 62-68.

2673 WILDER, A. N. "Literary Sources," in Johnson, F.
      Ernest, ed., Institute for Religious and Social Stud-
      ies, Foundations of Democracy. New York: Harper,
      1947. Pp. 87-108.

2674 WILEY, Autry Nell. "Reiterative Devices in Leaves of
      Grass." American Literature, 1 (May, 1929), 161-
      170.

2675 WILLARD, Charles Borromeo. "The Growth of Walt
      Whitman's Reputation in America after 1892." Ph.D.
      diss., Brown, 1948.

2676 _____. Whitman's American Fame: The Growth of
      His Reputation in America after 1892. Providence,
      R.I.: Brown University Press, 1950.

2677 _____. "The Saunders Collection of Whitmania in
      Brown University Library." Books at Brown, 18
      (May, 1956), 14-22.

2678 _____. "Whitman and Tennyson's 'Ulysses.'" Walt
      Whitman Newsletter, 2 (March-June, 1956), 9-10.

2679 _____. "Ezra Pound's Appraisal of Walt Whitman."
      Modern Language Notes, 72 (January, 1957), 19-26.
      See Bergman, ed., American Literature (1955).

2680 _____. "Ezra Pound and the Whitman 'Message.'"
      Revue de Littérature Comparée, 31 (January, 1957),
      94-98.

2681 _____. "Ezra Pound's Debt to Walt Whitman."
      Studies in Philology, 54 (October, 1957), 573-581.

2682 WILLCOCKS, M. P. "Walt Whitman and Edward Carpenter," in Between the Old World and the New. New York: Allen and Unwin, 1926. Pp. 315-330.

2683 WILCOX, L. C. "Walt Whitman." North American Review, 183 (August, 1906), 281-296.

2684 WILLIAMS, F. H. "Individuality as Whitman's Primary Motive." Conservator, 11 (July, 1900), 71-73.

2685 _____. "An Appreciation of Walt Whitman." Columbia Monthly, 5 (May, 1908), 7.

2686 WILLIAMS, Mentor L. "Whitman Today." University of Kansas City Review, 14 (Summer, 1948), 267-276.

2687 WILLIAMS, Philip. "Whitman and Eliot: Two Sides of One Tradition." Hikaku Bungaku, 15 (1972), i-xxv. In English; Japanese publication.

2688 WILLIAMS, Stanley T. "The Adrian Van Sinderen Collection of Walt Whitman." Yale University Library Gazette, 15 (January, 1941), 49-53.

2689 WILLIAMS, William Carlos. "Essay on Leaves of Grass," in Hindus, ed., Leaves of Grass One Hundred Years After (1955), pp. 22-31. Reprinted in Pearce, ed., Walt Whitman: A Collection (1962), pp. 146-154.

2690 WILLINGHAM, John R. "The Walt Whitman Tradition in Recent American Literature." Ph.D. diss., Oklahoma, 1953.

2691 WILLSON, Lawrence. "The 'Body-Electric' Meets the Genteel Tradition." New Mexico Quarterly, 26 (Winter, 1956-1957), 369-386.

2692 WILSON, Edmund. Patriotic Gore. New York: Oxford University Press, 1962. Whitman, pp. 479-482 et passim.

2693 _____, ed. The Shock of Recognition. Garden City, N.Y.: Doubleday, Doran, 1943. Reprints "Emerson and Whitman: Documents on Their Relations (1855-1888)," pp. 208-228.

2694 WILSON, Harry B. "Psychological Projection in Five
      Romantic Poems, English and American. " Ph. D.
      diss. , California (Davis), 1976. DA, 37 (1976),
      3631A. Includes "When Lilacs..., " by Whitman;
      "Resolution and Independence, " by Wordsworth; "Ode
      to a Nightingale, " by John Keats; "Ulalume, " by Poe;
      and "The Idea of Order at Key West, " by Stevens.

2695 WINN, R. B. "Walt Whitman, " in Winn, ed. , Ameri-
      can Philosophy. New York: Philosophical Library,
      1955. Pp. 262-264.

2696 WINTERICH, J. T. "Walt Whitman and Leaves of
      Grass. " Golden Book, May 1929, pp. 79-96. Re-
      printed in Winterich, Books and the Man. New York:
      Greenberg, 1929. Pp. 1-17.

2697 WINTERS, Yvor. "The Significance of The Bridge by
      Hart Crane, or What Are We To Think of Professor
      X?, " in In Defense of Reason. Denver: Swallow
      Press, 1947. Excerpt reprinted in Hollander, John,
      ed. , Modern Poetry: Essays in Criticism. New
      York: Oxford University Press, 1968. Pp. 219-242.

2698 WINWAR, Frances, pseudo (Frances Winwar Grebanier).
      American Giant: Walt Whitman and His Times. New
      York and London: Harper, 1941.

2699 _____ . "Whitman's Calamus Poems. " Princeton
      University Library Chronicle, 3 (February, 1942),
      66-68.

2700 _____ . "Walt Whitman's 'Dark Lady, ' " University
      Review, 9 (Spring, 1943), 191-197.

2701 WOLFE, D. M. "Whitman and the Ideal Man, " in
      Wolfe, The Image of Man in America. New York:
      Crowell, 1970. Pp. 137-160.

2702 WOLFE, Peter. " 'Song of Myself'--The Indirect Fig-
      ure in the Word Mosaic. " American Transcendental
      Quarterly, 12 (1971), 20-25.

2703 WOLFE, Theodore F. Literary Shrines: The Haunts
      of Some Famous American Authors. Philadelphia:
      Lippincott, 1895.

2704 WOLFSON, Leandro. "The Other Whitman in Spanish
      America." Walt Whitman Review, 24 (1978), 62-71.

2705 WOMACK, Judy. "The American Woman in 'Song of
      Myself.'" Walt Whitman Review, 19 (1973), 67-72.

2706 WOOD, Clement. "Walt Whitman: A Mystic Volcano,"
      in Poets of America. New York: Dutton, 1925.

2707 _____, and M. C. Wood. For Walt Whitman. New
      York: Dutton, 1923.

2708 WOOD, Frank. "Three Poems on Whitman." Compara-
      tive Literature, 4 (Winter, 1952), 45-53. Stephen
      V. Benét, García Lorca, Hart Crane.

2709 WOODBRIDGE, Hensley C. "Walt Whitman: Additional
      Bibliography in Spanish." Walt Whitman Review, 12
      (1966), 70-71.

2710 WOODHULL, M. G. "Walt Whitman: A Memory Pic-
      ture." Literary Era, 8 (March, 1901), 159-160.

2711 WOODRESS, James, ed. Ph. D. Dissertations in Amer-
      ican Literature, 1891-1966. Durham, N. C.: Duke
      University Press, 1968.

2712 _____, ed. American Literary Scholarship: An An-
      nual Survey, 1963--to date. Durham, N. C.: Duke
      University Press. See "Whitman and Dickinson," by
      different authors in each volume.

2713 _____, ed. Eight American Authors. New York:
      Norton, 1971 edition. See also Stovall, Floyd, ed.,
      Eight American Authors, 1956 edition.

2714 WOODRUFF, Stuart C. "Whitman: Poet or Prophet?"
      Walt Whitman Review, 14 (1968), 35-40.

2715 WOODWARD, F. L. "Walt Whitman: A Prophet of the
      Coming Race." Theosophical Review, 32 (August,
      1903), 508-515.

2716 WOODWARD, Robert H. "The Journey Motif in Whit-
      man and Tennyson." Modern Language Notes, 72
      (January, 1957), 26-27.

2717 _____ . "Davy Crockett: Whitman's 'Friendly and
        Flowing Savage.'" Walt Whitman Review, 6 (1960),
        48-49.

2718 _____ . "Whitman on Records: Addenda." Walt
        Whitman Review, 8 (1962), 91-92.

2719 _____ . "Voyage Imagery in 'Terminus' and 'O
        Captain! My Captain!'" Emerson Society Quarterly,
        27 (1962), 37.

2720 WOOLF, Virginia Stephen. "Visits to Walt Whitman,"
        in Woolf, Granite and Rainbow. New York: Har-
        court, Brace, 1958. Pp. 229-231. Reprinted in
        Woolf, Collected Essays, 4 vols. New York: Har-
        court, Brace, 1967. Pp. 51-53.

2721 WORKMAN, Mims Thornburgh. "The Whitman-Twain
        Enigma." Mark Twain Quarterly, 8 (Summer-Fall,
        1948), 12-13.

2722 WORTHAM, Louis J. A History of Texas, 3 vols.
        Austin: Steck, 1924. Vol. III, pp. 239-265, relates
        to Section 34, "Song of Myself," the Goliad massacre.

2723 WORTMAN, William A. "Spiritual Progression in 'A
        Sight in Camp.'" Walt Whitman Review, 14 (1968),
        24-26.

2724 _____ . "The Troubled Self: Romanticism and
        Leaves of Grass." Ph.D. diss., Case Western Re-
        serve, 1971. DA, 33 (1972), 1751A.

2725 WRIGHT, James A. "The Delicacy of Walt Whitman,"
        in Lewis, R. W. B., ed., The Presence of Walt
        Whitman (1962), pp. 164-189.

2726 WROBEL, Arthur. "Walt Whitman and the Fowler
        Brothers: Phrenology Finds a Bard." Ph.D. diss.,
        North Carolina (Chapel Hill), 1968. DA, 29 (1969),
        2232A-2233A.

2727 _____ . "A Poet's Self-Esteem: Whitman Alters
        His 'Bumps.'" Walt Whitman Review, 17 (1971),
        129-135.

2728 _____ . "Whitman and the Phrenologists: The Divine

Body and the Sensuous Soul." <u>PMLA</u>, 89 (1974), 17-23.

2729 WYATT, E. F.   "With Walt Whitman in Camden, " in Wyatt, <u>Great Companions</u>.   New York: Appleton-Century, 1917. Pp. 158-176.

2730 _____ . "A Peace-Lover's War Epic. " <u>New Repub-</u><u>lic</u>, 11 (June 30, 1917), 242-244.

2731 _____ . "The Answerer: Walt Whitman. " <u>North</u> <u>American Review</u>, 209 (May, 1919), 672-682.

2732 _____ . "Whitman and Anne Gilchrist. " <u>North Amer-</u><u>ican Review</u>, 210 (September, 1919), 388-400.

2733 WYLLIE, J. C.   "The Barrett Collection of Walt Whitman. " <u>American Book Collector</u>, 11 (May, 1961), 33.

2734 WYMAN, Mary A.   <u>The Lure for Feeling in the Creative</u> <u>Process</u>.   New York: Philosophical Library, 1960. "Burroughs and Whitman--Naturalist and Mystic, " pp. 104-128.

2735 XIQUES, Sister Donez, M. C. N. D.   "A Descriptive Anal-ysis of Selected Elements of Walt Whitman's Prose Style in the 1855 Preface to <u>Leaves of Grass</u>. " Ph. D. diss. , Fordham, 1972. <u>DA</u>, 33 (1973), 3608A.

2736 _____ . "Whitman's Catalogues and the Preface to <u>Leaves of Grass</u>, 1855. " <u>Walt Whitman Review</u>, 23 (1977), 68-76.

2737 YALAN-STAKELIS, Miriam, and S. Halkin.   "Poems of Walt Whitman. " <u>Israel Argosy</u>, 7 (1960), 120-131.

2738 YARMOLINSKY, Avraham.   "The Russian View of Amer-ican Literature. " <u>Bookman</u>, 44 (September, 1916), 44-48. Whitman, passim.

2739 YENAWINE, W. S.   "The Hier Whitman Collection. " <u>Courier</u>, 6 (January, 1960), 1.

2740 YERBURY, G. D.   "Of a City Beside a River: Whitman,

Eliot, and Thomas Miller. " Walt Whitman Review,
10 (1964), 67-73.

2741 YESTADT, Sister Marie, S. B. S. "Two American Poets:
Their Influence on the Contemporary Art Song. "
Xavier University Studies, 10 (1971), 33-43. Whit-
man and Langston Hughes.

2742 YORKE, Dane. "Whitman in Camden. " American Mercury, 8 (July, 1926), 355-362.

2743 ZANGER, Jules. "The Twelfth Newberry Library Conference on American Studies: Whitman and the Influence of Space on American Literature. " Newberry
Library Bulletin, 5 (December, 1961), 299-314.

2744 ZAREK, O. "Walt Whitman and the German Poetry. "
Living Age, 316 (February 10, 1923), 334-337.

2745 ZEIGER, Arthur. "In Defense of Whitman. " Tomorrow,
9 (June, 1950), 54-56.

2746 ZIMMERMAN, Lester F. "Walt Whitman and the Tradition of the Organic," in Zimmerman and Weathers,
eds. , Papers (1970), pp. 44-55.

2747 _____, and Winston Weathers, eds. Papers on Walt
Whitman. Tulsa: University of Tulsa Press, 1970.

2748 ZOCHERT, Donald. "A Note on Whitman's 'Port of
Destination. ' " Walt Whitman Review, 21 (1975), 76.

2749 ZUEBLIN, Charles. "Walt Whitman, Prophet and Democrat. " Ford Hall Folks, 2 (December 28, 1913),
50-51.

2750 ZUNDER, Theodore A. "Walt Whitman and Hawthorne. "
Modern Language Notes, 47 (May, 1932), 314-316.

2751 _____. "Whitman Interviews Barnam. " Modern
Language Notes, 48 (January, 1933), 40.

2752 _____. "William B. March: The First Editor of
the Brooklyn Daily Eagle. " American Book Collector,
4 (1933), 93-95.

SUBJECT INDEX

"Aboard at a Ship's Helm" 1874
Adams, Henry 1312
Adams, John Quincy 367, 1647
Aeolian Harp [The Correspondent Breeze] 57, 1332
Alcott, Bronson 2195, 2634
Allen, Gay Wilson [about] 518, 1701
America [includes Americans, Americanism] 9, 129, 234,
    317, 325, 418, 530, 556, 567, 568, 571, 624, 697,
    714, 718, 723, 815, 849, 887, 930, 975, 1027, 1062,
    1101, 1124, 1144, 1168, 1215, 1233, 1251, 1289, 1303,
    1313, 1350, 1381, 1395, 1414, 1463, 1464, 1469, 1549,
    1571, 1595, 1629, 1631, 1752, 1754, 1792, 1822, 1863,
    1876, 1968, 1986, 2011, 2075, 2161, 2206, 2207, 2282,
    2344, 2351, 2415, 2430
American Literature [Histories of; includes histories of
    American Poetry] 488, 495, 505, 662, 769, 872, 874,
    1059, 1142, 1193, 1199, 1203, 1208, 1227, 1276, 1299,
    1300, 1396, 1397, 1442, 1473, 1509, 1529, 1592, 1593,
    1628, 1907, 1916, 1921, 1922, 1923, 1924, 1925, 1934,
    1964, 1990, 1999, 2003, 2055, 2111, 2118, 2138, 2285,
    2286, 2287, 2288, 2289, 2302, 2308, 2309, 2311, 2362,
    2400, 2455, 2456, 2496, 2498, 2500, 2531, 2548, 2690
Anthologies [American literature; Whitman included] 176,
    599, 873, 1467, 1750, 1755, 1963, 2190, 2191, 2192,
    2310
"Apple-Peelings" 2409
Arnold, Matthew 273, 694, 1566
Arnold, Sir Edwin 238, 1109
Art [Artists] (see also under individual names) 288, 1957,
    2017, 2113
"As I Ebb'd with the Ocean of Life" 141
Asia (see also under specific countries) 525, 557, 1898,
    2127
Astronomy (see also under Science) 770
Australia [includes New Zealand] 1304, 1305, 1578, 1580,
    2386, 2463, 2464

Birds   472, 1979, 2561
"Black Lucifer"   1323, 2246
Black Poems   1654
Blake, William   917
The Blue Book   108, 344, 987, 988, 994
Bly, Robert   1315
Boehme, Jacob   2424
Booth, Edwin   1689
Boston   922
"A Boston Ballad"   1127, 1607, 1622
"A Broadway Pageant"   1761, 2365
Brooke, Rupert   2278
Brooklyn   335, 2549
Brooks, Van Wyck [about]   71
Browning, Robert   799, 2458
Brownson, Orestes   929
Bruno, Giordano   441, 1505
Bryant, William Cullen   963, 2052
Buber, Martin   1677
Buchanan, Robert   294
Bucke, Dr. Maurice   206, 260, 354, 448, 452, 1264, 1266,
      1267, 1268, 1510, 1511, 1512, 1515, 1518, 1521, 1522,
      1523, 1524, 1573, 2619
Burroughs, John   6, 197, 198, 199, 940, 941, 1556, 2734
"By Blue Ontario's Shore"   259, 693, 1789
"By Emerson's Grave"   499
Byron, Lord   2100

Calamus [Japanese Whitman publication]   491, 1791
Calamus Poems   339, 450, 1041, 1069, 1243, 1399, 1522,
      1602, 1643, 1735, 1850, 1851, 2338, 2699
Camden (see also Traubel, Horace)   8, 375, 378, 592, 593,
      1053, 1356, 1357, 1808, 2407, 2438, 2450, 2729, 2742
Canada (see also Bucke, Dr. Maurice)   23, 429, 1367, 1513,
      1583, 1585
Carlyle, Thomas   651, 1303, 1908, 2099, 2261, 2508, 2653
"A Carol of Harvest for 1867"   340
Carpenter, Edward   21, 2682
Casseres, Benjamin de   1713
Catalogue [device in poetry]   564, 619, 1632, 2167, 2376,
      2736
Catel, Jean   1093
Cather, Willa   2252
Catullus   1541
"Cavalry Crossing a Ford"   722, 741, 903
Cendrars, Blaise   324

Dunbar, Paul Lawrence 2235
Duncan, Robert 406, 407

Eagle (see also under Birds) 472
Eakins, Thomas 2113
Early Poems (see also under Uncollected Works) 390
Editing Whitman 101, 104, 306, 370, 1722, 1915, 2334
Editions (Leaves of Grass, Selected Prose, Selected Poems,
    Selected Prose and Poetry, etc.; listed in checklist
    under editor's name) 43, 47, 48, 69, 115, 116, 130,
    133, 309, 313, 374, 377, 405, 460, 514, 673, 674,
    680, 850, 928, 946, 1013, 1188, 1191, 1192, 1277,
    1324, 1370, 1393, 1411, 1710, 1722, 1748, 1789, 1790,
    1828, 1938, 1981, 2004, 2024, 2090, 2133, 2208, 2218,
    2352, 2354, 2355, 2477, 2478, 2488, 2552, 2590, 2611,
    2630, 2646, 2648, 2651
Editor [Whitman as editor] (see also Journalism) 382, 1699,
    2245
Education [includes Teaching Whitman, schools, Whitman as
    a teacher, etc.] 136, 368, 890, 899, 1081, 1143,
    1179, 1245, 1293, 1314, 1444, 1667, 1772, 1773, 2529
"Eidólons" 526, 690, 1084, 2117, 2527
The Eighteenth Presidency 540, 927, 1036, 2572
Elegy (see also "When Lilacs ...") 66, 691, 1005, 1141,
    1714
Eliot, T. S. 1144, 1146, 1325, 1386, 1418, 1445, 1736,
    1833, 2687, 2740
Ellison, Ralph Waldo 1664
Emerson, Ralph Waldo 185, 193, 315, 316, 403, 417, 442,
    498, 499, 525, 529, 632, 658, 898, 972, 1047, 1146,
    1287, 1304, 1361, 1366, 1539, 1556, 1617, 1785, 1888,
    1931, 1943, 1988, 2047, 2078, 2087, 2169, 2262, 2371,
    2506, 2693, 2719
Encyclopedia [American] 1145
English [England, British] 2, 4, 291, 292, 296, 934, 952,
    973, 1018, 1026, 1211, 1278, 1283, 1355, 2016, 2053,
    2325, 2533
Epic 195, 1741, 1879, 1932, 1984, 2433
Epistemology 1082
Europe (see also under individual countries, including English)
    11, 160, 169, 182, 187, 191, 230, 264, 302, 794, 814,
    860, 861, 1042
Evolution (see also under Science) 637
"Excelsior" 876, 878
Eyre, Ellen 1692

"Faces" 147
Fast, Howard 1797
Father [Whitman's] 360, 1588, 2640
Feinberg Collection 49, 402, 413, 1647, 2602, 2607
Ferlinghetti, Lawrence 1330, 1477
Fiction [includes short stories and novel] 394, 662, 751,
        1152, 1190, 1184, 1249, 1530, 1531, 1545, 1889, 2129,
        2150, 2401, 2414, 2576, 2585, 2596, 2608, 2659
Films [includes Television and Movie] 72, 891, 1017, 1497,
        1788, 2108, 2215, 2480
Finland 1817, 1982
Folklore 321
Foreign Critics (see also under individual names and coun-
        tries) 100, 102, 114, 322, 557, 597, 794, 907, 908,
        909, 910, 912, 913, 919, 932, 1063
Form [in Whitman's poetry] 127, 1016, 1037, 1856, 1973,
        2534, 2535
Franklin Evans [Whitman's 1842 novel] (see also under Fic-
        tion) 662, 751, 1152, 1190, 1249, 1531, 2129
Fraternity 1592
Freiligrath, Ferdinand 2292
French [critics; includes French authors and articles in
        French] 33, 135, 150, 152, 167, 168, 211, 324, 420,
        772, 807, 884, 912, 1307, 1308, 1309, 1310, 1311,
        1427, 1484, 1485, 1527, 1672, 1673, 1797, 1880, 1971,
        1978, 1994, 2023, 2093, 2096, 2156, 2203, 2301, 2383
"From Far-Dakota's Canóns" 2313
Frost, Robert 877, 2055

García Lorca, Federico 1433
Garland, Hamlin 462, 1564
General comments [brief items, includes "A Note on Whit-
        man, " "Whitmaniana, " "Walt Whitman, " etc.] (see also
        Biographical items and Contemporary comments) 3,
        10, 12, 33, 38, 46, 63, 79, 174, 227, 274, 277, 551,
        566, 591, 663, 664, 699, 773, 778, 779, 782, 789,
        790, 841, 852, 897, 945, 970, 981, 1019, 1100, 1110,
        1125, 1259, 1603, 1627, 1652, 1730, 1731, 1775, 1776,
        1783, 1786, 1793, 1794, 1795, 1799, 1801, 1815, 1836,
        1862, 1869, 1892, 1893, 1899, 1900, 1903, 1953, 1958,
        1960, 1961, 1966, 1980, 1985, 1992, 2014, 2038, 2059,
        2069, 2070, 2173, 2220, 2225, 2327, 2381, 2462, 2489,
        2540, 2588, 2683, 2685, 2731
German [critics; includes German authors] 597, 814, 902,
        908, 909, 910, 919, 1118, 1119, 1263, 1437, 1459,
        1460, 1461, 1471, 1480, 1550, 1613, 1962, 2008, 2009,

Joyce, James   2370
Jung, Carl   229, 266, 267
Justice [as a theme in Whitman's poetry]   702, 719
Juvenilia   737, 1616

Kennedy, President John F.   1244, 1330
Kennedy, William Sloan   1111
Kent, Charles   855, 1940
"Kentucky"   35, 2578
Khayyám, Omar   1572
Knortz, Karl   908, 909

Laforgue, Jules   808
Language [Whitman's interest in]   125, 257, 258, 580, 676,
      758, 759, 760, 761, 934, 1016, 1155, 1156, 1206,
      1297, 1380, 1384, 1537, 1604, 1641, 1883, 1976, 2084,
      2085, 2086, 2280, 2546
Lanier, Sidney   2300
"The Last Invocation"   1272, 2001
"The Last of the Sacred Army"   60
Latin America [see also individual countries]   77, 78, 287,
      746, 805, 999, 1000
Lawrence, D. H.   134, 1149, 1734, 1747, 1766, 1866, 2018,
      2315
Leaves of Grass [discussion of; includes all editions]   72, 99,
      162, 226, 228, 246, 299, 310, 345, 404, 424, 449, 467,
      468, 475, 519a, 537, 539, 555, 559, 581, 582, 617,
      621, 650, 667, 669, 678, 679, 695, 787, 975, 1007,
      1009, 1092, 1096, 1138, 1154, 1200, 1201, 1258, 1289,
      1318, 1334, 1363, 1365, 1373, 1389, 1452, 1526, 1568,
      1570, 1805, 1820, 1858, 1879, 1891, 1911, 1912, 1913,
      1970, 1998, 2004, 2005, 2033, 2041, 2065, 2066, 2071,
      2135, 2137, 2170, 2172, 2255, 2314, 2334, 2335, 2346,
      2349, 2350, 2375, 2390, 2391, 2392, 2405, 2459, 2472,
      2486, 2490, 2510, 2523, 2570, 2592, 2674, 2689, 2696,
      2735, 2736
Lecturer [Whitman as; includes Oratory, Public Speaking]
      179, 180, 682, 853, 1769, 1774, 1989, 2226, 2490,
      2491
"Lesson of the Two Symbols"   1043
Letters [Collected and Uncollected]   34, 40, 45, 151, 185,
      206, 411, 414, 450, 451, 483, 610, 612, 631, 730,
      738, 896, 909, 910, 982, 989, 1071, 1077, 1174, 1224,
      1512, 1515, 1520, 1523, 1524, 1533, 1581, 1584, 1613,
      1686, 1687, 1688, 1689, 1690, 1694, 1695, 1696, 1702,